# *12 faith journeys*
## of the **minor prophets**

### NATHAN JONES & STEVE HOWELL

Lamb & Lion Ministries
P.O. Box 919
McKinney, Texas 75070
lamblion@lamblion.com
www.lamblion.com

Cover design by Nathan Jones & Steve Howell.
Cover photo used under license from Shutterstock.com.

Unless otherwise noted, Scripture quotations are from the New King James Version of the Bible, copyright © 1982 by Thomas Nelson, Inc. Used by permission. All rights reserved.

Printed in the United States of America.

# Acknowledgements

God, of course, deserves all the glory and credit, for without His source material and the blessings of health and mental fortitude none of this would be possible. If our book is nothing more than a sacrificial offering to Him, we hope He finds it pleasing. If it becomes something more and can make a real difference in the reader's life, even better!

We'd like to thank Dr. David Reagan for his wisdom and support in this endeavor and the team at Lamb & Lion Ministries for their encouragement and keen eyes.

To the church family at Tonganoxie Christian Church, thank you for the encouragement, support and willingness to be engaged as students so that the teacher can learn.

To those accomplished authors—Dr. Ron Rhodes, Carl Gallups and Warren Smith—we so appreciate your learned feedback and direction.

To our chapter-by-chapter review team of Gary Gaskin and Jay Saunders, your passion for the Bible, clarifications of what we meant to say, and fresh perspectives make us better writers.

And last, but certainly not least, to our wonderfully supportive wives, Heather and Deb, and to all our children—you mean the world to us!

# CONTENTS

# INTRODUCTION

Outside Nathan's upstairs office stands a tiny, three-foot tall door. It's not this little, rarely used aperture to a dusty attic that really catches his eye, but the laminated paper sign pinned to the top of its frame. It simply reads: "Minor Prophets".

This strange sign is likely the result of someone's wry wit, but to us it speaks volumes about how people perceive the 12 books of the Bible labeled just like that sign—the Minor Prophets. Minor. Strange. Little. Unimportant. Unused. Dusty. These are all words so many people of the Christian faith think of when they encounter these Old Testament writings. And so, therefore, let's state the obvious, the Minor Prophets don't get much attention.

The excuses for skipping these books are plentiful. For starters, the Minor Prophets' writings are short, merely a brief few chapters or just a chapter, hence the designation "minor." The Old Testament is comprised of thirty-nine books, but the combined 12 books of the Minor Prophets comprise less than 7% of the entire Old Testament. So, when compared to the massive writings of the Major Prophets such as Isaiah, Jeremiah, Ezekiel and Daniel, the writings of the Minor Prophets can seem miniscule and unimportant. Because of their short length, these books are often deemed of little value, and so are easily overlooked.

Then there's the fact of popularity. They are "fringe" by almost any definition of the word, trapped on the outskirts of the Old Testament and written by a dozen guys who would be considered by today's standards strange and unpopular. Sure, since grade school we've all learned about the runaway Jonah who was swallowed by a "whale." But, other than Jonah, who has heard of these other oddly named men: Hosea, Joel, Amos, Obadiah, Micah, Nahum, Habakkuk, Zephaniah, Haggai, Zechariah and Malachi? Try even pronouncing Habakkuk! And so, because we believe we cannot possibly feel any connection to such "fringe" men, their names are never spoken of from the pulpits.

In addition, while other well-known Bible heroes have compelling stories, a number of the Minor Prophets seem to have missed the memo when it comes to personal narrative. From the opening line of Scripture, God paints a compelling story and immediately builds in suspense and mystery. We see cosmic forces at play like in the Flood faced by Noah. We follow the Exodus from captivity boldly led by Moses. The stories of Abraham and David and Ruth and Samson are exciting and filled with colorful personalities. But, what can we say about Malachi? Where does the personality of Amos shine through? With the exception of a few brief examples, the Minor Prophets can seem like faceless mouthpieces for God, not interesting individuals in their own right. They end up being treated as Minor League players, stuck in God's dugout, fervently wishing to ascend to the Majors.

Oh, what a tragedy! How wrong we would be to ignore the Minor Prophets. When we just take the time to understand their stories, the Minor Prophets and their messages turn out to be amazingly profound. They fill us with hope and wonder, all the while convicting and challenging us to faithfully follow God.

## MEET THE PROPHETS

To better appreciate these spokesmen and their impact, let's start by understanding their role. At certain periods of time, Yahweh God made clear both His intentions and plans through the work of individuals He called in the Hebrew *nabi*, which we today call prophets. While that job title currently causes most people to think about telling the future, a prophet's main role wasn't prediction. Prophets were simply individuals who would receive and then declare God's messages. These twelve authors were, as the Apostle Peter explained, "holy men of God [who] spoke as they were moved by the Holy Spirit" (2 Peter 1:21).

Some prophets spoke God's messages. Nathan, for example, confronted King David regarding his sin with Bathsheba (2 Samuel 12). Elijah challenged evil King Ahab and the false prophets of Baal (1 Kings 17).

Other prophets acted out God's messages, communicating by deed. The deeds could range from the mundane (naming a child), to the eye-catching (wearing an oxen's yoke), to the outrageous (walking about naked), to the miraculous (calling down fire from heaven).

Still other prophets wrote down God's messages for people to read. The majority of our information about prophets comes from the books written by the "classical" or "writing" prophets who flourished during Israel and Judah's political turmoil with the Assyrian, then Babylonian, and finally the Medo-Persian Empires. Using their experiences and personality, the writing prophets translated their visions and oracles from God into amazing poetry and prose that shared a perspective different from the rest of Scripture.

Some of the books in the Bible tell us about the actions of God and His people. These books of history are filled with facts and stories that tell us the "what" of God's actions. Other biblical books tell us about the reactions of people to the work of God in their time. These books of poetry, also called Wisdom Literature, are filled with songs and poems and proverbs that remind us of how we should respond to what God has done. But, the books of prophecy are different. While they sometimes mix in "what" and "how" thoughts In their writing, their bigger concern is the "why." In the prophetic books, we best find God's motivations for the actions He takes involving justice, as well as His nature of compassion and forgiveness. As God is speaking through these men, we are granted a breathtaking, bay window-sized view into our Heavenly Father's heart.

Yahweh called the prophets to share important messages because He cares about His people. There were messages for the nations of Judah, Israel, and the surrounding nations of their time. They contained dire warnings of coming judgment for their moral failings and emphatic calls to repentance. God even pointed out events that would occur in the far distant future, such as the coming of the Messiah and the events of the end times. Each message was delivered through the filter of the prophet's language, style and situation, but all of the messages poured forth God's heart.

## PROPHETS OF FAITH

When one truly digs into the lives of the Minor Prophets, one will discover not something minor, strange, little, unimportant, unusable and dusty, but the real-life stories of 12 men who were thrust into quite perilous situations. They will discover that these guys were everyday people just like so many of us. They hailed from diverse backgrounds such as farmers and construction workers, some clergy and few aristocrats, and a mix of ages from teen up to senior citizens. What tied them all together was a specific call by God to wear the burdensome mantle of prophet and deliver His messages. And what messages they were! So full of fire from the pain of betrayal and the joy of fatherly love that their ears must have burned upon hearing them.

Those impassioned messages revolved like the planets around the sun, all around one key subject—faith. Faith is that strong or unshakeable belief in something, especially with little or no proof or evidence. The Bible itself defines faith simply as "the substance of things hoped for, the evidence of things not seen" (Hebrews 11:1). Faith is primarily tied to the idea of trust and confidence, for as King David pled, "Preserve me, O God, for in You I put my trust" (Psalm 16:1). When it comes to daily living, we're told "the just shall live by his faith" (Habakkuk 2:4), and that followers of God "walk by faith" (2 Corinthians 5:7). And then there's the warning that "whatever is not from faith is sin" (Romans 14:23).

Confidence. Reliance. Credence. Belief. Trust. We could all use some of that in our relationships with God. And so, too, did the Minor Prophets. The Minor Prophets needed a healthy dose of faith in God, for despite their position of honor in being chosen to relay the Lord's oracles, these messengers were often treated quite badly by the very people God had sent them to.

> *"Some faced jeers and flogging, while still others were chained and put in prison. They were stoned; they were sawed in two, they were put to death by the sword. They went about in sheepskins and goatskins, destitute, persecuted and mistreated—the world was not worthy of them" (Hebrews 11:36-38).*

Because of this treatment, the prophets gained a unique perspective into the challenges surrounding faith, and that makes them highly relevant to us today. The tremendous faith these men had to demonstrate was sometimes rooted in their situation, as they had to learn to trust in God and obey His calling, even if it meant being dropped into life-and-death dilemmas with little hope of survival. Other times their faith was revealed as they boldly trusted God and proclaimed a surprising or challenging message, knowing that it wouldn't be popular. Faith is shown as they wrestled with questions, as they observed injustice, as they saw devastation, and as they anticipated the future.

These men didn't start as super-soldiers of the faith, but instead as humble men who painstakingly had to learn its meaning. Their faith journeys were in no way dull, nor were they insignificant, but exciting and insightful and very applicable to us today.

It doesn't matter that these books are often overlooked. What matters is that they are in our Bibles, and their lessons of faith are available to us if we'll just take the time to look. We should strive to have a faith like that of the Minor Prophets, for we too need to learn how to have that kind of faith and benefit from its spiritual riches.

## GOALS FOR THE READER

In the following pages, you'll have the chance to meet Hosea, Joel, Amos, Obadiah, Jonah, Micah, Nahum, Habakkuk, Zephaniah, Haggai, Zechariah and Malachi. All of the introductory stories you'll read are elaborations on Scripture, imagining scenarios that the text hints at but doesn't necessarily describe. We ask that you take these stories as intended—as historical fiction to illustrate historical fact. We want to use narratives to help you fall in love with these prophets and see them as humans, instead of merely hard-to-pronounce names. We want to show their diverse backgrounds, their unusual settings, and their varied experiences in a way that would spark your imagination.

We also want to take some time to explain their messages. Each prophet wrote with a specific audience in mind, and each dealt with issues that requires some background information to understand. We'll walk you through each message and cover the important points. Our goal is not to provide an academic assessment or a full-blown comprehensive commentary. We simply want to help you get the most out of each book and hear God's message with fresh ears.

Finally, we want the information to be practical. In ministry we encounter so many people who each and every day experience challenges to their faith in God. We believe we can help, and we can do that by learning from how the Minor Prophets reacted to the challenges they faced and the lessons they learned, and then applying that wisdom to our own lives. So, in each lesson, we have applications for Israel, the Nations, the Church, and for you. Our hope is that the applications learned will change the readers' walk with our Heavenly Father into something so much deeper and richer.

We welcome you to come along with us on the 12 faith journeys of the Minor Prophets!

# FAITH JOURNEY 1
# HOSEA: FAITH WHEN YOUR HEART IS SHATTERED

## THE AUCTION

She stood motionless and forsaken atop the high wooden platform. Stripped of all clothing, hands held together by a loosely tied rope and hanging limply before her, she made one last futile attempt to search her well of emotions and to no real surprise found its depths too dry to stir up any care. The indignity of the public display no longer held any horror for her, for long ago she had shed whatever dignity she once possessed.

Darkened, murky images of her life over the last few years played out in her mind's eye. Head hung low, gaze empty, staring down upon the roughhewn boards below her bare feet, she tried to remember the face and features of the man she had once known long ago as her husband. How old were her three little children now? Puzzled, she couldn't quite remember. She had left them all behind. They had offered her nothing but stress and embarrassment and poverty.

Oh, the poverty! She had wanted so much more than a provincial life. She had desires. Her beauty was widely admired and so she believed worthy of rich adornment in fancy clothes and expensive jewelry. She had wanted to know the joys of wine with friends at parties in the evening and with various lovers at private parties throughout the night. She had craved the attention and high position in society that she had believed she rightfully deserved.

*There were always many, many men who could fulfill her heart's desires. A long litany of suitors cascaded across her memory, and like her abandoned husband, she could no longer quite clearly picture them now. How many men had she given herself to procure these favored gifts? She could no longer remember that either. These lovers all seemed the same, so full of promises for a better life, yet each one eventually failed her, proving empty once they had gotten what they'd wanted out of her.*

*It started out so wonderfully with pleasures untold she had thought, but over time the procession turned into a nightmare. With every bit of her body she sold for fancy baubles, a piece of herself was ultimately lost. The parties and the pleasures and the hard living rapidly took their toll. She found her soul was dying on the inside as rapidly as her body was aging on the outside. Face worn and cold, eyes empty of life, hair streaked with grey, shoulders slumped, the young woman appeared decades older than her true age. To her horror, as she declined she found she had less to offer, and so too dropped the quality of her lovers. She finally resorted to paying them for just an inkling of the attentions she had once received. And then the abuses and neglect had begun.*

*So there she stood atop that platform—cold in both body and soul, friendless and oh so utterly lonely; face dirty and cheek bruised, long hair bedraggled, eyes bereft of the spark of life, reeking of prison stench—absolutely desolate. She remained somber, utterly crushed and defeated. And, also indebted beyond all hope of repayment.*

*The sweaty auctioneer began the call for bidding.*

*Across the busy market center of the capital city, hidden among the colorful merchants selling their various wares, stood a man used to being completely alone even in a bustling crowd. Head covered, cloak pulled tightly around him, the man attempted to be company with only his thoughts. For hours he'd been there waiting, pacing and wringing his calloused hands. Strong and powerful* emotions assailed him, wave after wave, until he was quite sure he could stand against them no longer. Then she was standing before him on the auction block, and his strength almost caved.

Taking in the crowd with only quick and furtive sidelong glances, the man took measure of the people around him. While some seemed more interested in the pungent smells of the exotic spices and fine textures of the fabrics the market had to offer, a greater number seemed intent on ogling the latest procession of slaves being sold to market, hoping to be titillated by some sordid, tragic story from the auctioneer. They were to be disappointed by this sad creature of a woman now brought before them, for in her worn condition, the auctioneer knew she would fare little to no value, so he barely made any effort to up-sell her.

Some knew who she was though. She had a past. He noticed cliques of women whispering and laughing to one to another, spiting bitterly without pity: "Good-for-nothing man stealer." "Adulterous!" "Her own husband couldn't control that wretch." "Deserved what she got." The watcher cringed inwardly, for painfully he knew the words were all too true.

At the booming call of the auctioneer for the first bid, the milling crowd responded with skeptical silence. He called again, this time dropping the bid even lower, but was met only by pockets of quiet laughter. A third time the auctioneer called out the lowest possible price, yet still nothing.

Gathering his fortitude, the man took down his hood and revealed his face. Eyes fixated only on the woman, voice cracked with emotion, he called out. "I bid 30 pieces of silver! But, all I have is 15. Will you, uh, take the other 15 in barley?" The words having escaped his lips, the man self-consciously believed all eyes were now boring into him. And so they were. Who would pay even pittance for such a treacherous and defeated creature, much less the full price set by their law for a healthy slave? It seemed like a preposterous offer. And then, with looks of absolute shock revealing recognition, they knew. The people began to whisper one to another. "Isn't that her former husband?" He paid no attention to the unkind words that flowed around him. The auctioneer was quick to respond, knowing he'd get no better price. "Sold!"

The woman couldn't look up—didn't dare look up—for where once was emptiness, there was now mortal fear rising up within her at the sound of her husband's voice. As a slave she was property, and her former husband and now master had the legal right to stone her to death for her infidelities. Would he take his revenge? Her mind was a torrent of panic as the man paid the auctioneer. And now he stood before her on the auction block, all eyes hungrily watching for the drama to unfold.

She braced herself for the inevitable blow, only to be confounded by the sensation of a warm cloak being slipped around her slight shoulders. The man—the husband she had betrayed and abandoned time and again—now her master, lifted her trembling chin gently in his hands and tenderly spoke. "You are to live with me now for the rest of your life. You will no longer cheat on me. I forgive you, and I love you." Her eyes darted up to meet his and was utterly stunned by the warmth within them. Like a marionette whose strings are cut, she collapsed as an ocean of guilt washed away from her soul. To the stunned silence of the market crowd, the husband caught her in his strong arms, lifted her off her feet, and carried her back home.

## A SHATTERED HEART

Have you ever had your heart shattered into a million painful pieces? Maybe the cause was betrayal by a loved one such as a wayward spouse or rebellious child. Possibly it's by a failed career, crushed dreams, lost hopes, or personal failure. The experience is rather like running through an obstacle course of emotions. One minute we feel such stabbing emotional pain that it attempts to overwhelm us. The next minute, we experience an uncontrollable rage at the injustice of it all. We cry, we plead, we call out, we lose sleep and our health diminishes, but in the end we're ultimately left feeling hollow, bitter and, oh, so very alone.

The book of Hosea, the first of the twelve Minor Prophets recorded in the Old Testament part of the Bible, introduces us in the first three chapters to two people who have also had their hearts shattered, though for very different reasons. They were real people. They may have lived long ago, well, very long ago, approximately 740 years before Christ's birth. They may have lived in a nation very different than your own, which was the ancient Northern Kingdom of Israel set on the eastern side of the Mediterranean Sea. The culture may have also been very different, being the Hebrew people whom we now call the Jews or Israelis. They ate different foods, they lived in a farming and livestock-based economy, they rode donkeys and mules, their clothes were made of a coarse, woven fabric, and their footwear consisted of sandals.

But, as for the heart, they were as human as we are today. They had thoughts, emotions, desires and dreams and yearned to be loved and accepted. Where it matters most, people are people no matter where and when they may be found. And, like us, they suffered pain and the subsequent trials of maintaining faith in God when their hearts were shattered.

The shards are lying all scattered about us. Therefore, let's learn why the trials in life happen, as well as discover how to gain the faith that repairs the broken pieces of your heart. We'll do that by delving into the lives of these two iconic characters from the book of Hosea. Though long deceased, their life stories continue to be lived out by so many of us today.

## Gomer, the Faithless Bride

Though the book is called Hosea, and that is the name of the man in our story and the author, the life experiences of Hosea revolved around his wife, so we'll start with her.

We find in chapter one that Hosea's wife was named Gomer. Not a great name by today's standards, nevertheless she caught Hosea's eye, though possibly not for the right characteristics one may look for when choosing a wife. You see, Yahweh God had told Hosea to find a wife who at first may have been just as pure as the infant nation of Israel was upon entering the Promised Land, but who also had a wandering eye which would eventually get her into serious moral trouble. So, whatever virtue Gomer may have had when their relationship began, she also started out with some serious character flaws.

In that ancient culture, Hosea would have gone to Gomer's father, Diblaim, and paid the bride price for her. Then Gomer, after an engagement time and wedding ceremony, would become Hosea's wife. The women of that time rarely had a say in who they married, so a wild-hearted woman such as Gomer may have during the engagement period already begun exhibiting the unfaithful behaviors that would spell trouble for their coming marriage.

Not too long into Hosea and Gomer's marriage, we discover in chapter two that Gomer had other major character deficiencies. For starters, she was quite vain, which lead to a self-centered materialism that ached for the finer things in life. Her era's Saks Fifth Avenue was where she'd be at each day, window shopping the expensive fashions and jewelry. She was totally greedy and never satisfied, incessantly nagging her husband to pick up that third job to provide her with more fun money, which she then had the nerve to spend on her boyfriends. The life of the all-night party, Gomer was the crazy drunk dancing it up on the tabletops. Her wandering eye turned into full-blown adultery, and like a dog in heat, she chased after her long list of boy toys who could give her the goods she craved. For a gold anklet or the next high, Gomer prostituted her body as payment.

On the home front, Gomer bore three children, but it's questionable whether the second and third were actually even Hosea's children. With all the affection of Cinderella's stepmother,

Gomer thought of her babies as brats who stole precious time away from her parties and attentions, and so she abandoned them for her latest lover's house. In between hook-ups, she managed to make fleeting appearances back at home, but was always quickly out the door again when she thought the next best offer beckoned.

Hosea and his God repulsed Gomer, so to be spiteful she chased after the pagan gods of the land. These demonic gods demanded she ritually burn incense and feast and prostitute herself before their stone altars used in the heinous practice of child sacrifice.

Two things happened to Gomer by chapter three. First, after a wild ride of a life, she was doused by the cold, hard reality that living in such a manner provided her with absolutely no joy whatsoever. No matter how much she had filled her life with material and sexual pleasures, she still felt utterly miserable. Nothing seemed to fill that empty hole in her heart. Second, hard living had taken its toll on her body, and only the dregs of the back alleys wanted to be with her.

Eventually she owned nothing but debt. In that culture, a person would have to work off the payments as a slave, and that's where we find Gomer. She'd sold her body for mere pleasures and trinkets, and then eventually to survive, because that's all that she had left to offer. She became impoverished, hopeless, pitiless, defiled and unwanted by all those around her. Gomer had made herself toxic to her own people, and they rightly wanted nothing to do with such a wretched individual. Having betrayed everyone in her treachery, and inevitably now all alone, she was left with nothing but a broken, shattered heart, and all of her own making.

## Hosea, the Faithful Servant

Whereas Hosea's wife Gomer was utterly faithless, those same first three chapters show Hosea was the complete opposite. He was a man whose life was dedicated to being totally faithful.

Hosea placed Yahweh God first in his life, and so lived defined by his faithful service to Him. One would think Hosea's father, Beeri, may have had an inkling of his son's destiny, for he named Hosea "God is salvation." God called Hosea to be a Nabi, which in Hebrew means Prophet, to his own people in that Northern Kingdom of Israel. As a prophet of God, Hosea would share God's messages to the people. Sometimes God would have Hosea write out His messages in letters, sometimes shout them from the balconies in speeches, and at times even more dramatically—act out God's messages using his own life as a type of living symbol.

In living out these messages, God would ask Hosea to do some of the most difficult things in order to get His messages across. Regardless of how drop-dead gorgeous Gomer may have been, it must have worried Hosea when God asked him to marry a woman such as her, but Hosea obediently did so. It must have caused no small resentment from Hosea's children towards their father, by God's command, to give them names with prophetic implications. The name of Hosea's oldest son, Jezreel, meant "God scatters; the threatened judgment." His daughter Lo-Ruhamah's name meant "not pitied; mercy not obtained." His youngest son Lo-Ammi's name meant "cast out; not my people." And, when Hosea's life crashed upon the craggy shoals of his wife's endless betrayals—the woman God had commanded him to marry—Hosea refused to divorce her. He then without question obeyed God yet again and bought his wayward wife out of slavery.

In such acts of obedience, Hosea showed how deep his relationship with God was and how totally selfless his faith was towards his Lord. Should God have asked Hosea to hop into a wheelbarrow He was pushing across a tightrope that spanned the raging Niagara Falls, Hosea would have jumped right in, no questions asked. That's how strong Hosea's faith and trust in God was. Even with his heart shattered into a million pieces by his failed marriage, and also by his own people who could care less about his prophetic warnings, Hosea knew that the only real choice was to keep the faith and just trust in God's divine purposes.

## ISRAEL, THE FAITHLESS NATION

On the surface it appears that Yahweh had set His messenger up for failure. That's led some readers to conclude that God is some kind of sadistic monster who enjoys seeing His children suffer. "God is the source of all our suffering and shattered hearts!" they conclude. Those are actually viable observations about His character and motive, but Hosea dispels them in chapters 4-14 by explaining God's relationship with the nation of Israel.

The culture in which Hosea was called to proclaim the Lord's messages existed during a very difficult time politically for the people of Israel. Internally, the people of the Northern Kingdom suffered through an ever-changing list of unstable kings who rose to power through assassination. The leaders were as self-serving and corrupt as any banana republic dictator.

External political pressure came from the ruthless Assyrian Empire, based in what is today Iraq. They were constantly breathing down the necks of Israel's kings, demanding allegiance and extorting protection money. If the oppressed nation didn't submit, in Mafioso style the cruel Assyrians would then ride down into Israel's lands and have their thugs beat up mercilessly on the people. As Israelite kings waffled from paying the demanded tribute to outright rebellion, Assyrian kings with challenging names would come breaking down the doors. This time period is quite succinctly described as: "Anarchy, chaos, feuds and broken covenants were visible on every side."[1] This is the tumultuous political atmosphere in which Hosea had to survive to serve as God's "prophet of Israel's zero hour."[2]

Ironically, despite all the corrupt politicians and flying arrows Israel was ducking during that time, according to 2 Kings 15-17, the nation was doing pretty well financially. Go figure!

Economically the nation was prosperous, but spiritually it was their darkest hour.[3] Israel may have been as prosperous as any Western nation is today, but its soulless people were continually shaken by ceaseless turmoil and frequent foreign attacks. Corrupt leaders have always been a symptom of a corrupt people, and Israel's people had by then devolved morally. When that happens, inward corruption in a nation is more dangerous to its existence than their external enemies.[4]

God explained how the people of Israel got into such a dire predicament by comparing Israel to Gomer. In personality they were one and the same. Gomer suffered a shattered heart of her own making, and so too did Israel, bringing about her own suffering and heartbreak. What a sad situation.

After all, like Gomer was to Hosea, Israel as a people group have always had a very special place in God's heart. The steadfast faithful obedience of their forefathers—Abraham, Isaac and Jacob (called Israel)—in a world that had shunned God had touched His heart. In response, God made Israel and his descendants a special covenant, meaning a sacred agreement one makes with another. In this eternal covenant, God promised the people of Israel that if they just kept His righteous law and remained faithful to Him, God would shower His loving blessings all over the Promised Land (Genesis 17:7-8; 26:2-5; 28:1-4,13-14; 1 Chronicles 16:17-18; Psalm 105:8-11).

Listen to the great love by which the Lord describes His covenant people Israel, found in Deuteronomy 7:6-8:

> *"For you are a holy people to the Lord your God; the Lord your God has chosen you to be a people for Himself, a special treasure above all the peoples on the face of the earth... because the Lord loves you, and because He would keep the oath which He swore to your fathers."*

As this passage proves, Israel was chosen by the Lord God Himself. He even called them a "special treasure." In agreement to the covenant, Israel was to be pure, holy and dedicated to the One who loved them. Such love and commitment, bound by a life-long agreement, sounds rather like a marriage vow. That was and still is how God views His covenant.

God in Deuteronomy 7 commanded His Chosen People when they entered the Promised Land to utterly destroy the heinously evil tribes—the Hittites, Girgashites, Amorites, Canaanites, Perizzites, Hivites and Jebusites—who occupied its hills and valleys. Long having rejected Yahweh God, they instead worshiped the gods of metal and wood that their own hands had crafted. These idols represented the demon "male" gods El, Baal and Dagon and "female" gods Asherah, Astarte and Anath. These pagan people believed their fertility gods had to be enticed to mate, so that man, animal and field would become fertile. To arouse these gods, these tribes performed various horrific acts including sacrificing their own children in the fires, reveling in drunken orgies, and openly having sex with temple shrine prostitutes and even animals.

God was deeply troubled that if the Israelites didn't destroy these evils, they'd become captivated by them and succumb to their temptations. As Deuteronomy 7:4 explains, "For they will turn your sons away from following Me to serve other gods." Tragically, the Israelites failed miserably in following God's command. Many of the evil peoples and practices remained throughout the land, and so God's concerns became quite realized. For Israel, just like Gomer, did not remain faithful to her "husband" for very long.

## Israel, a Profile in Faithlessness

The parallels of Gomer to Israel in personality and behavior were remarkably uncanny, as in truth they were meant to be, for Gomer was a living symbol of Israel. Marvel at the comparisons!

**Vanity.** The more Yahweh blessed Israel the more the Israelites began to think of themselves as too good for everyone else, even for God. They stopped thinking of Him as their provider and instead pridefully patted themselves on the back for their good fortunes. Just like a socialite with a titanium MasterCard, Israel's focus was solely on what new things they could buy for themselves. As God dejectedly bemoaned, "Me she forgot" (2:13; 5:5; 7:10; 13:1).

**Greed.** It wasn't enough for the Israelites that God had given them their own lush land, rich agricultural bounty, military protection, good health, and most importantly a special place in His heart. No! Never having enough to satiate their cravings, Israel had the gall to ask their evil enemy neighbors for more of those things and pretended the bill would never come due (2:5,12; 10:1).

**Drunkenness.** Israel partied like the world was coming to an end. The people didn't just drink, they were inflamed with wine morning, noon and night, and so were often were found staggering past the Betty Ford Centers of their day (2:11; 4:5,11; 7:5,14).

**Shamelessness.** The lack of inhibition and stupidity that drunkenness invariably produces caused the people to behave shamefully, just like the wild donkeys to which Hosea compared them. The people, even their own supposedly holy men—the priests—debased themselves with public nudity and engaged in every form of lewdness (2:5,9-10; 4:7-9; 6:9; 8:11).

**Lustfulness.** The people's passions burned without any marital or social constraint whatsoever. The old taboos of fornication, adultery, homosexuality, pedophilia and bestiality were torn down and replaced by San Francisco-style gay pride parades. Israel went after her lovers, and when she couldn't find any consenting parties, she hired lovers. The people made love openly on every threshing floor for all to see. The rampant sexual promiscuity resulted in begotten pagan children who rarely knew who their fathers were. So defiled were the people, and so unable to quench their sexual lusts, they devolved into kissing calves, both beast and graven image. The people had degenerated into nothing more than wild, rutting animals (2:7,13; 5:3,7; 8:9; 9:1; 13:2).

**Wickedness.** The question when playing the game Limbo is, "How low can you go?" And, for Israel, there was just no low to their rottenness. Hosea compared their stubborn hearts to an oven that burned for every kind of wickedness. Every one of them were cursing liars who brazenly bragged that they were in reality "good" people. They voted in or bribed leaders who would let them skirt the laws so that they could sin as often as they wanted and with great abandon (4:16; 5:11; 6:8; 7:1,3,6; 8:3; 9:7,9,15-16; 10:9,13,15; 12:8; 13:2; 14:4).

**Murderous.** To satiate their selfish desires, treachery was business as usual. What they wanted they got; most often by committing fraud, through lying, moving property lines, swearing false testimony, breaking covenants, or just plain murdering. The populace were killing, stealing, committing adultery and engaging in bloodshed upon bloodshed until they were "utterly defiled with blood." Even their own priests were murderers! All laws were broken, and any judge who took a stand was found hanging on his own gallows. Murderous bands of thieves lay in wait on every road seeking their next victim. Nobody helped those in need, and anyone who dared act righteously were openly mocked. Never sorry for whatever treachery they engaged in, the people absolutely refused to repent, and so continued committing every dirty deed possible under the sun as if some Clint Eastwood Western B-movie bad guy (1:4; 4:1-2,8,18; 5:1-2,10; 6:7-10; 7:1,5,7,16; 10:4; 11:5; 12:1,14).

**Idolatrous.** Israel was set apart for Yahweh God alone, but the people quickly dumped Him to engage in the pagan acts that Gomer was so frequently found committing in her vindictiveness towards Hosea. They left God in the dust and instead put all their energies into worshiping the abominable Baals. The more they worshiped the Baals and other false gods—these false lovers—the more the people shamed themselves by burning incense on the hills, asking counsel from their wooden idols, constructing shrines and temples, and participating in cruel human and animal sacrifices on stone altars atop the mountains. Instead of joining in a mutually loving relationship with the one true living God, the people cratered into becoming pagans enslaved to loveless blocks of wood (2:8,11; 4:12-13,17; 5:4; 8:4,13-14; 9:10; 10:1; 11:1).

**Adulterous.** There didn't appear to be a good marriage among the Israelites. Adultery was rampant. The divorce rate must have been up in the high 90th percentile. Even the brides were committing adultery on their own wedding day!

Despite all the references to female prostitutes in Hosea's messages, God didn't leave out the men. They could be found after hours up at the Baal shrine red light district offering "sacrifices" by having sex with the temple harlot, the very job Gomer took as her fortunes declined.

Adultery committed against one's spouse is bad enough, but the people as a whole committed greater harlotry by cheating on their Lord. By going after man-made idols fashioned in the form of demonic forces and creatures of nature, the "bride of God" played the harlot against her husband. God compared Israel's faithfulness to a morning cloud, which like the early dew, evaporates away (1:2; 2:2; 4:12-13,18; 6:4; 7:4; 8:9; 10:2).

**Rebellious.** God gave His cherished Israel the Ten Commandments and other precepts in the Mosaic Law so right and wrong and good and evil could easily be identified. Knowing how to choose what's right would save them from heartbreak. But, for Israel to engage in their sinful desires and then attempt to justify their evils, they would have to do away with God's Law and the boundaries that it set. Ultimately, so too must the Lawgiver be done away with. And so, for the sake of their sin, Israel treacherously rebelled against their Heavenly Father.

Much of the book of Hosea is filled with tear-stained page after tear-stained page as Yahweh God in first person explains the rebellious nature of His covenant "bride" Israel. In fitful pains of mournful agony, wailing and weeping and raging, and at times even seemingly disjointed ranting, the reader can only be struck by how staggeringly hurt God truly was by the devastating betrayal by His people.

Read the very words God bemoaned to Hosea when describing Israel's rebellion. The reason God's people "ceased obeying the Lord" and "transgressed My covenant and rebelled against My law" was because they considered the "great things of My law... a strange thing." God's law didn't fulfill the selfish desires, lusts and impulses of their sinful hearts, so in response Israel from peasant to prince rebelled against their Heavenly Father (4:10,18; 7:14; 8:1,12; 9:1,15; 13:16).

Dealing a devastating blow, Israel in their desire to reject God's law also rejected Him personally. Like the chest-thumping Atheists of today, they even went as far as pretending God no longer existed. In response, God cried out, "They forgot Me!" Yes, Israel had "forgotten his Maker" (4:1,6; 7:7; 8:14; 11:3; 13:6).

Deeply wounded, God, like a parent who's just heard their tween yell "I hate you!," lamented over Israel's betrayal. "They do not return to the Lord their God, nor seek Him." No longer having a healthy respect for the Lord, they did not obey Him and so "did not cry out to Me" in their distress. Craven and ungrateful, "they have fled from Me" and "transgressed against Me, though I redeemed them." The betrayers were only ever "bent on backsliding from Me." God just wouldn't go away, so the people went on the offense and sought to "devise evil against Me." They have "spoken lies against Me," and "encircled Me with lies and deceit" so as to tarnish and smear the name of the Lord (5:7; 6:7; 7:10,13-15; 9:17; 10:3; 11:7,12).

Rejecting God as their king, Israel installed their own flawed and worthless leaders, an act hauntingly parallel to today's nations which leave us with presidents who make confusing decisions, congresses being stuck in gridlock, and activist judges who just make up laws as it suits them. Israel had put all their trust in their military and endlessly tried to appease their two-faced enemies by making peace treaties not worth the clay tablets they were etched on (8:4,14; 10:13; 12:1).

As the rejection of God progressed over the decades, soon a youth culture arose who barely even knew the name of the Lord as anything but a curse word. Those who did know God held Him in absolute contempt and tried to provoke Him to anger most bitterly by their language, music and lifestyle choices. They could care less if God was offended, forgetting that in His all-knowingness the Omniscient always remembers (7:2; 11:7; 12:14; 13:1).

**Unhappy.** Israel thought a rebellious heart would bring them all God had ever denied them, but other than a fleeting kick, they just couldn't feel a contentment and satisfaction that lasted. None whatsoever! For, like Gomer, Israel after a life of committing every evil possible under the sun could only heave a dejected, "For then it was better for me than now."

Their response seems strange, but only at first, for when one realizes that without God's knowledge and the wisdom He provides, mankind becomes trampled down by our own lack of discernment until finally we're destroyed. When selfishness enslaves the heart, senseless people can only blindly stumble about through life making bad decisions. As Hosea so colorfully stated, "When one sows the wind, they reap the whirlwind."

Rebelliousness in reality is a sickness that devours one's strength. The very sinful pleasures the people of Israel craved were sapping their youth and vitality, essentially destroying them. And, crazy enough, the people didn't even realize their emaciated condition until they were too far wasted away. God's denials were in truth protection, not sadism (2:7; 4:6,11,14; 5:5,13,15; 7:9,11; 8:7; 14:1).

## GOD, THE FAITHFUL KING

Doubts about the goodness of God's character can come to mind when one first begins reading the book of Hosea, for on the surface it appears as if Yahweh had set poor Hosea up for failure by dooming him to a terrible marriage with a wayward woman. The reader can then jump to the conclusion that God must be heartless, even believing He is even now deliciously plotting our own eventual downfall and subsequent shattered heart.

As one reads deeper into the life story of Hosea, though, it becomes abundantly clear that Israel was the heartless one, and not God, for in every conceivable way she was at fault for shattering her own heart. Then we've got to remember that Gomer was the living embodiment of the faithless nation of Israel. Every wicked desire Gomer craved and evil deed committed was a reflection of Israel's heart. The faithless bride Gomer was the living symbol, a type, of the faithless bride Israel.

This is where it can get difficult, for God can at first seem uncaring for asking Hosea to marry Gomer. But remember, Hosea's job was messenger for Yahweh. For Hosea to most effectively share the heartache God was enduring with His wayward people, Hosea needed to also experience the same betrayal firsthand. As one commentator explained, "Not until a heart is crushed by love's indescribable sorrow is it truly fitted to preach the deeper things of God's matchless love."[5] Hosea relating to his Lord's suffering actually imbued him with the ability to effectively communicate God's heartache. Yahweh's and Hosea's hearts were bound together by the same heartache, and united together by the same love for a wayward wife.

Hosea was willing to take this plunge into pain for His Heavenly Father and obeyed. By doing so, this faithful messenger's life emerged as one of the greatest types of symbolic Bible prophecies ever to walk this earth. After all, who so willingly gives their life over to become a symbol of misery, and who because of obedience chooses to have their life become a "succession of sobs"?[6] Hosea became a living symbol, just like Gomer, for he modeled the very faithfulness and forgiveness that God was demonstrating to Israel. Hosea was, of course, merely a man, but his character and heart are a beautiful reflection of the character and heart of God, and that's precisely why God chose him.

## God, a Profile in Faithfulness

To better understand the vastness of the Divine's heart, let's experience who Yahweh really is as portrayed in the book of Hosea.

**Communicative.** The heart of God communicates. One of the most common complaints from skeptics today is that God, if He's real, is distant and never talks to His creations. Even the Deists of the early years of America thought this, believing God had wound up the universe and then stepped away. Not true! We find ample examples throughout the Bible where God has communicated about who He is to Man.

God actually wants to communicate with us, but sin stands in the way. When the eternal state comes, mankind will be reunited with God once more. There we'll walk, talk and fellowship one-on-one with our Heavenly Father, just as Adam and Eve did in the Garden of Eden before sin separated humanity from Him. God sent His own Son, Jesus Christ, to do the Good Work of restoring that relationship. But, while we wait for that heavenly state, God uses other avenues to communicate to us about who He is and what good He desires for us.

One such avenue is through the speeches, writings and symbolic lives of Israel's prophets, such as Hosea. Many times the rebuking messages given to Israel were to help keep them from making the wrong choices, but more often it was to reveal the person and character of Yahweh. Those messages to Israel became a conduit for revealing God to the larger world, so that every person in every land in every age since can know about our Creator. When God commanded Hosea and the other prophets to hear the words of the Lord, He was speaking not just to the prophet or Israel, but to you and me as well. Our Father God communicates to us through these messages, and when we call out to Him, He responds, "I will answer" (1:2; 2:21; 3:1; 4:1; 5:1-2,9; 6:5; 9:8; 12:4,10,13).

**Loving.** The heart of God is loving. It's easy to think that Almighty God would be altogether self-sufficient, and yet the book of Hosea reveals that God is loving and seeks those who will love Him in return. Drink in the poetry of God's love for His people when verse after verse He proclaimed, "When Israel was a child, I loved him, and out of Egypt I called My son," and "I drew them with gentle cords, with bands of love, and I was to them as those who take the yoke from their neck. I stooped and fed them" (11:1,3-4).

**Faithful.** The heart of God is faithful. When Yahweh makes a promise, He is faithful and will never, ever, ever break it. When God says, "I will make a covenant," the recipient can be 100% absolutely sure that the promise of God will never be altered, stretched, forgotten, or rescinded. So, for God to declare, "I will betroth you to Me in faithfulness," His loving character remains totally faithful to the covenant He has established. All 66 books of the Bible pour forth testimony of God forever remaining faithful to the promises He has made. Promises matter to God (2:18,20).

**Pained.** The heart of God can be pained. That so massive a deity concerns Himself over being betrayed by so small a people is because God also has the most massive of hearts. God's giant heart tears and shatters greatest of all. As unfathomable to us mere mortals is God's capability for love, for God is love, so too is His susceptibleness to pain. Those who love the most feel pain the hardest.

And so, in hair-pulling and teeth-clenching fiery, righteous anger, the Broken-Hearted handed down a series of judgments upon Israel. For that generation, "I will drive them from My house; I will love them no more." And yet, even though Israel provoked Yahweh to anger most bitter, God through His anguished rage cried out as from the heart of a parent forced into disciplining His wayward child, "How can I give you up, Ephraim?... My heart churns within Me; My sympathy is stirred." As an anonymous wise man once shared, "By chastening, the Lord separates the sin that He hates from the sinner whom He loves" (9;15; 11:8; 1 John 4:8,16).

**Sovereign.** The heart of God is sovereign. That God had the right to be angry over Israel's backstabbing betrayals should by now go without saying, but then that brings up the matter of His right to be angry over our own rebellion today. It's easier to understand God's anger over past wrongs, but oddly so much harder when we ourselves today are personally committing those very same wrongs. We then begin to question just what kind of authority God holds.

First, the authority God holds dwells within the very nature of who God is. "For I am God, and not man, the Holy One in your midst... I will be your King, the Lord God of hosts." So, as King of the Universe, there's nobody higher, and so therefore God possesses ALL authority.

Second, Hosea reveals God's power is supreme. Yahweh has all knowledge and power. Nothing is hidden from God, for He sees all. Nothing—nothing—can stand against God's might!

Third, because of God's holiness and sovereign position, He invariably holds the only right to judge us. God's decision to end the kingdom of Israel was indisputable, for God reigns supreme (1:4,5; 4:6; 5:3; 7:2; 11:9; 12:2,5,9; 13:4,10).

**Just.** The heart of God is just. Not only is God a loving God, but He is also a just sovereign. Hosea revealed that God rules with righteousness and justice because the ways of the Lord are right. What a blessing! For every evil committed, every wrong deed done, every injustice that escapes man's earthly justice, the Righteous Judge will deal with each in fairness, either in the present or at time's end during the Great White Throne Judgment (Revelation 20:11-15).

At least 35 judgments are stated within the book of Hosea, too many to list here, but they pour forth justice for the wrongs Israel committed against God and His universal moral law by their refusal to repent. "My God will cast them away, because they did not obey Him; and they shall be wanderers among the nations." And, God did just that. By 722 BC, within Hosea's own lifetime, God had allowed the Assyrian King Sargon to conquer and carry off Israel into exile (2 Kings 17:24). Foreigners were brought in to settle in Israel's abandoned homes. The Northern Kingdom of Israel was destroyed and its people forced to become wanderers among the nations, exactly as God warned Hosea would happen. Many believe God to be an impotent judge, but He's only being patient, for judgment inevitably comes as swiftly and destructively as a Category 5 hurricane (1:4; 2:13,19; 3:4; 6:5; 9:3,9,17; 10:2; 14:1,9; 2 Peter 3:9).

**Forgiving.** The heart of God is forgiving. If only Israel had heeded Hosea's messages by asking for forgiveness and repenting of their rebellion and other evil deeds, God would have been merciful. Loving-kindness and mercy are at the heart of our Heavenly Father. The Righteous Judge declared, "I will have mercy on her who had not obtained mercy." If Israel would have repented, God promised, "I would have healed Israel" (1:7; 2:19,25; 3:5; 6:6; 7:1).

**Saving.** The heart of God saves. God's mercy towards Israel has not been extinguished, even to this day, for He promised His people: "Then the children of Judah and the children of Israel shall be gathered together, and appoint for themselves one head; and they shall come up out of the land." In that future day, God will turn His anger away and the "fatherless" people of Israel will be regathered back in the Promised Land to proclaim, "For in You the fatherless find mercy." This very day, we are first-hand witnesses of the beginnings of that promised time of mercy, for the Lord God declared with total absoluteness, "For there is no savior besides Me." God alone saves (1:7,11; 2:1,17-18; 13:4,14; 14:3-4; 6:1).

34

**Generous.** The heart of God is generous. When one is restored to a right relationship with God, they are continually bathed in His generosity. When a believing remnant of Israel is fully restored to Yahweh and the Holy Land once more, "O Judah, a harvest is appointed for you, when I return the captives of My people." No longer will Israel be under constant attack by world powers, for God will make them lie down safely, for God will be refreshing "like the dew to Israel." When God's Son, Jesus Christ, returns to set up His Kingdom on earth, great will be the day for those who have accepted Him as Savior! "The earth shall answer with grain, with new wine, and with oil." A believing remnant of Israel will finally dwell in their houses in peace and safety (1:10-11; 2:18,22; 6:11; 14:5).

# HOSEA'S FAITH LESSONS

The book of Hosea offers invaluable life lessons concerning how to maintain faith when the heart is shattered. These lessons can be applied to four groups: Israel, the Nations, the Church, and you personally.

## Lessons for Israel

The nation of Israel today can maintain faith when its heart is shattered. For many Jews who've made *aliyah* back to the land of Israel, they continue to feel the sting of the nations raging against them. In their dismay they wonder why the Jews over the centuries have been so hated. It just seems so illogical. And so, they wonder if God has totally abandoned them.[7]

Israel must realize that God continues to see their nation as a wayward wife, like Gomer, who broke her covenant relationship. The modern day nation of Israel continues to lack the very faithfulness, devotion and knowledge of God which condemned her in Hosea's time. Every day Jews are coming out of exile and back to the Holy Land just as the prophets said they would, but the nation remains wholly uncommitted to God. It wavers suspended in that purification time Hosea described before she can be reunited with her husband (3:3-5). Though Israel was reborn as a nation on May 14, 1948, she awaits that glorious day when God will move her to have a heart that will truly and fully love Him once more.

And what a day that will be! Hosea described that future day, the "latter days" as he called them, when the nation of Israel will be once again reconciled to God and remain faithful to their covenant: "Afterward the children of Israel shall return and seek the Lord their God and David their king. They shall fear the Lord and His goodness in the latter days" (3:5). No longer rebellious, they'll know the ways of the Lord are right and walk righteously in them. They shall love the Lord, pursue the knowledge of the Lord, prosper in His goodness, and finally understand how to keep His covenant.

Once redeemed and restored to a right relationship with Yahweh God, Israel in these not-so-distant days Hosea so colorfully describes will have God's love lavished upon them once more. They'll know joy, for "she shall sing there in their land as in the days of her youth." True safety will finally exist, for Israel will "lie down safely" and "live in His sight." Spiritual growth will define them, for the people of Israel will "grow like the lily," "lengthening her roots" and their "branches shall spread." Israel will be a thing of beauty to the whole world, like a fragrance whose "scent shall be like wine" (1:11; 2:15,18; 3:5; 6:2; 14:1,5-7,9).

By embracing Israel's promised, glorious and soon to be realized future, the nation of Israel today can survive the shattering and place their faith in their God.

## Lessons for the Nations

The nations of today can maintain faith when their collective hearts are shattered by natural disasters, wars, financial problems, social unrest and other traumas. Hosea gives no comfort when reminding the nations that their days are numbered. No matter how powerful or successful, or how many centuries a nation has stayed on top, God's prophetic word reveals that all human nations are in rebellion against Him and so will not last. One day human government will be supplanted by the coming Kingdom of Jesus Christ, and the nations as we know them today will cease to be. As long as the nations remain in rebellion, so too will they continue to experience a shattering.

But, citizens of the nations can have hope by becoming citizens of a kingdom not of this world—the spiritual kingdom Jesus now reigns, culminating in the day when He will return to set up His Millennial Kingdom here on earth. They can embrace that eternal citizenship and the hope that brings by accepting King Jesus as Savior.

## Lessons for the Church

The Church can maintain faith when its heart is shattered by external persecutions and inward troubles. While God in the book of Hosea compares Himself to a groom and Israel to a bride, so too does His Son, Jesus Christ, compares Himself to a groom and the Church to a bride. The Church is, as Ephesians 5:22-33 explains, the universal body of believers who have accepted Jesus as Savior, from the day of Pentecost up until the coming day when the Church is raptured up to Heaven. This special group of believers, which if Jesus is your Savior you belong to, are set aside by Him and for Him, like a bride is for a groom.

Knowing this, Hosea would warn that we must be very careful that in our privileged position of redemption we not grow proud and self-reliant. Doing so will cause the Church to fall into the same trap as Israel did when they forgot God's sustaining hand and believed they could cut themselves off from the power that sustained them.

Church brethren, remember your condition when you were saved. Heed the command of Jesus in John 8:11 to the woman caught in adultery: "Go and sin no more." Never forget how terribly low we had once fallen, and only through salvation in Christ how we are now lifted up to such incredibly new heights. Only when the

Church is fully connected to our Lord can it maintain its faith and effectively do the Good Work as a messenger bearing Good News.

## Lessons for You

You can remain faithful to your Heavenly Father when your own heart is shattered and all hope seems lost. To understand how, let's look at the broken heart as if it was a physical condition. When your body gets hurt, you go to the doctor, right? The doctor then performs two actions: 1) discerns the problem, and 2) prescribes a cure.

So, first, let's discern the problem. God and Hosea both suffered because of what was done to them, but in contrast, Israel and Gomer both suffered because of what they did to themselves. In all cases, though, the underlying cause of all their suffering was a disease most today loath to even whisper—SIN. Sin is the problem. Sin erodes the foundation of your faith until nothing more is left than a few grains of sand. Sin tears, it washes away, it shatters your heart and all the hearts of those your sin collides against.

Now, let's prescribe the cure. Hosea teaches us the cure to healing both our broken heart and our tattered faith is the restoration of the relationship back to its former mutually loving and trusting condition. That is accomplished through our repenting of our sins and by God granting forgiveness, which is called reconciliation.

Once reconciled, great will be the day of your salvation! Hosea compares it to passing through a door of hope. We are promised by God that mercy will be shown. "And I will have mercy on her who had not obtained mercy." Forgiveness will be granted, made possible through Jesus' sacrifice which He bought at the cost of His own life. We are restored into a mutually loving and trusting condition with God. The relationship transforms from enmity to affinity. We become sons of the living God whom He calls "My people." As God promises, "And it shall be in that day you will call

Me 'My Husband,' and no longer call Me 'My Master'" (1:10-11; 2:1,15-16,20; 3:2).

Maybe, like Hosea, you are going through a painful marriage ordeal that challenges you to maintain your faith in God. Maybe you find yourself in the same disastrous marriage as Hosea and Gomer had which was battered by unfaithfulness and failed trust, leaving your heart broken and shattered. If that is the case, look to how both God and Hosea handled it. Remember that as faithless as Gomer was, no matter how badly she betrayed Hosea, Hosea remained faithful and loving to her. Likewise, Jesus Christ has always remained faithful and loving to you and is ready to forgive any lack of faith.

When it comes to marriage, remain as faithful as Hosea was, even if you are in a terribly difficult situation. Show God's unconditional love to your spouse no matter what. When others are faithless, you remain faithful and committed, just like your Heavenly Father. Wait patiently and expectantly for when God restores the shattered heart, for when faith is restored, the blessings will follow.

## QUESTIONS FOR DISCUSSION

1.  Do you know people who are like the faithless Gomer? Can you see yourself in her at all?

2.  Do you know people who are like Hosea, who remain faithful even through the worst of trials?

3.  What lengths did Hosea go to restore Gomer?

4.  What lengths did God go to restore Israel to Himself?

5.  What lengths has God gone to restore you to Himself?

6.  Have you asked God to put the pieces of your life back together again by asking for that new life in Jesus Christ?

7.  Could you live your life as faithfully as Hosea, even doing the seemingly impossible when God asks? How so?

8.  If you have accepted Jesus as Savior, what joys have you experienced since?

9.  How do you maintain faith when your heart is shattered?

# FAITH JOURNEY 2
## JOEL: FAITH THROUGH DEVASTATING LOSS

## THE WHIRLWIND

The young woman stood just outside the door of her little farmhouse, hand to forehead to shield her eyes from the gathering morning light. She was scanning the horizon, looking for her husband's familiar form. "Ah, there you are." she said to herself, recognizing the silhouette of the man she loved located deep in the heart of their sprawling wheat field. She watched him walking softly along the workman's path so as not to snap any of the fully grown stalks, flattening his hands to his sides in order to feel the wheat heads slide gently across his palms. His chest swelled as he inhaled deeply, savoring the richness of the summer harvest's aroma. Then he stopped, stood perfectly still, and soaked in the satisfying feeling of victory over long months of back-breaking work. The pride she felt in her husband lit up her face like the rays of the sun.

Knowing he'd likely be out there for quite a while reveling in the wonders of it all, the farmer's wife let out a small sigh, called her two rambunctious preschoolers to her side, and headed out to share in the experience. As she approached his position, the squeal of the children's laughter as they skipped down the path drew him out of his revelry. He turned to behold his loving bride eagerly approaching and returned her smile with equal warmth. Once together, his arm slipped around her petite waist and she rested her head upon his shoulder. The beauty of the morning coupled with the warm feeling of accomplishment added to the excitement of the harvest day ahead. With no possible words to express how content they were, the pair simply remained silent and watchful. Even the little ones appeared subdued as they beheld the growing sun redden their amber fields.

It was the older of the two children who first noticed it. Holding up a chubby little finger, he pointed at what appeared to be a tiny black cloud forming along the sun's lower radius and questioned his papa if rain was coming. With one eye buried by his wife's long hair, the farmer peered out of the remaining eye at the approaching cloud. No, the sky the last few days showed rain wasn't to be expected. That's why he'd picked this day to start the harvest. Curiosity snapped the family out of the revelry they'd all been enjoying. As the cloud swelled in speed and size, curiosity transformed into concern. And, when the cloud changed direction suddenly and eerily morphed its shape, concern was abandoned to sheer panic. Hurriedly scooping up a child in each arm and hastily pressing his wife back down the path, the farmer cried out, "Run! Now! Back to the house."

Only once they were ensconced in the farmhouse, door secured and sheets pulled over the window openings, did the couple dare to catch their breath. The children whimpered quietly, unsettled by their father's sudden alarm. Then they heard a sound that would haunt their dreams all of their remaining years. At first the noise started out as a distant hum, but as the light outside dimmed, the louder and more distinctive the sound became. The increasingly deafening noise chittered away like the upending of ten thousand rain sticks combined with the beating of a million hummingbird wings. When the din reached full cacophony, a dreadful chewing sound blended into the terrible mix to create a nightmarish roar.

The farmer leapt off the dirt floor where he was comforting his family and threw open the door. "No! No! No!" he yelled over and over again at the black cloud. It was pouring out of the sky and down into his wheat field like a waterfall that would never run dry. His wife shrieked in terror behind him. Whirling around, the farmer saw his wife clutching at her long hair as brown lumps tumbled down upon her through a hole in the ceiling. Frantically she used both hands to rake them off her head. Her children stomped on the chitinous masses, producing a sickening, crunching sound. The farmer despaired as he returned his attention back outside at a morning that had turned as murky as dusk. The worst fear of all those who worked the land had just came true—a locust invasion.

The farmer burst out the door, slamming it behind him to his wife's pleadings of, "Don't go!" He had to do something, anything, to save an entire season's worth of work. The locusts' voracious appetite would destroy months of labor in just mere hours. After that, his family would starve.

The scene was the stuff of nightmares. Everything was covered in a tide of movement. Not one plant, one tree, or one shrub was visible. Millions of empty, black eyes stared up at him as they hungrily consumed everything with their clacking mandibles. Neighbors in the distance were setting fires in the hopes that the smoke would drive the insect plague away, but the black tide continued to deluge out of the sky. The farmer's wife was out now as well, running back and forth and crying hysterically as she waved a sheet to disperse the swarm, only to have the locusts roll back in behind her like a river.

For an eternal hour the exhausted, despairing couple battled the swarm with sticks and fire, and lost. Once drained of all energy, the pair fell sobbing into each other's arms amidst the stripped and burnt remains of their harvest field.

Tear-filled eyes almost caused the couple to miss the peculiar change in the movement of the swarm. Spinning down the lane towards their house appeared to be a... tornado? To their utter surprise, the vortex wasn't made of wind, but a swirling storm of locusts. The farmer's wife let out a gasp when she realized that within the eye of the storm strode a lone man. Just as odd, not one insect dared land upon him. They moved out of his way as if he were on fire. Adding to the bizarre scene, a bedraggled crowd of neighbors

*and town elders, men staggering around like drunks, and towns-
people whom they'd never encountered before followed in the
tornado's wake.*

*As the freak of nature approached, out of the funnel a
powerful voice boomed out to all those it passed. "Blow the trumpet
in Zion, and sound an alarm in my holy mountain! Let all the
inhabitants of the land tremble; for the day of the Lord is at hand."
The mystery man bellowed on, "Consecrate a fast, call a sacred
assembly; gather the elders and all the inhabitants of the land into
the house of the Lord your God, and cry out to the Lord!"*

*Defeated and now destitute, there was only one thing left for
the stricken farmers to do—obey. The young couple gathered their
sniffling children, left the ravages that was their life behind them,
and joined in the line of people shuffling wearily after the whirlwind.*

## WHERE WAS GOD THE DAY SHE LOST EVERYTHING?

The six-man rescue team sifted through the debris of the
neighborhood assigned to them, searching for any sign of life. There
was little hope. The place looked like a bomb had gone off. The
wreckage appeared eerily reminiscent of scenes from old pictures
which depicted the blasted remains of Hiroshima and Nagasaki by
atomic weaponry. There was nothing man-made about this bomb,
though the damage had been made just as swiftly as if by an atomic
weapon. The cause of this destruction—a tsunami created by the
most powerful earthquake ever known to hit Japan.

On March 11, 2011, a staggering 9.0 magnitude earthquake
erupted under the Pacific Ocean, becoming the fifth most powerful
earthquake in recorded history.[1] The resulting 133 foot high tidal
wave of water crashed down upon northeastern Japan, instantly
erasing whole towns before washing everything—buildings, boats,
houses, livestock and people—all out to sea. After the water
receded, full-scale rescue and relief efforts descended upon the
devastated areas, only to discover an almost hopeless situation.

Relief workers reported back that nearly 130,000 buildings had totally collapsed and more than 690,000 buildings lay partially damaged. At a total of $235 billion dollars in damages, this was the most expensive disaster ever recorded. But, as bad as the property damage was, it was nothing compared to the death toll. The final number was 15,854 dead, with 27,000 injuries, and over 3,000 people missing due to being buried in mud or washed out into the Pacific Ocean.[2]

And yet, amidst all the death, destruction and supposed futility of searching for survivors, a little story of hope shone through this chaos. One of the rescue teams working to carefully remove a pile of debris discovered a young woman buried underneath. The men hastened to dig her out, throwing household wreckage left and right. Once they reached her, though, their enthusiasm drained away. The medic on the team announced what they all had expected, that she was dead. But, as they rolled the dead woman over, the rescuers were surprised to find secure in her lifeless arms a three-month old baby boy wrapped in a flowery blanket. The mother had paid the ultimate sacrifice—her life—in order to shield her son's little body with her own from the brunt of a collapsing house.

Then the baby cooed! To the amazement of the team, the little boy was still alive. He'd been sleeping peacefully somehow under his dead mother's body throughout the whole deluge. While the medic examined the baby and was relieved to see he was unharmed, a cell phone tucked inside his blanket with him slipped out. Curious, the medic activated it and discovered a text message still alight on the screen. After reading it he began to cry. He then passed the phone on to his fellow teammates. As the phone went from one rescuer's hand to another to another, the tears flowed freely down their cheeks. The mother's final message to her baby boy read, "If you can survive, you must remember that I love you." The men could only weep silently over the mother's love for her child.[3]

If there was even one man who believed in God on that team, they would have had to have been asking, "Where was God the day she lost everything?" Certainly the world was asking that very question as the news reports began to filter in over television and the Internet. Horrible pictures of dead bodies intertwined with the shattered remains of houses floating out into the Pacific Ocean made their way onto our screens. Videos captured by people trapped on top of sinking buildings and from inside submerging cars recorded the tales of many who did not live long past uploading their files to YouTube. The whole world could at some basic level share in the experience of living through one of the worst disasters in human history. The destruction, the desolation, the death, the loss, and the hopelessness of it could only truly be felt by those who were suffering. And yet, in this high-tech society in which we live today, the whole world was struck at some level by the shared horror of it all.

Like those people in Japan, maybe you also have suffered during your lifetime a devastating loss, or are even now suffering through one. When we suffer a devastating loss such as a death of a close family member, a bitter divorce, destruction of property, declining health, financial ruin, betrayal by a best friend and so on, we cannot help but wonder why God did not prevent the loss in the first place. We ask ourselves, "Why me?" Or, "Why didn't God stop it?" Or, "Where was God while it was happening?" Feeling neglected and abandoned, we can experience a hurt so deep that our faith in God is stretched to the point of snapping. For those whose faith has already snapped, the rage and bitterness they feel towards God becomes yet another devastating loss for them that lasts potentially for an eternity.

How then do we maintain faith in God through a devastating loss? The answer can be found in a little three chapter book from the Old Testament written by the Minor Prophet Joel.

# THE PROPHET AT THE CENTER OF A WHIRLWIND

## Time of the Prophet

Joel, the second in order of the books of the Minor Prophets, was a prophet of Yahweh God who lived during the time of…? Well, we don't know. Joel doesn't say. He mentions no king to give his readers any frame of reference. Because the Hebrew ordering of the books of the Bible puts Joel's message between Hosea and Amos, an early date of about 835-796 BC is suggested.[4] That date would place Joel's time period during the reign of the boy King Joash of Judah, about 160 years after King Solomon dedicated the Temple back in 960 B.C. The enemies Joel lists—the Philistines, Phoenicians, Egyptians and Edomites, with no reference to the Assyrians or Babylonians—also gives credence to a traditional early date.

Other historians would place Joel much later during the 400's BC, just after the Jews returned from captivity in Babylon.[5] Support for this later date recognizes that since the Northern Kingdom of Israel is not mentioned that it must have no longer existed. Joel also points out a plundering of the Temple, a people scattered, Jews having been sold off as slaves to the Greeks, and nobody practicing idolatry any longer, all of which would have been related to an exile (3:2,5,6). Some 27 out of the 73 verses that comprise the book of Joel parallel other prophets in their writings. And so, there's strong evidence for a late date.

Early date or late date? In Joel's mind timing was totally unimportant to his narrative. Joel lived during one of the most devastating agricultural and financial losses in all of Judah's history, and that's all that mattered to him. He was laser focused on the disaster at hand, and not on establishing when he fit into history's timeline.

## Construction of a Prophet

"The word of the Lord that came to Joel the son of Pethuel." This is how Joel 1:1 begins, and this is all that Joel left us about himself personally. Joel did give us his name which means "Yahweh is God." He also gave us his father's name Pethuel, or Bethuel in the Greek, which means "Persuaded by God." We can go to other books in the Bible and find 12 other men who shared Joel's name, but context shows they were clearly not this Minor Prophet.

The reading of Joel's messages provide clues which help us discern Joel's occupation. He was quite knowledgeable about the Temple and its worship programs. In Joel's first chapter he even led the people in prayer just as a priest would. So, maybe Pethuel had been "persuaded by God" to dedicate his young son into the priesthood.

Because Joel added some of his own suggestions to the messages God sent him to give to the people of Judah and Jerusalem, we can learn something about his personality. He was pious and godly, hating sin but loving the sinner. He was a bold and courageous preacher, literally letting no disaster stop him from getting God's message out. He obeyed God. He loved his people and wanted what was best for them all. In the capacity of a priest, he acted as an intercessor, seeking reconciliation between the Heavenly Father and His earthly children. His colorful writings show a deep heart and a faith in God that withstood any devastating loss. To his very soul, Joel was a man of deep faith. And, as we shall see, he probably wasn't afraid of bugs either, but that's just a guess!

## Call of the Prophet

Joel the prophet found his calling rather on-the-spot. There was no warning by God. He wasn't prepped ahead of time. When the swarm of locusts descended upon Judah, there was no time to even think. Disaster had come in the form of a locust invasion, and with it God's message of judgment, repentance and salvation.

Disaster is often like that. It comes suddenly and with little warning. Disaster barges into our lives and demands we drop everything and deal with it at that very moment. Disaster could care less about our plans. It mocks our aspirations. It seeks to crush our dreams. For many it requires the ultimate sacrifice. Disaster feels like the most selfish of events.

"Joel, are you my messenger or not?" God may have asked. Joel had to decide right then and there in the flash of a moment. He chose to obey.

Why were locusts such a terror to Joel's people? How could a bunch of grasshopper-like insects, that according to *National Geographic* are a mere half to three inches long and weigh a scant 0.07 ounces, present a real threat?[6] That's because just one locust or even fifty are not a threat. The true danger with locusts lie when exceptional environmental conditions produce lush foliage and excellent breeding conditions. Plentiful amounts of females will then dig little four inch holes and lay anywhere from 65,000 to 75,000 eggs concentrated in just a single square meter of soil![7]

After all these insects hatch, they then grow through four stages. Joel actually named them, for each stage causes a different types of devastation which combined left no scrap of plant in all of Judah. The young larval stage (Hebrew *yeleq*) creeps and hops along the ground because they haven't yet developed flight. The second nymph stage (Hebrew *gazam*) strip and cut the foliage down. The third adolescent stage (Hebrew *chasil*) gnaw away on every kind of plant. The fourth and final stage (Hebrew *arbeh*) are the great locusts of the adult stage.[8] These four life cycle stages of the locust when acting together combine into what Joel compared to as a great army (1:6; 2:4-5,25). This army of war horses rumble along like chariots and sound like the crackling of fire as they devour their prey with fangs fierce as a lion's. Crawling and swarming about, the army consumes every plant in sight, even the stubble.

When locusts get overcrowded they reach what's called the gregarious phase. The insects sort of go crazy and become driven by impulse to congregate into a thick, mobile, ravenous swarm whose mission it is to gorge themselves on every bit of vegetation in its path. Swarms of locusts have been known to cover 460 square miles in size and pack anywhere from 40 to 80 million locusts into less than half a square mile. Each locust eats its weight in plants daily, meaning a swarm could consume 423 million pounds of plants. [9] That's every single day!

Hundreds of years before Joel, back in Moses' day, God had punished the Egyptians with ten plagues to force them to free their Hebrew slaves. One of those plagues was by locusts, and it was terrifying. Exodus 10:15 describes the horror of a locust swarm:

> *"For they covered the face of the whole earth, so that the land was darkened; and they ate every herb of the land and all the fruit of the trees which the hail had left. So there remained nothing green on the trees or on the plants of the field throughout all the land of Egypt."*

When a locust invasion arrives to greedily devour everything in sight in a mere matter of hours, there's no stopping it. All hope is lost. But, such devastation provides a unique opportunity. As one commentator explained, "It was a tragic hour. Men were desperate in their plight and ready to listen to God's messenger as he interpreted the divine will. It was a great hour for the preacher."[10] Out of the hopelessness of stopping a locust invasion and the devastating loss it causes, with God's people facing starvation and a monumental crisis of faith, Joel found his calling as a prophet.

## A DEVASTATED PEOPLE

The world looked like it was coming to an end! One can only imagine what Joel could have been thinking, but surely it was something like this. He'd stepped out of the quiet protection of the Temple into a world plunged into utter chaos.

From the lofty heights of the Temple Mount, God's newly appointed prophet could only have gasped in dismay as he scanned the hills and valleys surrounding Jerusalem. The day was young, but the sky was black and convulsing, as was the ground. Armored locusts poured out of the air and onto the earth as if hail from a thunderstorm. The landscape crawled and churned with an unnatural movement. Frightened people and animals ran to and fro, shrieking and swatting off the insects skittering all over them. A deafening, chittering, crunching sound echoed off the hillsides. Fire barriers dotted the landscape as smoke billowing up into the sky, forming a temporary void in the onslaught of insects. The smoky air was permeated by the putrid stench of crushed bugs.

One can imagine the smoke would have given Joel an idea. His wits finally collected, God's prophet pulled down one of the massive torches used for lighting the sacrifices. Using the fire and smoke of the torch to blaze a path through the frenzy, Joel could then wade into the maelstrom. To avoid the fire the locusts would have swirled around him as if he were the eye of a tornado.

It was time to collect the battered people and get them quickly to the safety of the Temple. Joel's first destination was the gate where Jerusalem's elders held court. The city's leaders were hunkered down together in a cluster by the gateway, their robes pulled up over their heads for protection. Joel began yelling out to them from the center of the storm with this question, "Hear this, you elders! Has anything like this happened in your days, or even in the days of your fathers?" (1:2-4). From under the protection of their cloaks they replied with a muffled, "Never." Drawn out of their makeshift shelters by the spectacle and the authority of the prophet's voice, the elders heeded Joel's next command to help gather the people behind him.

Once they started to walk on together, Joel was anticipating a message from God that would condemn whatever sins the elders must have committed that surely brought about this disaster. To the prophet's surprise, there was no message of condemnation. To the leadership God had only this addition command, "Tell your children about it, let your children tell their children, and their children another generation" (1:3).

Joel's second destination was the taverns of the merchant district. Scores of men had flocked there to find temporary escape by drowning their sorrows in booze, only to find their bottles empty or their flasks swimming with half-drown locusts. The prophet thought that surely it was the people's drunkenness that had caused this plague. Again, to Joel's surprise, that wasn't the reason. God had His messenger instead call out, "Awake, you drunkards, and weep; and wail, all you drinkers of wine, because of the new wine, for it has been cut off from your mouth" (1:5-10). Realizing that whatever alcohol was left couldn't be replaced because the vineyards this year certainly would not be producing any grapes, the town drunks got off their bar stools and fell into procession behind Joel and the elders.

Joel exited the city out of one of the town's gates and headed down the road towards his third destination—the farmers who dwelled in the valleys. What he saw was a pitiful sight. Exhausted men and women sat in the ashes of their once fruitful fields, sorrowfully ripping their burned and bug-gut drenched clothing in defeat. Because their pastures were decimated, the cattle and sheep groaned pitifully. "Maybe they'd fallen into idolatry again, calling on idols like Baal to help produce their crops?" the prophet must have wondered as to the cause of the plague. After all, the punishment seemed directed at the farmers in particular. But, no, that wasn't it either. God instead had a lament for Joel to share with them. "The harvest of the field has perished. Surely joy has withered away from the sons of men" (1:11-12). With not a scrap of food left to save, the farmers fell in procession behind the whirlwind.

Long hours later, Joel ended his circuit, having returned to the Temple with his mass of followers. There he found the priests rocking on their knees and reciting prayers. It hadn't taken long for them to realize that with the destruction of the harvest there would be no grain and drink offerings to present to the Lord. "Well, then, my fellow priests must be at fault for this calamity. Maybe we haven't been devout enough?" the prophet despaired. To his relief, Yahweh said no. God instead ordered Joel to get the priests working to usher the people into the asylum of His house.

To the watchmen Joel yelled, "Blow the trumpet in Zion, and sound an alarm in My holy mountain!" (2:1). The shofars bellowed out their sonorous calls. To others he commanded, "Consecrate a fast. Call a sacred assembly. Gather all the inhabitants of the land into the house of the Lord your God, and cry out to the Lord!" (1:13-14). To the terrible, heartbreaking sound of the masses wailing in grief, the priests pressed the weary people into God's embrace.

## THE CHARACTER OF GOD

Once the people of Judah had been collected into the Temple courtyards and settled down, God let His prophet know that it was finally time to present His messages. From these three messages the people's faith in God would be tested as they learned the true character of their Heavenly Father.

We can imagine that as Joel looked out over the huddled crowd, what he saw must have broken his heart. He could actually feel the heavy burden of their pain from their devastating losses permeating the room. The people's new-found poverty and panicky fear of starvation had brought them to the brink of despair. They were tearfully crying out, "Why, God, why?" and "Where were you when I lost everything?"

# Lesson 1: God Will Use Disaster to Get People's Attention

Looking out over the crowd, a realization dawned on Joel. In the course of his priestly duties, he'd never once seen any of these people set foot in the Temple. Clearly then they had no interest in knowing God and so had been neglecting their relationship with their Heavenly Father. That, Joel understood, was yet another tragedy these people had been enduring. They'd willingly given up the opportunity to truly experience God's love and forgiveness. Tragic!

A second realization caused the prophet to shiver. These people would never have come to hear God's messages had this disaster not happened. Did that mean God had actually instigated this plague in order to gather His people to the Temple to listen to His prophet? No, surely this disaster was a coincidence of nature, right? Joel's heart told him otherwise. God was risking that if it was revealed He was the one behind His own people's anguish that knowledge would damage and even end whatever relationship they may have had with Him.

How could Joel explain that it was God Himself who had caused their suffering? It was time for him to share these new insights with the people, but it surely wouldn't be a popular message. The prophet needn't worry about defending God, though, for Yahweh Himself was more than ready to go right ahead and take full responsibility for the calamity.

Found in chapter 2 verses 1-11, God directed Joel in his colorfully descriptive way to paint a mental picture of the locust swarm as an invading army, and army so great and strong and disciplined that no opposing force could hope to stop its advancement. The army moved as swiftly as a wildfire. If the land was as fertile as the Garden of Eden, by the time the infantry crossed, it'd be a desolate wilderness. The earth quaked and the heavens trembled before its onslaught. In response, the people gasped at the comparison, for it perfectly described the horror they'd just experienced that day.

And then the boom fell. God directed Joel to cry out, "The Lord gives voice before His army, for His camp is very great; for strong is the One who executes His word. For the day of the Lord is great and very terrible; who can endure it?" (2:11). One could image the look of shock and pain on the people's faces. So, it was true. God was behind their suffering. He was the cause of it all. Or, was He?

There was no denying that God was indeed behind the plague that had inflicted the people of Judah, but He didn't cause this disaster without reason. In chapter 2 verses 12-17, Yahweh confirmed Joel's realization—the people had grown apathetic in their relationship with Him. They had relegated their Heavenly Father to the backburners of their lives. He didn't matter to them anymore. The business of daily living made them forget God's continual goodness and guiding hand of protection. They'd neglected the single most important person in all their lives, and they were spiritually dying on the inside for it. God couldn't let this damaged relationship go on any further, and so intervened in the only method that would shake these people out of their lethargy— disaster. The tactic had worked very well.

"'Now, therefore,' says the Lord, 'Turn to Me with all your heart, with fasting, with weeping, and with mourning'" (2:12). Joel remembered what God through King Solomon promised all those decades ago in 2 Chronicles 7:14, "If My people who are called by My name will humble themselves, and pray and seek My face, and turn from their wicked ways, then I will hear from heaven, and will forgive their sin and heal their land." Joel added his own advice, "So rend your heart, and not your garments; return to the Lord your God, for He is gracious and merciful, slow to anger, and of great kindness; and He relents from doing harm" (2:12-13).

God wasn't looking for "no washing of the outside of the cup affair," as one commentator so colorfully described concerning that era's practice of ripping one's clothes as an outward expression of grief.[11] No, God was seeking a truly inward, genuine, heartfelt repentance from His people for breaking their relationship with Him. They were to, as one pastor wrote, "understand that the Lord looks for far more than external signs of sorrow over sin. His eyes penetrate right through to the heart of reality. He listens for the ring of truth in our profession of repentance."[12] God was looking for real faith in the midst of crisis, and a heartfelt sorrow that embodies the hallmark of true repentance.

## Lesson 2: After True Repentance, God's Blessings Flow

As the Apostle John would write centuries later in 1 John 1:9, "If we confess our sins, He is faithful and just to forgive us our sins and to cleanse us from all unrighteousness." And that's what the people huddled there in the Temple must have done—rended their hearts—for God's next message was all about the gracious outpouring of His love towards His faithful and penitent people.

God in Joel 2:18-32 and 3:17-21 made some amazing promises. He first promised to be zealous for His land by recalling the locusts. He would then be sending Judah grain and new wine and oil to replace what the insects had consumed. The dry period they were also experiencing would end with gentle rains. The lost years of food would be restored and the people would know nothing but plenty. A time of great rejoicing would replace the people's great sorrow, and it would come without delay. Maintaining faith granted the people hope of better times ahead.

With Judah's material losses covered, God then promised in Joel 2:28-32 something even more wonderful—spiritual riches by the outpouring of His Spirit. Because the people actually responded in faith and repentance, the barriers between God and man would be lowered. A much better relationship would now be possible. Judah's people would know God's love in a personal way like no other nation. And, the faith of this group of penitent people demonstrated in Joel's time would serve as an example for a people still yet to be born.

Joel could only have been staggered by the prophetic vision God was giving him as He extended the prophetic telescope down through time. Did God actually show Joel a glimpse of a day hundreds of years later when the Church would be born? Acts 2 records the birth of the Church on the Day of Pentecost, when the resurrected Jesus sent the Holy Spirit down to His followers to indwell them with His power. With a sound from heaven of a rushing mighty wind, the Apostles were given the Holy Spirit. From that amazing day until our day nearly 2,000 years later, those who respond by faith in God's Son, Jesus Christ, and in repentance accept Him as Savior would be redeemed. They too would be given the Holy Spirit to guide them. On Pentecost, God lowered even further the barrier that separates God and Man.

The Apostle Peter on that great day of Pentecost confirmed in Acts 2:17-21 that what God had revealed to Joel about spiritual blessings being poured out by the Holy Spirit had found its fulfillment. Whoever calls on the name of the Lord Jesus Christ shall be saved and be granted the indwelling of the Holy Spirit. The saving work of Christ would provide spiritual blessings for all of His people throughout the life of the Church. And then, when the last days of the Church's work on this earth had finally come, the Holy Spirit would pour out His power in even greater amounts. Young and old, women and men, will all receive amazing prophecies, dreams and visions as proof of His saving work "before the coming of the great and awesome day of the Lord" (2:28-32).

How could Joel possibly understand just how long-term God's prophecies were for extending His blessings down through the ages? For God wasn't just talking about just blessing those faithful Jews in Joel's day, but all faithful Jews and Gentiles in the millenniums to come.

## Lesson 3: Final Judgment of the Unrepentant on the Day of the Lord

God was now going to in this next and final prophecy address the unrepentant. If only the prophet could have fully understood just how much road the Jewish people would have to travel over the centuries for this prophecy to find final fulfillment, his mind truly would have been blown! God was about to introduce the world to a new concept—the Day of the Lord.

The horrific encounter by an unstoppable insect invasion which Judah had endured would become an object lesson God would use for centuries to come. Since the prophet penned his prophecies in his book, people have been able to read Joel 2:1-11 and 3:1-17 and the writings of other Minor Prophets such as Amos, Zephaniah and Malachi and compare the devastating losses from the locust invasion Judah endured to a future period of catastrophic judgment.

Also called "The Day of Yahweh," this final end time judgment by God has been defined as "a day in which [Yahweh] will break silence and intervene in history to judge both Israel and the gentile nations."[13] The Apostle Paul would later in Acts 17:30-31 describe this judgment day as the time when God would "judge the world in righteousness by the Man whom He has ordained," that Man being Jesus Christ. "He has given assurance of this to all by raising Him [Christ] from the dead." Another commentator compared this final judgment to "like waters collecting behind a great dam, God's wrath has been gathering and increasing as it awaits the day when it will be released in fury against individuals and nations."[14] The world identifies this coming time of God's wrath in literature and movies as Judgment Day, the End of the World, the Tribulation, and Armageddon.

When will the Day of the Lord come? Joel tells us it'll be when the "captives of Judah and Jerusalem"—the Jewish people who since 70 AD have been dispersed throughout the world—are fully regathered back into the land of Israel (3:1). Joel prophesied that while the Jews would be scattered among the nations, they'd never be forgotten by God. Yahweh would certainly regather the Children of Israel back into the Land He promised them. The Jews have been regathering as a people since the late 1800s to become the nation of Israel once more, officially in May of 1948. We today are the generation seeing this prophecy in the process of being fulfilled right before our very eyes!

God provides two main reasons why He will gather all the nations of the world together for judgment in the Valley of Jehoshaphat. For this Valley of Decision is, as translated, "where the Lord judges."

The first of the two main reasons God gives is due to how the world has mistreated the Jewish people, whom He tenderly calls "My people" and "My heritage Israel" (3:2). All throughout the past 1,900 years while the Jews have been in exile, they've been mistreated as outcasts.

The second reason pertains to the world's obsession with trying to divide up God's Holy Land. God promised those weary people huddled in the Temple, driven by calamity to hear His messages, that His blessings would extend so far as "Judah shall abide forever, and Jerusalem from generation to generation" (3:20). The world over the centuries has tried to thwart these blessings from God by mistreating the Jews and their spiritual children, the Church, and trying to steal their promised land. God admits He's not been happy about it.

As an example of those who try to prevent God's blessings, Joel uses Judah's national enemies at that time. Tyre and Sidon (today's Lebanon) and Philistia (today's Gaza) looted Israel and sold a number of their people into slavery. Sidon would later be destroyed and its people enslaved by Artaxerxes III in 354 BC, and Tyre would be captured by the Greeks under Alexander the Great in 332 BC.[15] Those who persecuted the Jews would receive the exact same treatment in kind by God. Likewise, Egypt and Edom (today's Jordan) committed violence against the people of Judah, and do so even to this day, and so Yahweh promises those countries will become a desolate wilderness on the Day of the Lord (3:4-8,19).

Not just these nations, but all the world has blood on its hands. God cannot allow this corrupt system to go on forever. And so, the Day of the Lord will soon come upon every nation of the world. The Lord will drive the nations into a war fury against Israel, rather like a locust's gregarious phase, gathering them from the four corners of the world to rain down upon the land of Israel. Revelation 16:16 has a name for this gathering of the nations into judgment—Armageddon.

Like the sky on the day of the locust invasion, the Day of the Lord will see the sun and moon grow dark and the stars diminish in brightness. The armies will cringe in terror as the Lord roars from Zion and shakes the earth with His righteous anger. Due to the wickedness of the nations, God's Son returns to this earth to harvest the nations. Jesus will swing His sickle and cut down the invading armies, and so judge the nations (3:13,15-16).

On the Day of the Lord, God's people—both believing Jew and Gentile—will witness the Lord being "a shelter for His people" and "the strength of the children of Israel." Because God's righteous fury punishes His enemies and protects His people, the world will finally know "I am the Lord your God." And when that terrible yet wonderful day comes to pass, God's blessing will flow down on His faithful people whereby the "mountains shall drip with new wine, the hills shall flow with milk, and all the brooks of Judah shall be flooded with water... from the house of the Lord" (3:16-18).

## JOEL'S FAITH LESSONS

The spiritually apathetic in Joel's time received a hard-knocks lesson about just how far God is willing to go to get His people's attention. Yahweh would go as far as even afflicting them with devastating losses in order to pull their focus away from the mundane and onto the divine. Should the people "rend their hearts" in heartfelt repentance, God would relent, blessings would flow, and God's enemies would be destroyed. Such loving yet terrifying attention given by the Heavenly Father demonstrates just how intimately God longed for the hearts of His people. Such a display of unconditional love, coupled with the joyous hope of future blessings and justice, were meant to buoy hope and solidify a rock-solid faith through life's devastating losses. Four different groups will now learn just how this lesson revealed by the Prophet Joel applies to us today.

## Lessons for Israel

How can the nation of Israel maintain faith through devastating loss? For the nation of Israel today, which suffers through continual and painful losses at the hands of its enemies, the faith lesson Joel has for it should be obvious. God has a brilliant future in store for the nation. The suffering of Israel as a nation will end upon her Messiah's return, and she will finally know the peace and blessings of God. Israel can maintain faith through devastating losses when it knows that history will end with Israel victorious.

But, that promise of victory is for a believing, penitent, faithful population. Israel exists today in a state of unbelief, preferring the man-centered religion of Humanism. Therefore, it'd be wise for the individual Jewish Israeli to ask themselves, "What is the condition of my own heart?" Just because you're born a Jew doesn't mean that you're necessarily "His People." The nation will live on, but not necessarily all the people who dwell within it. The Bible reveals that the Jewish people throughout history have felt secure in their belief that their heritage somehow exempted them from having to have a penitent heart for God (Matthew 3:9; Luke 3:8; John 8:39). Remember that Joel's people suffered continual tragedies to remind them of that mistaken conclusion, just as the people of Israel today suffer as God tries to get their attention.

The true hope of the Jewish people today is to heed what King Solomon advised in 2 Chronicles 7:14, "If My people who are called by My name will humble themselves, and pray and seek My face, and turn from their wicked ways, then I will hear from heaven, and will forgive their sin and heal their land." Accept by faith Jesus Christ as your personal Messiah and you will be forgiven. Be in a right relationship with Yahweh so you can be a victor when Jesus returns on the Day of the Lord.

## Lessons for the Nations

How do the nations maintain faith during tragedy? Take to heart the undeniable fact that God is sovereign. God could stop disasters from happening, but He at times chooses not to because we as a people have told Him we neither desire His presence nor need His protection. God has obliged us. We're on our own.

A nation hit with disaster can actually be thankful because it shows that God still has an interest in its welfare. Ironic, yes, but disaster wakens us from our prideful spiritual stupor. Our national hearts have become so hardened that at times God has to slap us hard with a destructive storm or financial collapse or other such disaster to make us hear His call to restore a right relationship with Him. Under fresh calamity the heart of a nation will be broken.[16]

God wants to heal our sorrows and sicknesses, but will do so only when we as a people surrender our pride, in remorse give up our sin, and in sincerity place God in charge of our nation. Make "In God We Trust" not just a motto, but a reality, and a nation can maintain faith through disaster.

## Lessons for the Church

What does Joel have to say to the Church today concerning maintaining its faith during devastating loss? After all, Joel of all the Old Testament prophets is especially pertinent to the Church, for one of his prophecies foretold the Church's birth on the Day of Pentecost. Joel prophesied that the Church would, by the indwelling power of the Holy Spirit, perform such amazing miracles that the world could not help but know there is a God. By its godly testimony to Christ resurrected and in supernatural deeds, the Church would be God's witnesses to the people of this world. The Church exists to bear witness to Christ's love so that the spiritually lost will repent of their sins and so be saved. That is the purpose of the Church.

But, is the Church really living up to its purpose? Could it be that the locusts of disaster and persecution are descending upon our congregations in order to get us into the temple and force us to listen to God's marching orders? God could be trying to tell us something. We clearly are not doing something right.

To be a spiritually fit body of believers who can weather the storms of life and still maintain their faith through devastating trials, famed preacher G. Campbell Morgan advised, "For life and service it is of the utmost importance that the heart should be warned and comforted by being constantly reminded of the present and overruling of God, and the sure certainty of His final victory."[17] Our churches need to keep Christ central, remain focused on the job, and direct our eyes ever hopeful towards the eternal prize, never leaning on our own strength. By doing so, our congregations will maintain the faith through trials.

## Lessons for You

**You're not alone.** How can you personally maintain faith through devastating loss? Keeping our faith in God can be so hard, we all know, for who on this earth hasn't experienced some kind of terrible tragedy? No person who has ever walked this earth has been exempt from suffering through the storms of life. Like the ravaged people of Judah in Joel's time to the tsunami victims in Japan today, nobody is exempt from tragedy.

So, firstly, Joel teaches us that you should understand that you're not alone in your suffering. Even God was betrayed by both angels and Man, and had His Son sacrifice Himself on a cross for our sins, to become "a man of sorrows and acquainted with grief"

(Isaiah 53:3). We've all ridden in the same wind-tossed boat of suffering. God can relate to our pain. Find comfort in that truth.

**God is in control.** The second lesson Joel has for us, and the one that can challenge our faith the most, is understanding that God is in control. It's easy for some to look at calamity as a mysterious accident of coincidence in which we have no control over, or chalk it up even to a demonic attack by Satan. Living in a fallen world, those certainly can play a part in our suffering. But, God is still sovereign, and therefore He is in control of everything that happens. From our perspective, life appears to be chaos, but if we could see from God's perspective, we'd learn that there really is order to the big picture.

God can stop what's hurting you, or He can allow it. Either way, and particularly when we're really hurting badly, it's a reality that's very difficult to swallow. Realization of this truth often can destroy a person's faith in God, turning some into bitter haters of God who give up on Him and live in indifference. The true test of faith is in how you will respond to this realization. Keeping your faith is a decision. Joel made that decision, and he chose to trust in God. Decide now if you will continue to trust in God's sovereignty and His perfect plan for your life.

**Loss teaches lessons.** The third lesson Joel taught us is that God uses loss to teach a lesson. Sometimes our Heavenly Father has to wake us up from our spiritual stupor in order to build a better relationship with us. It took the destruction of their food supply for Judah's people to actually make the time to listen to God.

At other times, God is strengthening our resolve to trust Him and live by faith. A martial artist will beat their knuckles on a board day after day so as to develop calluses that are resistant to pain. So, too, will the pain of trials forge us into someone tougher and better fit to deal with the more difficult circumstances which often lay ahead. At other times, loss prepares us to help others through their own difficulties, just as Joel helped. We learn through experience to echo God's voice of compassion and healing.

**Keep an eye on the eternal prize.** The fourth lesson for maintaining faith Joel taught us is to keep your eyes on the eternal prize. God wanted to unleash the unfathomably rich bounty of His spiritual and material blessings on His people, but He couldn't because the people just weren't ready. God was ready to pour out His love, but the people needed to make a personal sacrifice to demonstrate that they still loved Him in return. The sacrifice God was looking for can be found in Psalm 51:17, "The sacrifices of God are a broken spirit, a broken and a contrite heart—these, O God, You will not despise."

Ask yourself, "Is my heart in God's hands?" If not, repent and cry out like the people of Judah did. A heart that loves the Lord will maintain faith through devastating loss, and do so joyously in the hopes of being showered by the blessings of God's love.

## QUESTIONS FOR DISCUSSION

1.  What kind of devastating loss am I now experiencing, or have experienced in the past?

2.  Why does it feel at times as if God is not there for me and just doesn't care?

3.  How can God be sovereign and yet still allow bad things to happen?

4.  When God's presence is evident in the pain I'm experiencing, how do I respond?

5.  What did I learn from going through hard times?

6.  Have I been able to help others who have experienced the same losses as I have?

7.  How have I been blessed by God since the loss?

8.  When Jesus returns at the Day of the Lord, will He be my blessed hope or my holy terror?

9.  What future blessings has God promised me?

# FAITH JOURNEY 3
# AMOS: FAITH THROUGH THE FIRES
# OF INJUSTICE

## THE RIVAL

The man's yell split the stillness of the night. He awoke with a start, leaping up from the coarse woolen mat he'd been tossing about on for the past few fitful hours. With ragged breath, racing heart and fully soaked with sweat, he tried to clear the fog from his head. "Was I really asleep?" he asked confused. The empty air within the goat-skinned tent offered no reply. "Couldn't be," he realized as the confusion lifted from his mind. "Dreams? No, visions rather. Visions? Visions from Yahweh God!"

Realizing what just happened to him, the man began tearing through his worn travel bags, upending their contents hastily onto the mat. "Where? Where is it?" he asked in a panic while rummaging through his meager belongs. "Ah-ha!" The rolled up leather parchment and writing kit were quickly unfurled on the ground. Gripping the reed and dipping it into a murky inkwell, the man knelt on calloused knees and began to print furiously. He must write down the visions he was given before the images were lost to the dark recesses of his mind. For hours the only noises in the little tent were the frantic scribbling sound of reed to parchment and the pleading mumblings, "Oh, Lord, forgive... Lord, forgive... please forgive them."

The rip of the tent flaps being torn asunder shook the man from his frantic reverie. Snapping his head in the sound's direction, his gruffly bearded face felt the blast of the cold morning air that proceeded two hulking figures. With no loss of stride, the large men flung themselves upon the stooped writer. Well experienced in a fight, he clamored valiantly to defend himself, but was laid low by a violent uppercut to the stomach. Falling to the ground winded, he attempted to try and protect his vitals as blow after blow landed upon his body. The beating mercifully stopped when the assailants each grabbed an arm and dragged the man kicking and flailing out of his travel home.

Dumped unceremoniously onto the ground, the beaten man raised his head painfully to gaze blearily at the finely sandaled feet standing before him. Rich in his tasseled robe, imperious posture, and a sneer of outright contempt as if he was looking down at a mangy dog, the figure could only be the high priest of the Bethel shrine. Spitting out of his mouth his own salty blood mingled with dirt, the accosted man let out a bitter chuckle, then stated plainly "Amaziah." The imperious man standing above him replied in the same. "Amos." Falling back on his haunches, Amos squinted contemptuously at the stately figure framed by the blinding morning sunlight.

After what seemed an eternal stare down, Amaziah finally spoke in his supercilious tone while wagging a finger. "Amos, oh, Amos. Jeroboam, king of Israel, doesn't take kindly to threats against his life and his nation. Israel will be taken away as captives? Indeed! What fantasy." Amaziah lifted an eyebrow and waited for a response, but the only reply was the look of pitying disdain on Amos' swollen face.

Seeing he had not stirred his rival, Amaziah nodded to his two temple thugs. Grabbing Amos' arms a second time, they dragged him roughly up onto his bare feet. Amaziah continued speaking, this time with a hint of vehemence, his calm veneer cracking just a bit. "Go, you seer! Flee to the land of Judah. There eat bread, and there prophesy. But never again prophesy at Bethel, for it is the king's sanctuary, and it is the royal residence."

Another punch to the stomach from a burley arm and Amos went down to his knees again. Catching his breath for a second, Amos jerked his head up to reveal eyes of molten steel. "Seer, you say?" growled Amos. "I was no prophet, nor was I a son of a prophet, but I was a sheep breeder and a tender of sycamore fruit." Working his jaw, Amos continued unabashed, "Then the Lord took me as I followed the flock, and the Lord said to me, 'Go, prophesy to my people Israel.'"

Clearly unimpressed by Amos' claim to a divine mission, Amaziah countered, "And so here you are, though not for long." Nodding again, the guards replied to Amaziah by grabbing Amos by the hair and yanking him backwards, dragging him towards his tattered little mule. He struggled heroically, but the men were too strong and only laughed derisively at Amos while they bound his hands with a rope to the animal. "Grubby farmer," one spat, "get out of here!"

The crowd that had gathered during the interchange watched disconnected and unfeeling. None rose to Amos' aid, rather some used the spectacle to cover their plunder of Amos' tent. A slap to the hind side of the mule propelled it forward and Amos was yanked off his feet and onto his back. The crowd burst into laughter at the sight of God's prophet being dragged down the street. Not moving from his spot, Amaziah looked on, betraying his calm with only a cruel smirk.

Bloodied, dirty and derided, Amos was not yet finished. Rolling onto his back as he was being dragged away, Amos called out. "You say, 'Do not prophesy against Israel, and do not spout against the house of Isaac.'" A piece of rotting filth smacked him in the face, cutting him off. Shaking the stench out of his nose, Amos thundered on undaunted. "Hear this, Amaziah, thus says the Lord: 'Your wife shall be a harlot in the city; your sons and daughters shall fall by the sword; your land shall be divided by a survey line.'" The crowd booed and heckled. "You will all die in a defiled land; and Israel shall surely be led away captive from his own land!"

*Once the prophet of God was dragged well outside of town and was finally out of sight, Amaziah let out an imperceptible sigh of relief. The smirk disappeared from his face, replaced by the cold shudder of foreboding.*

## WHERE CAN JUSTICE BE FOUND?

That was the question the Nineteenth Century author, Joseph Ignatius Kraszewski, cried out from the depths of his pain concerning the treatment of his defeated and scattered people—the Jews. He lamented, "The only rights accorded, or, rather, dearly sold, to the Jews can at any moment be revoked, suspended, or torn in shreds by the tribunal of the clergy. Where can justice be found? To whom can they complain?"[1]

The Jews of Kraszewski's time were treated just as their ancestors had treated God's prophets and Israel's servant class during Amos' time. As wanderers for centuries in countries not their own, with no land to call home nor place where they were welcome, the Diaspora Jews had few and often untenable rights. Their property and even their lives could be taken at any moment. Local officials merely turned a blind eye to their persecution. Very few people cared enough to lift a finger to help them in their distress. The general public disdained these inconvenient people. Where can justice be found? To Kraszewski, the answer was obvious. Nowhere!

Injustice. How does one define it? Injustice can be defined in the tear-stained face of the bedraggled woman who in a back alley tries to stay warm under a pile of old newspapers. Injustice can be defined in the glazed-over eyes of the nine year old boy who has been sniffing glue to kill the pain of being unwanted. Injustice can be found in the rat-a-tat sound of semi-automatic weapons ripping apart a classroom of teenagers. Injustice can be found in the blood seeping out of a peaceful villager hacked down by the machete of an insurgent. Injustice can be found in the defeated look of the desperate father who cannot provide food for his family. Injustice can be found on the smug grin of the murderer who yet again escapes a prison sentence.

Wherever the inalienable, God-given rights of people are violated without legal recourse, there's injustice. Wherever the law of the land is cast aside for convenience or ignored due to position and wealth, there's injustice. Wherever the needy are trodden down to burgeon the lifestyle of the greedy, there's injustice. Wherever crime goes unpunished, criminals run rampant, laws are skirted, freedoms are denied, property is taken wantonly, decisions are made based on biases and innocence is stolen, there's injustice.

Label injustice by another name such as inequality, unfairness, unjustness, selfish malevolence, cruelty, or call it what truly in essence it is—Evil—the results are the same. Injustice hurts people, leaving them angry, defeated and often broken. Injustice hurts the human condition, degrading humanity to its baser and more violent instincts. Injustice hurts society, leaving it dysfunctional and decaying. Injustice even hurts the earth, destroying the natural systems God has created.

And, injustice seems to be everywhere. A scan of the news headlines on *AP* becomes unbearable under the onslaught of daily injustices. As King Solomon once said in, "Moreover I saw under the sun: in the place of judgment, wickedness was there; and in the place of righteousness, iniquity was there" (Ecclesiastes 3:16).

You yourself know injustice. Never has a single person escaped the sting of injustice, though some suffer under it in greater degrees. Maybe your job was outsourced to someone overseas. Maybe you couldn't get into that club because of the color of your skin. Maybe you lost that court case over a ridiculous legal loophole the other side exploited. Or, maybe you were teased by your classmates for standing up for your beliefs. You fill in the blank. You know the pain firsthand, and wonder like Amos must have often wondered, "Why, God?"

Fortunately, the questions surrounding "Why, God?" when it comes to maintaining one's faith through the fires of injustice are at the very heart of the message of the Minor Prophet Amos.

# THE FAITHFUL FARMER

## Time of the Prophet

"The words of Amos, who was among the sheepbreeders of Tekoa, which he saw concerning Israel in the days of Uzziah king of Judah, and in the days of Jeroboam the son of Joash, king of Israel, two years before the earthquake." Thus Amos 1:1 introduces the third Minor Prophet named Amos and helps pinpoint the times in which he lived.

King Uzziah of Judah ruled from 783-742 BC. King Jeroboam II of Israel ruled from 786-746 BC. Due to Amos' mention of an earthquake and later an eclipse (8:9), scholars have placed Amos' date of writing precisely at 763 BC.[2] The prophets Micah, Isaiah and Jonah would then have been contemporaries of Amos. Hosea would follow in ministry a decade or so later.

Amos lived during Israel's golden age of economic stability and tranquility. From 805-740 BC, Israel's enemies, such as the mighty aggressor Assyria, were stuck in a temporary time of decline.[3] During that intermission, the Jewish kingdoms both north and south expanded back into the old Solomonic boundaries outlined in 2 Kings 14. It was a golden age historians described as "a period of expansion, freedom, activity, prosperity and peace. Money poured in; the armies were always victorious. The people were filled with pride... nothing interfered to chill the popular spirits."[4]

The devolution of human society which the Prophet Hosea would later have to endure found its roots a decade earlier here in Amos' time for, as human history repeatedly demonstrates, serenity often is an illusion, and a false sense of peace inevitably becomes a breeding ground for human vices. The golden age was about to transform into their darkest hour.

Since fallen human nature during times of blessing forgets God's benevolence, a human-centered form of worship arose in Israel's Northern Kingdom that replaced the true worship of God. Worship of Yahweh in the Temple in Jerusalem was replaced by the worship of golden calves in the cult shrines in the towns of Bethel, Beersheba and Gilgal (1 Kg. 12:26-33). Samaria's shrine towns and their calf idols were never authorized by God, and He despised them as abominations.

As the false, idolatrous worship of God arose in Israel, the people were no longer taught who the real Yahweh God was and His moral law as revealed in the Torah. Ethics and morality were replaced by empty rituals and man-made ceremonies. The consequence of this godless, human-centered religion combined with a new ethically-lacking upper class fostered a fertile breeding ground for terrible acts of injustice. These injustices defined the time in which Amos lived.

## Construction of a Prophet

Thus in this spiritual climate of apathy and empty religion which defined the Northern Kingdom, Yahweh turned his gaze far south to the little town of Tekoa in search of a faithful messenger. If Bethlehem was considered an "O, little town," then Tekoa just six miles south of Bethlehem and 12 miles south of Jerusalem was equally insignificance. This fly-speck of a village overlooking the Dead Sea was nestled among the barren limestone hills of the Judean wilderness. Like America's old El Paso in Texas, Tekoa was the frontier town burned by the sun and dried hard as the clay. What the town lacked in size and culture, though, its harsh setting more than made up for it by producing a stock of ruggedly hearty people.

One of these iron men was Amos. Built tough like the herdsmen of old, Amos lived the harsh life of wrangling an ugly, stunted breed of sheep which had a fine wool called *noked*.[5] When the seasons got too dry, he'd pull up his tent pegs and head for the coastal plain or Jordan Valley to tend sycamore-fig trees. He'd set to the tedious task of ensuring good fruit by slicing or pricking the top of each fig with all the great patience one would need in doing such mind-numbing labors. And, when the wool and fruit were ready, Amos would likely travel a few miles to join the busy caravan route linking Jerusalem with Hebron and Beersheba to sell his goods up in the Northern Kingdom of Israel.

Wealthy merchants who attempted to swindle Amos thinking him an ignorant bumpkin were in for a big surprise when they discovered to their dismay his sharp tongue spoke "a purity and vividness of language that at once made their words burn."[6] Amos was hardly illiterate, for his writings show he spoke not in the slow slang of a rural field hand, but with a fine Hebrew that denoted a quick, literate and well-ordered mind.

It is likely that in those northern trade markets Amos got to witness first-hand the bitter taste of the religious and social corruption that dominated the North. He was a humble man of the earth with no stated lineage, cut from the same hairy cloth as Elijah and John the Baptist, and just as much a devoutly faithful follower of Yahweh. The rampant materialism and harsh oppression of the poor he would have witnessed could only have galled him. What he saw became a burden on his soul, fitting for a man whose name means "burden-bearer." Amos, weighted down by such a burden that would have crushed the faith of a lesser man, still must have questioned time and again, "Why, God?"

## Call of the Prophet

Few would want God's call to become His messenger the way Amos received his calling. "The Lord roars from Zion and utters His voice from Jerusalem; the pastures of the shepherds mourn, and the top of Carmel withers" (1:2). What a call! Amos, the lowly shepherd, heard the ear-splitting shout of the Lord roaring with a voice so loud it would have withered one of the highest mountaintops in the land.

From the lowest pastures with his ugly sheep, Amos responded to that mighty voice with, "Surely the Lord God does nothing unless He reveals His secret to His servants the prophets. A lion has roared! Who will not fear? The Lord God has spoken! Who can but prophesy?" (3:8). The Lion of the Tribe of Judah had found His messenger in Amos.

Amos could not absolve himself from God's call by using the excuse that he was not formally schooled in theology (7:14). God wasn't looking for a doctoral student. Instead, He had forged a faithful servant utilizing the spiritual disciplines of hard labor, prolonged meditation in the harsh wilderness, long stretches of silent time in the hills communing with God, and a dependence on the benevolence of the Heavenly Father that only comes when one knows deprivations. It was the irony of God to use a peasant to bring His message to the wealthiest in society. The contrast was perfect. And Amos, he had no choice but to respond to God's command to go. Amos didn't volunteer; he was drafted![7]

And so, by God's roaring command, Amos quickly left his little town of Tekoa in Judah to travel by mule to the Northern Kingdom of Israel, to its religious center at Bethel some 22 miles north. He was going to put on his own Occupy Wall Street. He would be to the North the "calamity howler" calling out God's righteous anger on the injustices that he saw.[8] He was positive the cowed noblemen and debutantes would naturally respond in weeping and repentance. They would all turn back to a right relationship and worship of God, and finally "let justice run down like water, and righteousness like a mighty stream" (5:24). Instead, Amos was in for quite a surprise.

# THE UNJUST NATIONS

Amos, considered the first of the writing prophets, proved he was one of the "epoch-making men of the Bible" by the might of his pen over sword.[9] His writings reveal a mind as wily as a wartime general and as crafty as any D.C. politician. Ironically, for a guy who spent more time with sheep than he did with people, he also possessed the skills of the most degreed psychologist in understanding how to initially work his way into the sympathies of his audience.

This is how Amos did it. Imagine the rugged prophet approaching the shrine at Bethel, too much a commoner for the noblemen arriving to pay their respects to "God" to notice him climbing up the chiseled marble steps. Once at the top, blocking the parishioners' way into the grand entrance, Amos exclaimed in chapters one and two with all the thunder he could muster, "Thus says the Lord, 'I will punish your enemies!'" That surely got the parishioners' attention!

## Damascus

"For three transgressions of Damascus, and for four, I will not turn away its punishment," began Amos. Using this Jewish idiom meaning "for multiplied sins," Amos started with God's message against their northeastern neighbor—Syria. "They have threshed Gilead with implements of iron." The Israelites all knew about the bloody war atrocities and back-stabbing betrayals inflicted upon them by Syria for generations. It was about time God did something about those barbarians. Amos revealed God would indeed act by sending a fire to devour their palaces, break down their city gates, and cut off their inhabitants and king by sending the people of Syria into captivity (1:3-5).

"Hey, this is good news!" the people must have thought. Now excited, the shrine visitors had begun to give this prophet their undivided attention.

# Gaza

Amos continued, "For three transgressions of Gaza, and for four, I will not turn away its punishment." The Philistines of Gaza, the enemies of Israel since the time of the Judges, "took captive the whole captivity to deliver them up to Edom." For centuries the hated Philistines raided defenseless villages and sold their captives into slavery. Cheers whooped from the burgeoning gathering after Amos declared the Philistines would suffer the same dire fate as the Syrians (1:6-8).

# Tyre

For the inhabitants in the dominant Phoenician merchant city of Tyre in Lebanon, Amos accused them also of being slavers, for they "did not remember the covenant of brotherhood." For turning their fellow men into mere property and destroying their dignity, the seemingly impregnable island city of Tyre would be burnt to the ground (1:9-10).

Now Amos had a good sized crowd gathered around him. All eyes gazed expectantly at him and wondered, "Okay, who's next to get what's coming to them?"

# Edom

The next to fall under God's hatchet was Edom, Israel's cousins from Father Isaac's brother, Esau. Every Israelite knew how Edom pursued his own cousins with the sword. The Edomites were known for having no pity as they raided Israel's land to slaughter even the women. Their rage against Israel boiled perpetually, ever holding a grudge without end. For their years of hostility towards Israel, God would send a fire to consume their cities of Teman and Bozrah (1:11-12). The onlookers cheered uproariously at this great news.

## Ammon

The Ammonites east of the Jordan River were the savages who ripped open the pregnant women of Gilead so that they might enlarge their own territorial borders. The imagery forced the gathering throng of women to in unison put their hands on their stomachs. For the Ammonites acts of brutal genocide bred by territorial greed, Amos declared God would send the Assyrian army to burn down their walls and palaces in Rabbah and drag their people away into captivity (1:13-15). The crowd erupted in mass celebration!

## Moab

For Israel's cousins the Moabites, they stood accused of burning the bones of the king of Edom to lime as a way of desecrating the dead. "How dare the Moabites deprive a person's spirit of rest!" these ancient people must have thought. Because of their disrespect for the dead, Moab like the other nations Amos listed would know the fires of the Assyrian war machine as well as the bitterness of exile (2:1-3). By now all of Bethel was out standing on the stairs of the shrine, drinking in the messages of this gruff-looking prophet.

## Judah

"For three transgressions of Judah, and for four, I will not turn away its punishment," Amos announced, finger jutting southward to his own land. "Judah? Our own brothers?" the people asked each other in bewilderment. Amos had to pause due to a lump caught in his throat over God's coming revelation concerning his own tribe. Taking a moment to gather himself together, Amos finally forged on to declare Judah's sins. "Because they have despised the law of the Lord and have not kept His commandments. Their lies lead them astray, lies which their fathers followed." For rejecting God's law and worshipping false gods, Jerusalem would one day also know the fiery wrath of the one true God (2:4-5).

All of the parishioners inside the Bethel shrine had vacated in order to hear the fiery lashings of this uncompromising messenger from God. Worship there had totally ceased. The finely robed priests and even more luxuriously dressed shrine prostitutes would have filed out of the building as well, along with their high priest, the imperious Amaziah. Amaziah just had to know who would dare steal the attention of his acolytes away from him.

The crowd outside had been worked up into a frenzy that bordered on chaos. All eyes of the worshippers at Bethel were now riveted on the lone orator who shot out each judgment upon their enemies with such power and passion. And then, Amos spoke the name of the seventh nation that was about to face God's judgment.

## Israel

"Thus says the Lord: 'For three transgressions of Israel, and for four, I will not turn away its punishment'" (2:6ff). The cheering abruptly stopped. Bewilderment cast itself upon confused faces. The throng's energy drained away like a dead battery. There was nothing left but a weighty and uncomfortable silence. And yet, without losing any of his pace and furor, Amos recorded over his next four chapters in three categories his recitation of Israel's long, long, long list of sins.

**Social injustices.** Amos began his list of Israel's transgressions with the first category concerning social injustices. He boldly addressed his audience, all the while oblivious to the fact that they were a large and potentially hostile crowd of people encircling all about him. Before the watchers could catch their breath from what must have felt like a sucker punch, Amos marched on with one accusation after another, building in strength and intensity.

Pointing directly at those men in the crowd who were dripping with jewelry, Amos accused, "They sell the righteous for silver and the poor for a pair of sandals." Singling out an elegant man riding atop a litter carried by four bedraggled slaves, Amos stated, "They trample on the heads of the poor and pervert the way of the humble." Opening wide his arms to encompass the crowd, he chastised, "You lie on beds made of ivory and stretch out on your fine couches. You gorge yourselves on the lambs from the flock and the calves from the midst of you stalls. You lay around idly singing to the sound of stringed instrument." Thundering on, "You drink wine by the bowl full, and you anoint yourselves with the best ointments." Then, with great disgust Amos spat out, "But you are not even grieved by the afflictions of your own brothers!" (2:6-7; 6:3-6).

Unrestrained, Amos turned his verbal attack on the sodden women, the Mean Girls of his time. "Hear this word, you cows of Bashan, who live high up on the mountain of Samaria, who oppress the poor, who crush the needy, who say to your husbands, 'Bring us wine! Let us drink.'" The husbands in the crowd were not sure whether to be offended at the cow insult aimed at their wives or to secretly elbow each other in agreement. "You have built your summer and winter houses out of fancy hewn stone and planted your pleasant vineyards in order to drink all day long." Amos, holding his stomach accused, "To fill your bellies you tread down the poor by taking their grain taxes from them, make up fines in order to steal the poor's drink, and wear the clothes taken in pledge for the loans you grant at exorbitant interest." Lifting his eyes up towards the Beverly Hills neighborhood of his time, Amos revealed its dark secrets. "Your great mansions assembled on the mountains of Samaria are filled with great tumult and oppression. You abuse your servants with violence and rob them of their very bread, all within your own palaces" (2:8; 3:9-10,13; 4:1; 5:11).

Amos pulled from a fold in his tunic a fist-sized, semiprecious stone fashioned in the shape of a turtle that he'd earlier pulled off a trader's cart. Holding it high over his head, with two hands he broke the measuring weight into two pieces, revealing the stone was really not stone at all. "Your merchants falsify the scales by deceit!" (8:5). The Law of Moses in Leviticus 19 called for standardized weights and measures, but the people in their greed were cheating and stealing from each other.[10] Merchant carts began to topple over as fist fights broke out.

Abruptly turning with a shaking, outstretched finger toward the city gate, Amos declared, "God knows your manifold transgressions and your mighty sins!" Mesmerized, the crowd turned as one to look towards the city gate and the judge who held court within. The prominent man sitting high aloft the judge's seat looked shocked at being pointed out. "You!" said the prophet as he marched towards him. "You who turn justice to wormwood and lay righteousness to rest in the earth. Just look at the poor standing before you seeking justice! You afflict the just by taking bribes and divert the poor from receiving their justice at this gate. You've made it so bad for them that they prudently remain silent, for they know that because of you it is an evil time" (5:7,12-13). The peasant family standing before the unjust judge kept their eyes fixated on the dusty road, silently wondering when God would rise to their defense.

**Religious hypocrisy.** Amos next funneled the anger of God on the religious caste in his second category concerning religious hypocrisy. Stomping over to the high priest of Bethel, God's Prophet pointed his calloused finger mere inches from Amaziah's nose. "Why do you people look to them to know God? They certainly do not know how to do right." In a mocking tone, Amos pretended to be a Bethel priest. "Come to Bethel and transgress! Come to Gilgal to multiply your transgressions. Sure, bring your sacrifices every morning. Bring your tithes every three days. Offer a sacrifice of thanksgiving with leaven. Proclaim and announce the freewill offerings. For this you love, oh, you Children of Israel!" (3:10; 4:4-5). The priests all began to shout over one another as Amaziah looked on glowering.

"Do you know what God hates?" asked Amos unfazed. "He despises your feast days. He does not savor your sacred assemblies. God says, 'Though you offer me burnt offerings and your grain offerings, I will not accept them, nor will I regard your fattened peace offerings. Take away from me the noise of your songs, for I will not hear the melody of your stringed instruments'" (5:21-23).

Running up to the top of the shrine steps, Amos pointed through the door. "Is this how God desires to be worshipped? You priests, have you even read the Torah? Can Yahweh even be found in this building? You carry your pagan deities like Sikkuth in the tabernacle of Moloch and Chiun as your idols. You call the stars your gods, and these worthless idols you made for yourselves by your own hands." "And you," referring to the luxuriously but certainly under-clad shrine prostitutes, "A man and his father go in to the same girl and so defile God's holy name. Oh, the virgin of Israel has certainly fallen!" (2:6-8; 5:2,26). The harlots only giggled uncomfortably one to another.

Amos returned to Amaziah. "Do you really think this is how God wants to be worshipped, with shrines and idols and prostitutes? Where is the pure and undefiled religion our Heavenly Father desires, to visit orphans and widows in their trouble and to keep oneself unspotted from the world?" Stepping back to encompass all the shouting priests, Amos bellowed, "Hypocrites! No, Yahweh says He abhors the religious pride of Jacob and hates these places of worship" (6:8).

**Rejection of God.** Before the priests could scurry off in disgust, and while the crowd remained too stunned at having their sins paraded before them to react, Amos hit at the heart of the matter in his third category concerning their rejection of God. "Thus says the Lord: It was I who brought you up from the land of Egypt, who led you for forty years in the wilderness, who destroyed your enemies like the Amorites before you, and let you possess their land as your own." With almost a cry of anguish as the heart of God weighed so heavily on him, Amos cried out, "You only have I known of all the families of the earth, but you have rejected my blessings. Oh, woe to you who are at ease in Zion, you instead trust in the armies of Mount Samaria and not in me" (2:9-11; 3:2; 6:1).

Turning to point out an intoxicated man lying face-down in the shadows, Amos shook his head mournfully and declared, "God has been speaking to you. He has raised up some of your sons as prophets and some of your young men dedicated to me as Nazirites. But you gave the Nazirites wine to drink and commanded the prophets saying, 'Do not prophesy!'" (2:12).

"Wait a minute there," Amos must have paused to think to himself. "God had sent messengers to these people before and they had shut them up?" Reality finally dawned on this novice prophet as he realized this—his very first message—was not going to go over as well as he had naively expected. With alarm, He finally perceived that the crowd's mood had drastically shifted from confusion to indignation. Fists began to be waved in the air and shouting erupting in the fringes. The chill up his spine led Amos to back slowly towards the gate. The crowd as one surged forward at him.

Flustered yet undaunted, Amos implored, "Seek God and live, but do not seek Bethel, nor enter Gilgal, nor pass over to Beersheba." The shouting had become deafening. A sharp rock thumped against his chest. Exhaling sharply, "They hate the one who rebukes in the gate, and they abhor the one who speaks uprightly." Amos tore ahead of the crowd to gain some room, then spun upon them angrily. "Oh, how you grieve the Lord! He declares, 'I am weighed down by you'" (2:13; 5:4-5,10).

With that said, Amos ran for his life.

## THE JUST GOD

Israel was living it up in the lap of luxury, enjoying their greatest time of peace and self-indulgence, but all built on the striped backs of their suffering servant population. The nation functioned even when its government was corrupted by selfishly wicked kings and dishonest judges who heartlessly doled out injustice and class oppression. The prideful, thoughtless people gave no consideration whatsoever to any poor creature who starved for want of food. The people lived in a shallow spiritual stupor, participating in religious ritual without a concern for true righteousness, consumed by song and festivities without ever once thinking of the One whom they claimed to be worshipping. They cruelly manhandled God's messengers, like Amos, going so far even as executing the prophets. So, for all of this, it begs the question: "Why, God?"

## The Five Visions

The answer to the pertinent question of "Why, God?" is contained in five visions God sent Amos that cold, dark night. The true character of Yahweh—His sense of justice tempered by unconditional love—was to be revealed by the discourse between Maker and Prophet, recorded in Amos chapters seven through nine.

**Vision of the locusts.** "Thus the Lord God showed me," began the salutation of the first vision, and divulged an important characteristic about God (7:1-3). The very fact that the Lord recruited prophets reveals that He was not unaware of the spiritual deadness of His people. Nor did God wish His people to be ignorant of the fact that He knew of their crimes. Yahweh is not clueless or checked out, as some even to this day believe Him to be, just because He hasn't responded as fast as they'd like. No, God knows, and God wants us to know that He knows.

Sometimes God lets His people know how rotten their hearts have gotten and how terrible they've been behaving by sending various punishments for the purpose of chastising. The point of these chastisements is always to bring His people down to their knees in repentance and then back up to a right heart relationship with Him.

In Amos 4, God listed a number of these chastisements that He'd already earlier tried on Israel. He had hit their crops in some of the land hard with drought, holding back the drops to cause famine, but they would not repent. God caused flooding in other areas so their food would wash away, but they refused to turn back to God.

He blasted their gardens with mildew and a lesion-producing blight, but they did not repent and return to Him. A large number of men and horses had died tragically, but the people didn't seek God's consolation. The people would rather fashion a god out of wood to fit their own liking than love the one true Heavenly Father. The true God is the Lord of hosts, "He who builds His layers in the sky, who calls for the waters of the sea and pours them out on the face of the earth—the Lord is His name" (4:6-11; 9:5-6).

Because Israel had hit the snooze button on God's wake-up calls, refusing to give up their evil ways and return to a right relationship with Him, Yahweh would make it so they had no choice but to confront Him. "Prepare to meet your God, O Israel!" (4:12). And so, God showed Amos a vision of locusts swarming at the beginning of the late crop, devouring all of the grass of the land. Starving, the people would certainly cry out to God for help.

Clearly dismayed at the scope of the potential devastation, the farmer-turned-prophet pleaded, "O Lord God, forgive, I pray! Oh, that Jacob may stand, for he is small!" To Amos' utter amazement, the Lord considered Amos' intercessory prayer and cancelled this judgment by locusts. "It shall not be," said the Lord (7:1-3). What mercy both God and Amos showed to a people who had so vehemently rejected them both!

**Vision of the fire.** In the second vision, God changed tactics and showed Amos a vision of a conflict by fire, which "consumed the great deep and devoured the territory of Israel." Again, greatly dismayed, Amos cried out from his little tent, "O Lord God, cease, I pray! Oh, that Jacob may stand, for he is small!" And the Scriptures say the Lord relented (7:4-6).

**Vision of the plumb line.** In the third vision, the Lord showed Amos a plumb line. A plumb line is a construction tool that uses a cord tied to a lead weight that's pulled down by gravity. Builders use a plumb line to determine if their walls are constructed properly.

God set up a plumb line in the midst of His people Israel. The line proved Israel had settled just like a crooked and leaning wall, a disjointed danger that could not be shored up. Tearing down the crooked political and religious systems in Israel was therefore not only proper, but necessary. Amos, seeing Israel had failed the plumb line test, no longer had a defense to make on Israel's behalf. Israel was a building damaged beyond repair, too dangerous to be left standing, and so had to be condemned. The Builder rolled up His blueprints, took off His hardhat and declared, "In the midst of my people Israel, I will not pass by them anymore. The high places of Isaac shall be desolate, and the sanctuaries of Israel shall be laid waste. I will rise with the sword against the house of Jeroboam" (7:7-9).

**Vision of the summer fruit.** In chapter eight, a fourth vision was given. Amos saw a basket of summer fruit, which is a symbol of the end of the growing season. No more fruit is yielded past the summer fruit. The Northern Kingdom of Israel had yielded its last generation as a nation. For their sins of the oppression of the poor, injustice in the courts, sexual immorality, religious abuses, violence, idolatry and corrupt business practices, a dreadful harvest was about to be reaped. Israel rotted and stank like a moldy bucket of apples.

Amos knew the Lord could not relent this time and still be just, so seeing no last minute reprieve for these rotten people, he had no prayer to offer up on their behalf. There comes a time when the righteous can no longer intercede on behalf of a wicked, for when sin endures God's mind becomes as unmovable as Mount Everest.

**Vision of the destruction of Israel.** In chapter nine, God gave Amos his fifth, last and most frightening vision. Amos saw the Lord Himself standing by an altar. Suddenly, like a great wrecking ball about to swing, God smashes the false shrines and houses of Israel into splinters. Whoever doesn't get crushed by the collapsing debris flee to the farthest reaches in hopes of escaping God's wrath. Like a pack of hounds on a scent, the Lord's armies track the runners as high as Mount Carmel and as low as the Dead Sea. Sword-wielding marauders are called in to cut the Israelites down mid-run and poisonous snakes bite them as they pause for breath. Should any think they can hide from the living God, He reminds them who they are truly up against, for He is the One who "touches the earth and it melts" (9:5).

In the midst of this terrifying vision, with all this smashing and running and fleeing and pandemonium that Yahweh's unleashing, we learn of the people's very strange response. The people declared, "The calamity shall not overtake nor confront us" (9:10). Even as these morally bankrupt people were being destroyed, they genuinely believed no calamity could ever fully wipe them out. What prideful self-delusion!

The reason for their false confidence was because to them "religion was a cloak for their sin."[11] Nominally religious people think they are actually living for God because they do what they consider spiritually good deeds. They are "good people" who live by their own religious rulebook, but in truth what they're ultimately espousing is a self-created, self-centered religion. They make up and then live by their own moral standards, but never by God's standards.

How ironic it is then that the Israelites thought they were being religious and yet ignored God, His messengers the prophets, and His Word the Bible. They convinced themselves that God would just leave them alone to sin to their heart's content. But, they purposefully forgot that God hates evil and has a time limit on His patient call for redemption. As famed preacher Dr. G. Campbell Morgan once said, "The walls of doom close slowly, surely, around all those who forget God."[12]

With God's long-suffering patience finally expired, the Day of the Lord—the day of God's justice and wrath—was about to come down hard upon Israel with all its darkness, desolations and utter hopelessness of escape. Some forty year later, every prophecy God gave Amos concerning Israel came true. Using the newly empowered Assyrians as His instrument of justice, God unleashed one of the cruelest nations in history upon Israel and her wicked neighbors. By 722 BC, just like Amos warned, Israel's capital of Samaria was besieged and conquered. Their children were cut down by the sword. Amaziah's widow became a prostitute.

The defeated captives were lined up to have hooks pinned painfully through their lips or nose and then attached in tandem to other prisoners. With weary moans among howls of despair and the rattling of chains, the once wealthy oppressors became the oppressed. Hands tied behind their backs, they stumbled along the dusty road. No one dared to slow down due to the agony of pain in their pierced and battered faces.[13] For their sins, Israel marched north as one into exile to the echo of, "'Therefore I will send you into captivity beyond Damascus,' says the Lord, whose name is the God of hosts" (5:27).

Once these judgments were fulfilled against Israel, the nation's destruction would serve as an eternal reminder that God despises injustice and false worship. The fall of Israel would also serve as an example to the world, for God has reserved yet another Day of the Lord. The Bible promises such a time of God's wrath will occur again one day, but this time against every nation of the world for its evil, in the still future time period known as the Tribulation.

Destruction is never the end of the story with God though, for in Amos 9:11-15 the Almighty promised hope by restoring a believing remnant of Israel. God's overall plan for human history is about how He lovingly seeks to restore mankind's fellowship with Him. To achieve this restored relationship, the Heavenly Father in the process even sacrificed His own Son, Jesus Christ, to provide salvation.

Many will reject that fellowship, but a remnant will choose Christ. On a scale as large as all of humanity, God promised that the faithful remnant of Israel and the believing Gentiles of this world will be gathered like wheat to dwell in the Son's earthly kingdom, and then afterwards taken up to the magnificent city called the New Jerusalem which will reside on a perfected New Earth. Amos so wonderfully described the peace and bounty of this coming era as, "The plowman shall overtake the reaper and the treader of grapes him who sows seed. The mountains shall drip with sweet wine and all the hills shall flow with it" (9:13). And when the harvest is in, the great celebration commences!

# AMOS' FAITH LESSONS

## Lessons for Israel

Israel can have faith through the fires of injustice by embracing God's promise that the house of Jacob will never be destroyed. The Jewish people may have been defeated, exiled, and continue to this day to suffer through the fires of injustice, but they certainly have never been forgotten by God.

The Heavenly Father has a two-phase plan of redemption in the works for Israel. The first phase is a national restoration. This plan is woven into His promise to give the Jews the Holy Land as an everlasting possession ruled over by the Messiah Himself. Nearly 2,700 years later, we today are witness to the near fulfillment of those promises in a modern day miracle—the rebirth of the nation of Israel. As God promised, "On that day I will raise up the tabernacle of David, which has fallen down and repair its damages; I will raise up its ruins and rebuild it as in the days of old" (9:11).

The remnant of Jacob's children continue to be gathered from all over the world back into the restored nation. "I will bring back the captives of my people Israel. They shall build the waste cities and inhabit them... and no longer shall they be pulled up from the land I have given them" (9:14-15). If you are a Jew, you can see that Israel is a nation once more. Never in human history has a nation come back from the dead. This means a great deal, and is a boundless source of hope, for it is part of God's redemptive plan for you.

The second phase is a personal restoration. The nation of Israel today exists as a humanist state where few believe in God, much less His Son Jesus Christ. The parallels of Amos' Israel in its wealth and shallow spirituality built on man-made traditions directly parallels the modern-day nation. Therefore, the same warnings Amos had for ancient Israel apply to modern-day Israel. Another Assyrian-like chastisement is soon coming to the nation so that a righteous, believing remnant will arise out of the turmoil to claim this promise: "Judah shall abide forever, and Jerusalem from generation to generation" (Joel 3:20).

Israel can have faith through the fires of injustice this very day by heeding Amos' call. Respond to Yahweh's Son, Jesus Christ, in faith and repentance by asking Him to be your Savior and Lord.

## Lessons for the Nations

The nations can have faith through the fires of injustice. By studying the time of Amos, we can perceive that a remarkably frightening similarity exists between the affluent nations of today and ancient Israel. Warning! We have become the unfaithful Israel of the prophets' time who crazily thought themselves invincible. Realizing that, our nations must seriously take Amos' messages to heart. They must in faith embrace the fact that God is ultimately sovereign over the nations of the world and that our leaders are merely temporary stewards.

No national sin goes unnoticed or unpunished by the Omniscient. While the righteousness of the nation insures the blessings of God, the sins of the nation most assuredly ensures His judgment and curses. And, as the multitudes of extinct nations that litter the dustbin of history prove, God most certainly will cast down unfaithful nations. Therefore, the nations can maintain faith through the fires of their own injustices by heeding Amos' call for national repentance. There lay the hope that God in His merciful but limited patience may yet hold off judgment.

## Lessons for the Church

The Church can have faith through the fires of injustice. Remarkable similarities also exist between many modern-day churches and the shrine of Bethel in Amos' time. Israel had a special calling by God confirmed by a covenant relationship with Him. Israel had both the great privilege and responsibility of being a beacon to the world by being a conduit of Yahweh's love. That love would attract people to Him. Instead, they chose a spirituality that was totally devoid of faith and love.

The Church today also has a special calling given by God. It can be found in Acts 1:8, and it's called the Great Commission. We too have both the great privilege and responsibility of being the conduit of God's love by sharing both the Good News that provides the salvation of people's souls and in helping those in need. And yet, we fail to strike a balance between the two. We either are like the priest in the Parable of the Good Samaritan who are so busy looking out for men's souls that we neglect those who have been beaten alongside the road, or we are so focused on caring for their physical needs that their souls remain unchallenged over their inevitable fall into eternal judgment.

If you are a pastor or leader of a church that has lost its love for the Lord and for the souls and needs of your fellow man, then Amos has two lessons for you. First, as Pastor D. Stuart Briscoe has pointed out, "A simple rule applies here. If you don't *heed* the Word of God, it's only a matter of time before you will no longer *hear* the Word of God."[14] The more God's Word is ignored, the more God backs away until there's a famine of His Word. The Holy Spirit will no longer attend your services.

The second lesson follows. If ritual and religious form have replaced your communion and obedience to God, then embrace the warning of Dr. Kyle Yates:

> *...our worship will be as lightly esteemed by Him
> as was the worship of Israel long ago, and our
> sanctuaries will fall, as did the ancient high
> places. Our churches will be empty, their services
> despised, and the heart and mind of men will
> turn for sustenance elsewhere.*[15]

Jesus will do as He said He'd do to the church of Laodicea in Revelation 3:16, "I will vomit you out of My mouth." In other words, be warned, your church will die.

Therefore, "He who has an ear, let him hear what the Spirit says to the churches." Return Jesus Christ to the throne of your church. Make the Bible your only authority and a literal interpretation your unwavering method. Return faith in God and love for your fellow man to your church once more, and the Lord promises in Revelation 3:20 to "come in to him and dine with him, and he with Me." When that happens, your churches can endure the fires of injustice.

## Lessons for You

**Heed God's calling.** The first lesson to be learned is to heed God's call in your life. Since reading Amos, we shouldn't need God roaring from the mountaintops to wake us up to the fact that we've offended God's sense of justice. Built into human nature is the knowledge that, no matter how deeply we bury it, we are not right with God. That's why one writer stated, "When the evangelist speaks of sin and the need for forgiveness, it rings a bell in every human heart."[16] It's all about how we respond to that ringing bell that matters.

If you haven't accepted Jesus as your Savior, then heed the call this very moment and surrender to Him. "Flee to the place where judgment has already been poured out, that is, to the cross of Calvary. Only there may a guilty sinner find shelter."[17] And, once you've become a forgiven follower of Jesus Christ, and you feel that tugging on your heart to go where the Lord calls you to share His message of salvation, then like Amos heed that call without delay.

**Don't slip away.** As we've learned, Israel had an empty religion because they let their love of God grow cold and replaced it with empty ritual. Inevitably, their relationship with God just slipped away. The fast pace of modern-day living has caused our generation to push God aside to the margins of our lives. As one commentator so colorfully made this comparison in the way we treat the Almighty: "Maybe He is like a butler at a party who stands silently against the wall until his hostess needs him and beckons him with her eye to bring more gravy or clear the dishes."[18]

When we think of God only when we believe He can be useful to us, like some big Santa Claus in the sky, then our love of Him has truly grown lukewarm. Our relationship with our Heavenly Father has slipped away. Our perception of God's glory goes from Amos 4:13's "He who forms mountains and creates the wind, who declares to man what his thought is, and makes the morning darkness, who treads the high places of the earth" to a feeble god who exists to serve our beck and call. What a dangerous position to be in when we believe the all-powerful Creator of the Universe is our lapdog! And yet, we have all been guilty of that crime from time to time. Now is the time to repent and flip that relationship right-side up, placing God in command of our lives and we as His faithful and obedient messengers.

**Maintain faith during trials.** So, where can justice be found in the midst of our trials? How do we maintain faith though the fires of injustice while pleading, "Why, God?" First, rejoice in the knowledge that God's patient forbearance for the evil of this world has its limits. Our Lord hates injustice and false worship, and will only allow them to thrive for just as long as His wait for repentance lasts. Second, trust that God knows what's best for you, even when it seems contrary to what you feel is best. While enduring the trials life hurls at you, maintain your faith in your Heavenly Father with the same steel and grit that Amos demonstrated. God will at some point communicate His intentions to you if you like Christ are also patient to listen.

> *"Therefore be patient, brethren, until the coming of the Lord. See how the farmer waits for the precious fruit of the earth, waiting patiently for it until it receives the early and latter rain. You also be patient. Establish your hearts, for the coming of the Lord is at hand" (James 5:7-8).*

The coming of the Lord is indeed near at hand. So, where can justice be found? It can be found only in Almighty God. And, when Jesus returns, "justice will run down like water and righteousness like a mighty stream!" (5:24).

## QUESTIONS FOR DISCUSSION

1. How have you experienced injustice in your life?

2. Why does it seem so hard to trust God when you're under persecution?

3. With all the evil in the world, is God really in control of the universe?

4. Why do evil people seem to prosper?

5. Are injustices expected in a fallen world?

6. Did God ever endure injustice Himself?

7. Have the trials in your life made your love for Jesus grow cold?

8. In what ways does God promise to bring about justice in your life now? In the future?

9. How do you maintain your love and faith in God through the fires of injustice?

# FAITH JOURNEY 4
# OBADIAH: FAITH WHEN IT SEEMS LIKE GOD HAS FORGOTTEN

## THE ANONYMOUS MESSAGE

*Sun overhead. Dusty streets below. The stranger deliberately made his way through the sparse thoroughfares of Jerusalem. He earned barely a few glances from those standing by the market shops, the looks of appraisal one gives to those who aren't from "these parts." He was neither distinct nor remarkable, doing little to attract meaningful attention and apparently not interested in haggling with the local vendors. His presence went in one eye and out the other as the merchants who cared only about potential buyers soon returned to their latest news and gossip.*

*As the man continued on his way toward the east side of town, he paused at one of the large stones that littered the area. It no longer blocked half of the street but instead had been pushed to the side. The jagged edges had been worn down from use; conquered, no doubt, by an endless stream of energetic kids and their imaginations climbing to the top. Now just a plaything, the rock seemed as ordinary as the man looking at it. That hadn't always been the case.*

*Looking up, the stranger could see one of many gaps in the city's protective wall where the limestone jungle gym had once sat with confidence. The wall had served Jerusalem for years, keeping enemies at bay and giving those who lived here a sense of security...*

*until the day it didn't. The day when Zion was attacked. The day when Zion was defeated.*

*Years had passed since that day, and time's passing had softened the intensity of her defeat. Those residents who remained in the city—the handful not killed or captured—attempted to carry on as if little had changed. They bought and sold, made and repaired, talked and laughed. The duties of everyday life continued as they had and as they would.*

*But stones like this were a daily reminder that everyday life was not normal. Pretend though they might, life now was different. The people's routines masked heartache as survivors wondered why God had abandoned them; why God had pushed them aside like the boulder beside the street. The stones were ever a reminder of God's judgment on the city and its inhabitants. Life would never be normal for the remaining Jews, no matter how much they hoped. Jerusalem was defeated.*

*If anyone had been looking, they would have seen a mix of emotions on the man's face as he stared at the fallen rock. Maybe a little bit of sadness, maybe a wry smile. The look didn't last, though, and the man didn't linger to explain it. Unlike the boulder, he wouldn't be staying around this corner long.*

*Up the street, up some stairs, he found the home he'd been looking for and knocked to make his presence known. A man answered, polite but uncertain. The room behind the occupant was simple. Its only eye-catching detail being the priestly robes hung in the corner, clean and ready for duty. A few crumbs on the homeowner's beard were evidence of an interrupted lunch, but he showed no trace of irritation. Patiently, he waited for the stranger to state his business.*

*No words were said, though. The stranger simply reached into his cloak and pulled out a short scroll. Questioningly, the priest took it and unrolled enough to see the first few lines. His eyes widened a little, and he stole another peek at the stranger who stood calmly by his door. Without as much as a whisper, the priest stepped aside and allowed the man to enter, closing the door behind him.*

*If you asked any of the neighbors later, you would get a different story from each of them. Some thought the man was there for a few hours, while some guessed until after the day's end. No one could really remember him leaving. The only point on which everyone agreed was that he had quietly slipped away.*

*What of the paper delivered to the priest? That was a different story. It demanded more attention than the stranger ever did. As the priest shared its contents with his colleagues, and they with the residents of Jerusalem, a sense of hope and excitement gripped the city.*

*God had remembered them.*

## LONG-TERM MEMORY

As the reluctant owner of a Chihuahua, I (Steve) have discovered two things about dogs: 1) they can be very intelligent, and 2) they can be very stupid.

When my wife and children persisted in their request to bring home a dog for the first time, I didn't want to say "yes." The burden and responsibility of owning another pet far outweighed the potential blessings. Our cats, I reasoned, were more than sufficient for animal companionship. Why bother adding a new species to the mix? But when the energy of saying "no" to the sad faces and batting eyelashes became too much to bear, I caved. The little black terror, a.k.a. Ivy, soon pranced into our home and into our lives.

From day one, I've marveled at the way her mind works compared to our feline friends. Dogs are just different. On the one hand, she is full of spunk and intelligence. She can figure out innumerable ways to manipulate my wife into giving her the things she wants. From food to treats to the prime position on the couch, the dog has an ally in my spouse, and Ivy knows it.

On the other hand, the dog just doesn't seem to have any common sense. Maybe I'm expecting too much out of this animal, but she has yet to figure out the way things work in our house. For example, every single time we leave, we come back. It's a fixed pattern, and we've never forgotten to do so. Yet, every day, Ivy seems shocked that we return home, and she celebrates with a chorus of yapping that could wake the neighborhood. Also, every day we give her food and water. It shows up in the morning and the evening, thanks to my wife's keen powers of memory. Yet Ivy assumes that feeding time is not on the agenda, so a series of progressively louder whines and more pitiful stares come our way in hopes that it will prompt the end to our cruel neglect.

Ivy truly seems to think that we have forgotten her. I freely admit that there are days when I would *like* to forget her, but the plain and simple truth is that she is impossible to forget. As her owner, it is my duty to remember; as a resident in the house where she creates so much chaos, it is unlikely I'll ever fail to take notice.

Pets often give us insight into the nature of our relationship with our Heavenly Father, and my experience with this 11-pound bundle of nervous energy is no different. Her persistent doubts prompt me to ponder a question we sometimes ask of God:

*Will He remember?*

Such a question might elicit a chuckle from anyone who knows the Scriptures. The Bible clearly describes a God who is omniscient, the all-knowing being who perceives every inch of His creation from the number of stars in the sky (Psalm 147:4) to the number of hairs on a person's head (Matthew 10:30). To ask if God will remember is like asking if a mathematician knows the value of *pi*. God knows, and so God will remember.

Still, there are times when I am like my dog and I doubt God's memory. I worry that maybe I can be forgotten. Perhaps He will forget to provide my daily bread, or perhaps He will not remember my prayers. These doubts aren't doctrinal, they are emotional. But they aren't totally without reason.

The Bible does point out some instances in which God chooses to ignore information He knows. In Isaiah 43:25, God declares, "I, even I, am He who blots out your transgressions for My own sake; And I will not remember your sins." It seems that there are some actions which God may choose not to revisit; some sins that He may decide to disregard. The facts may be filed away, never again referenced. Known, but not considered.

And therein lies the question. If God can willingly overlook certain facts, what determines which facts He will overlook? Will He fail to notice a minor offense? A serious crime? A horrendous injustice? A life-altering assault?

Perhaps it is not just an action that He will ignore. Perhaps it is a person or even a group of people. After all, that's how the Israelites felt as they were languishing in slavery in Egypt. Though they were promised blessings by God, He seemed to be a distant memory as they toiled in the mud pits, making bricks while the whips cracked across their backs.

Theology may tell us about God's perfect memory, but it fails to quiet our worries when God grows silent. Our faith can sometimes struggle to stay positive in such moments. Will God choose to disregard us? Will He forget people He once showered with blessings? As time passes, our doubts become more pronounced. If God has not taken action yet, maybe He won't.

*Will God remember?*

Strong faith is needed to trust God when we feel forgotten, to believe in His eternal plans for our glorious future while we live a mediocre present. That is exactly the kind of faith we need, and it is exactly the kind of faith that our next Minor Prophet demonstrates. This prophet not only gives an affirmation that God remembers, but he also points out that God has a plan to put His people on center stage. Rather than being forgotten, they are being prepared for greatness!

How can we be so confident in God's message when so many others had given up? Let's investigate Obadiah, learn more about him, and be inspired by his trust in the Lord. Perhaps we'll see why he had faith that God would remember even when the people felt forgotten.

## THE PROPHET OF BREVITY

The prophecy of Obadiah is a quick read. At twenty-one verses, it is a tiny book that doesn't even warrant chapter divisions. Tucked between Amos and Jonah, Obadiah's message spans just one to two pages of text—the shortest book of prophecy in the entire Bible. He communicates an entire message in less than half the words of almost every other prophet in the Bible. By comparison, Jeremiah uses seventy-five words for every one that Obadiah writes.[1] If any prophet seems "minor," Obadiah surely qualifies!

Not only is the prophecy itself short, it seems oddly misdirected. At first glance, the message of Obadiah's writing is only distantly connected to the people of God. Obadiah addresses his message to the nation of Edom, a neighbor southeast of the nation of Judah. He is not the only one in history to address the Edomites; Joel, Amos, and Malachi all share prophetic words about this nation. However, messages to Edom were not the focus of their writing. These other prophets give their messages to Edom in an aside, directing the main message to the Israelites. Obadiah is exceptional in that his message is primarily given to the inhabitants of Edom, and not addressed at all to the descendants of Judah.

As much as this warning is directed *at* the Edomites, though, it really isn't *for* the Edomites. The real audience is the people of God. Though they aren't addressed, they would hear this message. Despite feeling forgotten, as they listened to the Lord's proclamation shared through Obadiah, they would have rediscovered faith.

So who is this prophet whose faith helped the people? To learn about him, we must do a little digging in the words of Scripture.

## Time of the Prophet

The text of Obadiah itself is surprisingly unhelpful in unravelling this individual's identity. Take a look at the list of personal information we have about Obadiah:

✓ His name

That's it! That's the extent of our knowledge.

Scholars, of course, have spent years trying to analyze and pinpoint Obadiah's identity. There are few tantalizing clues. Obadiah (which means "servant of Yahweh") is a fairly common name in the Old Testament. We can find at least a dozen men with the same name throughout Scripture, from the son of Azel in 1 Chronicles 8:38 to the steward of King Ahab's house in 1 Kings 18. None of these men are described with much information, though, and trying to connect any of them to our prophet based solely on a shared name is fruitless.

So, we are left trying to learn about Obadiah and his faith simply by knowing more about the period of time in which he lived and delivered God's message. But that's a problem, too. The message of the book, frustratingly, does not seem limited to one particular set of historical facts.

We know it was written sometime after an attack has been made on the city of Jerusalem. The attack involved a few elements that Obadiah describes: the enemy breached the city and took plunder (v. 11), the enemy destroyed life and property (v. 12, 14), and the enemy was assisted by Edom (v. 11, 14). Still, scholars have difficulty identifying the specific attack mentioned. The context seems to match the conquest of Judah in 586 BC by Nebuchadnezzar and his Babylonian army, but compelling arguments can also be made for an earlier assault.

Without other touch points such as the name of a current king, a reference to a specific and unique detail of the attack, or a mention of other contemporary nations, we have little to help us establish a firm timeframe for the book and its author. We can infer no more about Obadiah and his life in Judah than we can about a man named Smith who lived somewhere in America sometime between the American Revolution and today.

However, the lack of context might not matter.

## Construction of a Prophet

You may have heard an old, groan-worthy joke: "Three men walk into a bar... the fourth man ducks." The joke is funny, if you get it, but it is not specific. Who are the men? They could be cowboys or bikers or hipsters. What kind of bar do you assume it mentions at the beginning? It could be a Wild West saloon or an Applebee's. What kind of bar is it at the end? One could imagine a half-inch copper pipe or a piece of steel rebar. No matter your assumptions about the participants or the context, the joke can still make you laugh.

Consider Obadiah to be like that vague joke. Obadiah could be almost anyone—a business owner, a professional prophet, a shepherd, or a craftsman. Obadiah could have lived during the divided kingdoms of Israel and Judah, or the time after Israel had been devastated by the Assyrians, or after the Babylonians had humiliated Judah. No matter your assumptions about the author or the context, the message is still effective and still communicates God's truth.

Glance through this short message and you will find a theme that runs throughout all of the prophets: Destruction! Edom had been involved as a happy spectator and willing accomplice to attacks on God's people, so now Edom is going to face a thorough reckoning as punishment for her sins. When Jerusalem's gates were destroyed and her wealth plundered, Edom rejoiced and benefitted. Now, Obadiah says, Edom is about to receive the penalty for her behavior. God will remember to repay, and it will be severe.

## Call of the Prophet

We don't know any other details about this prophet, nor do we know the specifics of his call. We do know one fact: Obadiah heard God's message, and he communicated it. Though he is not significant enough to be discussed elsewhere in Scripture or history, he was faithful to the task God had given him. The vision provided by Yahweh was recorded, written, and delivered. The faith Obadiah demonstrated by sharing God's message of remembrance is a faith we can admire.

Obadiah must have known he might face ridicule claiming to have had a vision from God. He knew the content of that vision would win him no friends among supporters of Edom, and he knew the promises of future blessing for Judah might sound like wishful thinking to his countrymen. To be a prophet was in the people's minds to be different and odd. Common sense might tell Obadiah to keep the message to himself, to either enjoy the vision privately or simply ignore that it had happened.

Instead, Obadiah chose to believe that God *could* and *did* speak to him. He chose to believe that God *could* and *would* humble the land of Edom for their actions. He chose to believe that God *did*, *does*, and *will* remember his people, the Jews. Obadiah demonstrated tremendous faith in sharing this message. We may not be able to see the details of his life, but we can see the conviction he had in God. He showed faith in God, putting his own reputation on the line to deliver a message he was sure came from the Almighty One. The message: "God won't forget."

# THE MESSAGE OF JUDGMENT

You can imagine Obadiah crafting the vision into written form, sitting away from distractions and trying to accurately convey the words of God to a people who felt forgotten by God. His first task was to address the audience. "Thus says the Lord God concerning Edom..." (v. 1). We can imagine that Obadiah has some familiarity with the nation of Edom, based on his descriptions of it throughout this short book.[2]

Edom was mountainous wilderness. Its red sandstone dominated the terrain southeast of the Dead Sea. While there were some areas of land suitable to cultivate, most of it was desert. As a result, the population was comprised of semi-nomadic peoples, with the exceptions of a few centers of population in cities and villages.[3] The geography provided Edom with a lot of natural protection. Mountain ridges, steep canyons, and deep gorges coupled with manmade fortresses made Edom a difficult place to assault. Obadiah's reference to "those who dwell in the clefts of the rock" (v. 3) hints at the security that would come from living in this landscape.[4] Modern attempts to subdue fighters in mountainous Afghanistan should give us an idea of the difficulty involved in attacking such a territory.

The Edomites had a justifiably strong sense of protection. "Who will bring me down to the ground?" they ask with arrogance (v. 3). They "ascend as high as the eagle" and "set [their] nest among the stars" (v. 4), places that few would dare to approach. But the answer comes swiftly: God will bring them down!

There is a thoroughness and totality to the destruction Obadiah prophesies. In verse one, we see that God plans to use other nations to judge Edom as opposed to using a natural disaster. God employs the desires of free-will humans to work in concert with His own agenda. Their combined purpose is to defeat Edom militarily—not just to the point of submission, but to the point of elimination. In contrast to robbers whose thievery has limits, or grape-gatherers who leave some fruit still hanging, Edom's destruction at the hand of this military force is going to be total (v. 5). As one commentator mentions, the Lord always promised to protect a remnant of the Israelites when they faced destruction, but no similar assurance is given to Edom.[5]

Not only is a military force going to come against Edom, the force itself will be comprised of those who were once allies, or at least thought of as allies. There is a sense of deception here; the "men in [Edom's] confederacy" now "deceive [her] and prevail against [her]." They "lay a trap" for Edom that no one expects (v. 7). Set against the pride of Edom's fortifications, the coming destruction will be worse than anyone imagines. It is like a betrayal from a trusted friend. It is Brutus' blade to an unsuspecting Caesar.

Obadiah continues to make the total destruction known. God will eliminate the wise (v. 8) and the mighty men (v. 9). Edom— here called the two names Esau (a reference to the nation's ancestry) and Teman (a reference to the southern region of Edom)—would have no one left to lean on, no one to heroically rescue them through wisdom or strength.

The pride this nation had known would turn to shame. In location, they were to be brought down. In wealth, they were to be plundered. In friends, they were to be betrayed. In wisdom, they were to be destroyed. In military might, they were to be defeated. As commentator James Smith puts it, "None will be able to give a credible explanation as to how such a powerful nation could have been so completely destroyed."[6] None, except the Lord, who ordained it and chose to show that He would not forget.

Obadiah writes these words of punishment in certain terms. As he scratched out the words on his parchment, he now had the chance to share the reason for these calamities.

# Family Feud

Edom was not just a neighboring nation to the people of God. Edom was family.

In the book of Genesis, we find the story of the Patriarchs, the original ancestors of the nation of Israel. Abraham, Isaac, and Jacob are the three generations whom God promised to work through. Their descendants would be exceedingly numerous, and they would be given a specific parcel of land as part of God's promises. Abraham was given one son, Isaac, as fulfillment of the promise. Isaac was given twin sons, Esau (a.k.a. Edom) and Jacob, to continue the fulfillment of the promise. That promise would pass through only one of those sons, though. God chose the younger and weaker of the two boys to be carrier of His covenant. Jacob would go on to father twelve sons who would become the twelve tribes of Israel. Esau's future, however, was different.

God did bless Esau and his Edomite descendants. In Genesis 35, an account is given of Esau and his prosperous offspring settling in the hill country of Seir. The chapter goes on to fill out the family tree of Esau/Edom, including the chiefs of their tribes and the kings who reigned in that region.

The nation of the Edomites was related to the Israelites. They should have enjoyed a closer relationship. For example, Deuteronomy 23:7 says, "You shall not abhor an Edomite, for he is your brother."

That relationship, like in so many families, was neither a pleasant nor positive one. Edom played the role of antagonist to the Israelites for centuries. When the Israelites were being led to the Promised Land, Edom refused to let them pass through the land (Numbers 20-21), David and Saul later both fought against Edom (1 Samuel 14; 2 Samuel 8), and the Edomites eventually invaded Judah (2 Chronicles 20). Their relationship was neither close nor amicable.

As a result, the Edomites "became the cheering section" when Judah faced its worst conquest at the hands of the

Babylonians.[7] Obadiah describes Edom's sinful attitude in his next section of prophecy. The material is arranged in a "tightly structured series of seven parallel rebukes," building in intensity.[8] The first line of each rebuke informs Edom "You should not…" while the second line of each rebuke describes Judah's troubles "in the day…" The closing rebuke in the list has extra information in order to serve as a kind of emphasis.

- You should not… have gazed on your brother
  In the day… of his captivity. (v. 12)
- You should not… have rejoiced over them
  In the day… of his destruction. (v. 12)
- You should not… have spoken proudly
  In the day… of distress (v. 12)
- You should not… have entered the gate
  In the day… of their calamity (v. 13)
- You should not… have gazed at their affliction
  In the day… of their calamity (v. 13)
- You should not… have laid hands on their substance
  In the day… of their calamity (v. 13)
- You should not… have stood at the crossroads
  to cut off those who escaped
  In the day… of distress (v. 14)
- You should not… have delivered those who remained
  In the day… of distress (v. 14)

The callous attitude of Edom, watching their relatives suffer, was horrible and shameful. It was even remembered elsewhere in the Bible. Psalm 137:7 says, "Remember, O Lord, against the sons of Edom the day of Jerusalem, who said, 'Raze it, raze it, to its very foundation!'" Edom's survival in the face of Judah's defeat would have left many Jews hoping and pleading for God to remember.

Thankfully, God did.

As Edom watched and possibly even joined in the crimes against Judah, God's memory was active. He ordained that Edom would share a similar fate of destruction. In what is called a "day of the Lord"—a common prophetic statement indicating a day of judgment in the near future or in the end times, or sometimes both—punishment is shown as a forgone conclusion for Edom. "As you have done, it shall be done to you... for as you drank [the destruction of Israel]... so shall all the nations drink [your destruction]" (v. 15-16). God remembered, and Edom did not escape.

## Victorious Kingdom

Obadiah could have ended it there. He could have cleaned the ink off his quill, rolled up the parchment, and sealed it off, but he doesn't. Instead, he goes on to share God's intent for this punishment. The punishment will not just have consequences for Edom; it has consequences for Judah which will bolster their faith in God's memory.

If God's plan for Edom is destruction, Obadiah says, His plan for His people in Judah is glory. There will be deliverance and holiness (v. 17). The Jews will "possess their possessions" (v. 17), a clear reference to a full return to the land God had promised His people long ago.[9] Judah and Israel will be the flame, and Edom will be the flammable material that suffers (v. 18). This is God's plan, and it is presented with certainty.

In fact, the final portion of Obadiah's vision sets up a description of this change. Judah is no longer suffering and downtrodden; they are pictured returning to take the Promised Land in victory. Like a real-life game of Risk®, God lays out his plan for conquest. The south shall expand and take over the southern mountains of Edom, while those in the western hills will move victoriously to the coast of the Mediterranean. To the east, the land across the Jordan will be taken, as will the northern region around Samaria. Captives from Israel who likely had been displaced by the

Assyrian invaders long ago will return to claim territory even farther north than Israel's prior borders. Captives from far away in Sepharad (likely a city or region in Babylon, in modern-day Iraq)[10] will return to claim territory far to the south.

And in the end, God shall have His kingdom firmly established.

## THE GOD WHO REMEMBERS

For such a small book, the lessons of Obadiah stand tall among the prophets. You can't read his message without marveling at the God who plans such events. God orchestrates a total, thorough, and just retribution for the Edomites who had abandoned their family ties and brought shame and humiliation to God's people. Not only would Yahweh bring judgment, He would also reverse the fortunes of the Jews as an act of divine blessing.

*Will God remember?*

Anyone who reads this vision will have no doubt about the answer. Obadiah and the reader come away assured of God's steadfast care for His people, giving them a hope and promise that their future will be bright while their enemy's will be bleak. God did not forget.

Edom discovered this. Their judgment was not immediate, but history shows a series of events that lead to the downfall of their nation. Foreigners possessed the lands of Edom by the sixth and fifth centuries BC, and by the second century BC, it was ceded to the Maccabean Jews. For all practical purposes, the Edomites were gone.[11] While some may claim that this several-century delay in punishment was evidence of God's forgetfulness, the Bible emphatically confirms that God's memory was intact. He was able to tailor the punishment to the nation and to His own purposes, working the two in tandem for the greatest benefit to His own kingdom and His own glory.

Whether the Israelites had faith in Him to do so or not, God remembered.

## OBADIAH'S FAITH LESSONS

As Obadiah put the finishing touches on his written prophecy, he had no doubts. His faith was strong in the Lord, and he boldly proclaimed the message that Edom's fate was sealed and Judah's future was bright. He confidently used unambiguous language to make this point so no one could call him weak. Obadiah trusted that God would remember. And, so should we.

Can we share the spirit of Obadiah today? Can we boldly cling to the promise of God's long memory and His unswerving justice? Absolutely! We can and should have faith that God remembers, even when we feel He has forgotten us. Consider how such an attitude of faith could manifest itself in the following contexts.

### Lessons for Israel

The fact that God remembers applies to more than just judgment. God's long memory also extends to His promises. The Old Testament is filled with statements of intent and covenant that apply to Israel and her descendants. These promises are definite, and yet the fulfilment of them rarely happens in the expected timeframe.

For example, Abraham was promised descendants as numerous as the stars and a land in which they would dwell. Yet, by the end of his life, he had only one son and a small burial plot of land as down payments on that promise. Isaac received the same assurance, yet he died with only two sons. Jacob upped the average by having twelve boys, but twelve is a far cry from innumerable! In each case, the person had a promise, yet not a complete fulfilment. They had to have faith that God would remember despite the current lack of evidence.

Israel can today look with confidence at the Bible and remember the promises which have already been fulfilled. In faith, they can then look to the remainder of the promises which are yet to be fulfilled and know that God has not forgotten. Israel must continue to have faith that God will remember and fulfill every word He has spoken. They must have faith that God will not forget the glorious future He has promised.

## Lessons for the Nations

God remembers, and this should cause nations to have faith in His justice. There is no action which God will forget, and no injustice He will be unable to recall.

Like Edom, every nation on every map at some point engages in wrongdoing. Countries are comprised of people who sin, and their collective sins are exposed as national sins. Those sins may be economic, like financial policies that exploit the poor or lead to crippling inflation. Or, they may be acts of war, as men seek to expand their territory at the expense of their neighbors. Whatever the type of sin, no nation is guiltless.

Since God remembers, current nations should take heed and realize that they will not be forgotten. They will reap judgment for their sins. God's long memory should humble all nations. We may not know how God will punish or when He will punish, but we know He can and will.

Nations should consider the fate of Edom, and they should tailor their policies to make the best choices now (and by "best," we mean "godly"). While such policies will be imperfect and imperfectly implemented, they offer a chance for nations to delay the inevitable.

Have faith that God's mercy may supersede His memory. He may delay, even though He won't forget.

## Lessons for the Church

Christian history is filled with splits due to politics, preferences, and practices—and that statement is only referring to individual congregations! While some divisions occur for valid reasons, such as preserving truly essential doctrine, most divisions have been over things far more petty. Churches split over carpet color more frequently than they do over Jesus' identity. The results? Congregations that vilify their brothers and sisters in the Lord.

The conflict between Edom and Israel was one among brothers. Despite their differing paths, these two nations shared an ancestry and a connection to God's blessings. There should not have been animosity between them, but there was, and the results of that conflict show up in Obadiah.

We may feel that God has forgotten the sins of a church with which we split. Yet, more often than not, God just wants us to remember our connections. Obadiah should remind us of the imperatives of church unity. We can have faith that God won't forget those instances of congregational sin, and we can have faith that judgment is in His mindful hands.

In the meantime, we can stop worrying about those issues and instead work on being the Church together. Local congregations can do little to overturn centuries of church splits and denominations, but we have every opportunity to work together in our communities to spread the good news of Jesus Christ. There is no reason a Bible-believing plumber and a Jesus-loving accountant can't work together or worship together, even if their congregations of choice are meeting separately. In the name of God's Kingdom, we can promote united efforts like soup kitchens or adoption resources or fighting human trafficking. By working with those who sincerely belong to Christ, we can forget the pointless divisions that have hurt His cause in so many ways.

## Lessons for You

*Will God remember?*

Our answer to that question should come with confidence after reading through Obadiah. Rather than worry that God may have forgotten, we can have faith that God's memory is intact and sufficient.

That faith should make a tremendous difference in our prayer life. We can ask God to help us trust His timing and memory. We can ask Him to help us patiently wait for His justice to be made known. We can ask Him to empower us to love others while we wait. We can ask Him for wisdom to get us through the moments when we doubt.

Our perception of life tends to be too short-sighted. When we see injustice, we want the situation resolved before the judge's gavel can pound the bench. If we see illness, we want healing before the doctor finishes writing the prescription. If God doesn't act in that moment, the clock starts ticking and our questions of His memory may grow. Obadiah's faith instead reminds us that God's memory is longer than ours. A murderer may not be executed quickly, but God may remember his crimes and allow him to face the mental anguish of guilt for decades. A relentless cancer may not be healed by chemotherapy, but God remembers and heals the person with a newly resurrection body for all of eternity.

This short book of prophecy should give us the faith to trust that God remembers, even if we feel that He has forgotten.

*God will remember!*

## QUESTIONS FOR DISCUSSION

1.  What are some examples of God's memory in Scripture? How do they affirm God's long memory as shown in Obadiah?

2.  Why do you think the Edomites failed to treat their brothers (the Israelites) with concern rather than contempt?

3.  Edom's pride assured their downfall. How does pride blind us to God's will for us?

4.  A callous attitude toward God's people has negative consequences. What role can the Holy Spirit play in helping us avoid such an attitude?

5.  Why might God's timeline for justice be better than our own?

6.  How does faith in God's long memory grant us freedom?

7.  What things do we no longer have to worry about if we have faith that God will remember?

8.  What promises of God do you sometimes forget? (Thank God for His faithfulness, even when we are faithless.)

# FAITH JOURNEY 5
## JONAH: FAITH WHEN YOU DON'T FEEL LIKE IT

## THE PALE STRANGER

*"What's wrong with him?"*

Jonah was sick of the whispers and the pointing fingers, the awkward glances and the outright rudeness. This time the question was coming from a group of pre-teen boys who either didn't realize their voices carried across the bustling market square or simply didn't care. Jonah turned and stared at them, his expression a mixture of annoyance and anger. Their smiles and laughter trailed off.

Striding past the spices, slipping past the dates and figs, and ducking under the hand-woven rugs for sale, Jonah quickly approached the gang with a look of intensity none of them expected. One boy hastily began sweeping up a nearby vendor's stall, his sudden interest in tidiness fooling no one. Another scurried past an animated merchant next door as he haggled over the price of olive oil with an angry customer; their gesturing arms served as camouflage and protection from Jonah's apparent fury. But a few youths remained, calmly staring at the strange figure drawing near.

Jonah stepped close and addressed the ringleader. *"Something to say?"* he quietly asked the boy. His bleached skin practically glowed next to the dark tunic he wore, and a wrinkled hand clutched the walking stick he used as he ventured through the massive city. Stringy hair fell across his eyes, which gazed with fire at the lanky child who stared back.

Without hesitation, fueled by curiosity and a bit of daring, the boy repeated his question. "What's wrong with you?"

Jonah paused as the words piled up in his mouth. He stopped before an insult spilled out, checked his tongue at a sarcastic comment, and reeled in the truth. So many people in Nineveh during the past two days had asked variations of that same question. Time and time he had answered; sometimes in excruciating detail, sometimes with the briefest of replies. He was tired of the reactions, each one drawn from the imaginations of the crowd. No one could truly know what it was like to be abandoned in the ocean with the swells crashing around you, to feel the waters close in over your head perhaps for the last time, to feel the shock and horror as the water gave way to a gaping mouth. They couldn't know the terror and isolation of being inside that ghastly creature for days that felt like weeks, nor the jolt of being expelled to safety. The tale had earned him an audience, and each time the crowd of Assyrians clamored to hear more.

But, he always ended with the same few words. And now, as the boy stared at him with a smirk, mistaking Jonah's hesitation for weakness, Jonah decided to skip over the prologue and get right to the point.

As the bustle of the market continued around them, Jonah drew in closer until his brown eyes were level with the boy's.

"Laugh all you want, Kid," Jonah breathed. "Just know this. Forty days..." a white finger poked the boy's chest to emphasize each word, "...and Nineveh. Will. Be. Overturned."

## UNENTHUSIASTIC AFFIRMATIVES

My (Steve's) first girlfriend was an eighth-grader named Missy. Missy and I sat next to each other in band, at the intersection of trombones and baritones. We were friendly to each other; she attended our church youth group, and we occasionally made small talk. Then one day, things changed, and in the most Junior-Highish of ways. One of her closest friends approached me as I was sitting on the bleachers and informed me that she had a question to ask on Missy's behalf: "Would I go out with her?"

I struggled to answer. Not only was I completely inexperienced in the ways of women, but I didn't even like Missy! At least, not in *that* way. She was nice enough, and decent looking, but I didn't really want to *date* her. Regardless, I said I would give it some thought. A long bus ride home, some sleepless hours at night, and a long bus ride back did little to provide solace. Conflicted, I walked into school. I had no desire to say "yes," but I had no obvious reason to say "no." With little enthusiasm and a misguided sense of obligation, I reluctantly gave Missy's friend the message. By the end of the day, I was the talk of the middle school: Missy and I were an item.

I share this story with you to make a simple point: it's tough to say "yes" when you don't feel like it.

To this day, I can still remember the inner squirming and dread as that single syllable crossed my lips to Missy. I can recall the uncertainty as my answer sparked a flurry of eighth-grade gossip, and I can relive the sense of foreboding knowing that I just agreed to something I didn't really want.

Those feelings aren't limited just to middle school romance, though, nor are they limited just to me. It turns out that plenty of other situations elicit the same responses from all of mankind. They surface every time you say "yes" to your boss when he asks you to work on the weekend, or when you say "yes" to the Internal Revenue Service's polite request for an audit, or as you tell your dentist "yes" right before he fires up the drill for a root canal. Life doesn't always give you the chance to excuse yourself from participation. Like it or not, you're going to say "yes."

Still, it's tough to say "yes" when you don't feel like it! There is an innate human desire to resist, to ignore, to struggle, to retort, or to deny. We are either too busy, or too proud, or too stressed, or too comfortable to change our current course. We don't understand the need for our involvement, or else we don't care.

Perhaps no other situation highlights this principle like God's call in our life. Obedience to God's call often brings out a reactionary "no" from us. Not this person, not this time, not this action. No. No. No. NO. NO! Our aversion to saying "yes" may be with the reluctance of a ten-year old who rolls his eyes when asked to do a chore, or the defiance of a teenager when told he can't go out with friends. Yet, no matter the foot-dragging or the whining or the pleas, we eventually must have faith and say "yes" to God's plans.

Look through the pages of the Bible and you'll see example after example of people charging back-first into God's will.

Consider Moses at the burning bush. In Exodus 3, we read how God selected Moses to be His instrument to rescue the Israelites from slavery in Egypt. However, Moses comes up with every excuse he can think of to avoid this assignment. "Who will I say sent me? What if they reject me? I'm not talented enough to do it!" Moses' attempts to wriggle out of God's will failed. Even though he didn't feel like it, Moses eventually said "yes."

Or, consider the Israelites on their first approach to the Promised Land. In Numbers 14, the newly-formed nation struggled to say "yes" to God when He told them to enter and claim the land of Canaan. The Israelites balked, preferring to listen to the advice of those who said taking over the land was impossible. Though God had miraculously led them and fed them to this point, and though He had proven himself mighty in battle, Israel concluded that the inhabitants of Canaan were too big to fight. "Perhaps a return trip to Egypt isn't so bad after all," they reasoned. Despite their inclination to spurn God's commands, the Israelites eventually, though after a forty-year detour through the wilderness and the passing of an entire generation, said "yes."

Want further examples? Gideon needed a fleece before saying "yes" to attacking the Midianites (Judges 6). Peter needed a vision before saying "yes" to sharing the gospel with a Gentile named Cornelius (Acts 10). Paul needed a miraculous encounter with the risen Christ and a multi-day stint of blindness before saying "yes" to Christianity and a life on the mission field (Acts 9 and following). Men and women from Sarah to Saul to Esther to Thomas have shared the all-too-human hesitation to follow God when His requests seem tough.

None of those examples can hold a candle to Jonah, our Minor Prophet of choice here. His unwillingness to agree to God's will led to the astounding events in this short book that bears his name. His "yes" required some outrageous persuasion, but his struggle to obey (perhaps more than any other person in the Bible) can reveal some deep lessons about faith.

How do we say "yes" to God when He asks the impossible? How do we obey God when doing so feels like a burden or a sentence? How do we maintain faith when every fiber of our being resists? How do we have faith when we don't feel like it?

Let's read on for some answers.

## THE PROPHET IN FLIGHT

### Time of the Prophet

Jonah's story is undeniably a "whale of a tale." He may be the most well-known of the Bible's prophets, but there is more to him than a maritime adventurer inside a sea creature. The details just get swallowed up by the fantastic nature of his story.

Jonah, son of Amittai, was a prophet. Whether he was a prophet before this event or not is unknown. Jonah could have had a long history of sharing God's messages, or this could have been his first assignment. However, we know he was a prophet by this point because of the opening verses of the book were, "Now the word of the Lord came to Jonah..." (1:1).

While the book of Jonah itself gives us little background to his story, we learn a bit more about the prophet and his circumstances from connected references in Scripture. In 2 Kings 14:25, a "Jonah son of Amittai" is also described as giving messages from Yahweh. Reasonable people can infer that one prophet named "Jonah son of Amittai" is probably the same as another prophet with the same name and same father. Since these two Jonahs are one and the same, then the details of 2 Kings can fill in the gaps where our book is lacking. Two important pieces of information surface.

First, we find that Jonah's hometown was in the northern part of Israel, a town called Gath-Hepher. The town was located west of the Sea of Galilee; in fact, it was just a couple of miles from Jesus' future hometown of Nazareth. Jonah's connection to the Northern Kingdom of Israel is significant. His prophetic message is to the nation of Assyria, the nation that will conquer Israel in 722 BC. That Jonah's message is delivered to an enemy of Israel makes the content of that message even more compelling.

Second, we deduce from the passage in 2 Kings the timeframe of Jonah's life. The period of Jonah's prophetic ministry is during the reign of the Israelite King Jeroboam II. During this time, around 780-745 BC, the Assyrian capital city of Nineveh was at a weak point. Their previous ruler had passed away, and the power vacuum he left opened the door for Assyria's opponents to encroach on their territory. Mountain tribes from the north pushed their borders uncomfortably close to the city of Nineveh itself during this time of weakness, causing nervousness among the population and fears about Assyria's future. Jonah's message to Nineveh, with its warning of imminent destruction, would have found greater receptivity during this time of weakness than it would have at any other time in Assyrian history.[1]

Context helps us better understand Jonah's situation, but the rest of what we need to know about Jonah is tied to his person. The faith lessons come more from his character and experience than from his background, and such information is delivered to us in rich detail in this short book.

## Avoiding the Call of the Prophet

*In the port of Joppa, Jonah picked his way through crowds of seamen loading and unloading cargo from their ships. To his right, the briny Mediterranean waters lapped against the dock while the constant cries of seagulls carried over the breeze. On any other occasion, Jonah would have stopped to soak in the view and the warm sun, enjoying the occasional shade of a passing cloud. Today, though, he had no time for enjoyment.*

*Ahead, he spotted the vessel he had been looking for. It seemed small against the backdrop of open waters beyond the port, but it had been affirmed as seaworthy by the local traders and would certainly do its job. Jonah paused a few feet from the gangway, squinting up at the tanned men carrying boxes and jars into the cargo hold, dripping with sweat from their labor. Jonah hopped onto the ramp and approached the rigging of the boat's single mast, seeking out the only man who wasn't lugging freight. The captain paused from giving orders and directing men.*

*A few pleasantries ensued, followed by a bag of coins from Jonah and a nod from the skipper. Jonah found a corner of the ship where he was out of the way and set his belongings down, still gazing at the waves. Soon, he would be chasing the sun on its westward course and he would no longer feel the burden of ignoring God's call here in the land of Israel.*

In the opening of the book, God abruptly presents a call to Jonah: "Arise, go to Nineveh, that great city, and cry out against it; for their wickedness has come up before Me" (1:2). There is no preamble, no description of how the word came. The call is quick, concise and clear.

As soon as the reader hears that instruction, he expects the next verse to show obedience. The pattern of the Minor Prophets so far have conditioned us to assume that a call to proclaim will immediately be acknowledged and perfectly obeyed. However, Jonah's reaction breaks new ground. In the next verse, we read that Jonah did indeed arise, but he does not travel northeast toward Nineveh (located in modern-day Iraq). Instead, Jonah promptly heads west to the port city of Joppa (on the southwest coast of modern-day Israel). We soon discover that Joppa is only a stopping point so Jonah could find passage to a place even further west, the city of Tarshish (possibly in modern-day Spain or even England). His destination was about as far away from Nineveh as one could practically go in the ancient Mediterranean world and, thus, about as far away from God's call as one could possibly go.

Jonah is intent on saying "no" to God's command, and the language of the passage shows how decisively he avoids it. Jonah does not go *up* to Nineveh; instead he goes *down*: *down* to Joppa (1:3), *down* into a ship (1:5), and laying *down* in the bottom of the ship (1:5). The only thing that could make Jonah's deliberate ignorance of the call more obvious is if he were to cover his ears, close his eyes and scream like a toddler, "I'm not listening!"

Why was it so difficult for Jonah to say "yes" to God? The answer lies no further than the intended audience of God's message. Nineveh was the capital city of the Assyrians, one of the ancient world's cruelest peoples. Assyrian violence was well-known and feared. Whenever they won victory in battle, what followed was a parade of gruesomeness that's too hard to imagine. Dismemberment, flaying, decapitation and more were the standard practices of the Assyrian army, and they preserved a record of this violence in their written history. In fact, their fierceness was a matter of national pride.[2] If Jonah went to the Assyrians to proclaim their doom, he would likely be treated as bad as or worse than those the Assyrians routinely conquered. It would be safer to find a lion in a cave and poke it relentlessly with a stick!

While the danger of this assignment would have been enough to make any prophet pause, Jonah has another motivation for not wanting to go to Nineveh. He doesn't want the city and its people to be saved.

Later in the chapter, we read about Jonah's fear. "Ah, Lord, was not this what I said when I was still in my country? Therefore I fled previously to Tarshish; for I know that You are a gracious and merciful God, slow to anger and abundant in lovingkindness, One who relents from doing harm" (4:2). Jonah sees the evil and wickedness of the Assyrians and he doesn't want God to have mercy on them. As one commentator stated, "Not fear of failure, but fear of success prompted Jonah to run from his calling. He did not want these heathen to be saved from God's wrath."[3] Jonah was fully aware of God's fondness for forgiveness, and it was simply unacceptable for the evil people of Nineveh.

Not wanting to play any part in mercy, Jonah fled. As a prophet, Jonah understood that Yahweh was not a local deity. Jonah must have been aware of God's omnipresence and the fact that "fleeing" from God himself was an impossibility. However, in his defiance he chose to act as if God could be avoided. Jonah went away from the presence of the Lord, or at least from the place where God's presence was more closely associated. He tried to pretend that the call never happened, that God would write him off and would work out the details some other way.

## SURPRISE ON THE SEA

While Jonah certainly didn't feel like having faith, God would not be content to allow him to say no. The marvelously composed narrative of Jonah shows God pursuing him with gusto. The biblical story captivates us with its details and development of the plot.

We read that a divine wind finds Jonah's hired craft at sea, and the subsequent storm and swells threaten the safety of the entire crew. In fear for their lives, the sailors do all they can to save the vessel and keep it afloat, including fervent prayer to various gods. Their search for divine assistance leads them to Jonah, who sleeping is ignorant at the bottom of the ship.

The dialogue between Jonah and the crew during this time of stress and danger begins an interesting turnaround for our central character. When the pagan sailors gain nothing from asking their own gods for help in the storm, they plead for Jonah to consult his God. Despite running away from Yahweh, Jonah owns up to his identity. "I am a Hebrew; and I fear the Lord, the God of heaven, who made the sea and the dry land" (1:9).

There is a note of bravery in that statement. Jonah has done his best so far to distance himself from the Lord, to say "no" to God's call, but here he has the courage to face reality and to acknowledge his mistake. Jonah now allows the fear of God to surpass his fear of the Assyrians (both in the sense of "reverent worship" and in the sense of "being terrified for your life"). As the timbers creaked, the salt sprayed their faces, and the howling wind made it difficult to talk, Jonah's confession was a ray of sunshine that offered hope to the desperate deckhands. By owning up to his and God's identity, there was now a chance to fix the problem.

The solution Jonah proposes, though, was for him to leave the boat immediately and plunge into the sea. Jonah reasoned that God had little interest in the sailors, for it was him He wanted. But Jonah's newfound bravery falters yet again. Instead of valiantly jumping off the side of the boat himself, he instructs the men to throw him overboard. The impetus is on them. Jonah would sit and wait for someone else to act. It's hard to have faith when you don't feel like it!

The men try to find another option for safety by rowing toward shore, but when the waves get too intense, they accede to Jonah's proposal. Asking God for forgiveness, they chuck the prophet into the deep. Immediately the seas grow calm. The men are saved!

This sudden reversal of fortunes, from certain doom to miraculous security, leads the sailors to celebrate and worship the true Lord over the ocean. In one of the great ironies of this book, Jonah's reluctance to preach God's mercy to one group of foreign idolaters results in another group of foreign idolaters discovering God's goodness and mercy. Despite Jonah's hesitations, the will of God is accomplished through him.

What happens next is familiar to almost anyone who has heard this tale from Scripture. A "great fish," as the Bible calls it, swallows Jonah and rescues him from the waves, breakers and currents that threatened to drown him. While getting eaten by a giant fish would normally seem like the end of the road, God miraculously used the fish as an organic submarine. Inside, Jonah was safe and protected from drowning.

We hear few details from the experience. The fish keeps Jonah inside as it makes its way back across the Mediterranean Sea. The cramped quarters inside, the partially digested sea creatures floating around, and the sloshing gastric juices became an unlikely place of repentance for Jonah. Three days and three nights in the beast opened Jonah's eyes to some important spiritual truths.

With nowhere to run, Jonah recognizes God's provision. He sees the storm and his plunge into the ocean not as punishment, but as a catalyst for change. Setting a striking example for us to follow in the midst of our own hesitations, Jonah says, "I have been cast out of Your sight; Yet I will look again toward Your holy temple" (2:4). Faith trumps feelings. Jonah repents. In a moment of profound honesty, he observes that, "Those who regard worthless idols forsake their own Mercy. But I will sacrifice to You with the voice of thanksgiving; I will pay what I have vowed. Salvation *is* of the LORD" (2:8-9). Jonah sets aside his own feelings and his own fears and commits them to God, stating his willingness to do what God had asked. It's possible that Jonah may have regarded his changed heart as a deathbed confession, but God had other plans. The newfound faith wouldn't be hypothetical. It would be given a chance to act.

*The big fish broke the surface of the water yet again, gulping in the life-giving air that kept the man inside breathing as they swam around the sea. Jonah hardly gave it any thought, as it was just another one of hundreds of times the fish had done this in the past three days. Jonah's eyes remained closed as he prayed to the Lord. But he was distracted by the stomach muscles contracting and writhing underneath him. In the darkness, Jonah's prayer trailed off and then...*

*In a rush of confusion, Jonah felt himself squeezed and twisted and propelled forward. He was surrounded by the familiar hot stench and sting of acid, but then cold and salty water filled his mouth. Sputtering, Jonah extended his limbs only to discover that they weren't constrained by the fish's stomach. Instead, one hand touched sand and a foot broke the surface of the waves. Righting himself, Jonah put a knee on the sea bed and his head came clear of the water. He shook the wet hair out of his face and blinked and squinted in the sudden brightness. Gasping for breath, he stumbled his way toward the beach. The water grew shallower, first at his waist, then his knees, then his ankles. Wet sand gave way to dry and Jonah collapsed in jubilant exhaustion, lying among the shells and seaweed and rocks. He let out a mix of water-logged coughs and laughs, amazed at his good God and his unbelievable experience.*

*As he sat sand-covered on the beach, Jonah heard a familiar voice. "Go to the great city of Nineveh and proclaim to it the message I give you."*

*This time, Jonah nodded emphatically.*

## SURPRISE IN THE CITY

We don't know where the fish deposited Jonah, but the prophet next travelled eastward to Assyria (hopefully after a quick stop to change clothes and get cleaned up). The Jonah who arrived at Nineveh was a different man than the one who had run away to Tarshish. This Jonah was willing and bold, going to the city and stating God's message clearly: "Forty more days and Nineveh will be overturned!"

One can only imagine the strange sight this preaching would have been to the Assyrian residents. Here was a foreigner walking around town for three day (3:3), shouting the same message over and over again.

Not only were his actions strange, but his appearance was odd. We have little evidence to show exactly how an extended time in an aquatic tummy would affect a person, but we can speculate that his skin and hair could have been altered, at least temporarily. Jonah's strange appearance would have led to questions, and the even stranger tale that matched it would likely have provided extra incentive to truly consider the words Jonah pronounced.[3] Regardless, such changes were unnecessary, for if Jonah had gone when first called, Nineveh could still have reacted positively to God's message without Jonah's miraculous experience.

In a twist few would expect, the people of Nineveh received and accepted Jonah's words. Rather than kill Jonah, they repented! From the shacks of the peasants to the great gates that guarded the entrance to Nineveh, the residents believed God, turned to Him, and sought mercy. Even their king took the warning seriously, issuing a proclamation of fasting and mourning, and most importantly, repentance from evil and violence. Since their wickedness was the reason for God's message (1:2), this turning of hearts led to a reciprocating change in God's decision. "Then God saw their works, that they turned from their evil way; and God relented from the disaster that He had said He would bring upon them, and He did not do it" (3:10).

Some have doubted the sincerity of the city's response, but the Bible makes it clear that this was an actual change of heart. Jesus refers to this incident and says, "The men of Nineveh will rise up in the judgment with this generation and condemn it, because *they repented* [emphasis mine] at the preaching of Jonah; and indeed a greater than Jonah is here" (Matthew 12:41).

While the fate of Nineveh is key, the story moves on in chapter four and focuses more on Jonah's reaction than their repentance. Preaching at Nineveh certainly was a transformation for Jonah, but even in his obedience we discover that Jonah still didn't feel like following God. Rather than rejoice at the Assyrians' repentance and God's relenting from His threats, Jonah is sullen and angry. Saying "yes" was hard enough, and now his reasons for saying "no" are confirmed. He actually prefers death to the sight of his enemies' pardon!

Still holding out hope that God might destroy the formerly evil Assyrian city, Jonah camps out to wait and watch. East of the city, he constructs a shelter where he can have some shade. If this scene were in modern times, you could almost picture him with a fold-up camping chair, an umbrella for shade, some sunglasses and a bottle of Coke, all ready for the show.

Jonah still doesn't feel like following God. If he did, he could have been down in the city proclaiming God's mercy, celebrating with her citizens, and instructing them how to develop this opportunity into a lifetime of devotion to Yahweh. Instead, he waits for vindication of the message of destruction he has so enthusiastically preached.

During this pouting session, God takes the opportunity to teach Jonah. He provides an "object lesson" of sorts involving a quick-growing, shade-producing vine. On the first day, God causes the vine to grow and provide additional relief for Jonah from the sun. On the second day, God provides a worm that chews through and withers the vine. He also provides a scorching wind and a blazing sun. The lack of shade and the increased heat cause intense suffering for Jonah, and he again prefers death to his current circumstances.

The interchange between God and Jonah that follows, though, is revealing. Jonah shares his anger about the vine's demise, but God has a pointed reply:

> *"You have had pity on the plant for which you have not labored, nor made it grow, which came up in a night and perished in a night. And should I not pity Nineveh, that great city, in which are more than one hundred and twenty thousand persons who cannot discern between their right hand and their left—and much livestock?" (4:10-11).*

With that question, Jonah's tale ends.

## POINT OF THE TALE

After reading the book, we are left with a strong sense of its purpose. The emphasis, contrary to every children's Bible ever illustrated, is not on a man being swallowed and saved by a big fish. No, the structure points us in another direction.

God's lesson in the closing section of chapter four serves as the focal point of the entire book. One can divide Jonah's book of prophecy into parallel sections:

- A commission to go to Nineveh (disobeyed in 1:1-3 and obeyed in 3:1-3a)
- His experience with pagans (sailors in 1:4-16 and Nineveh in 3:3b-10)
- His prayers (positive inside the fish in 1:17-2:10 and negative outside the city in 4:1-4)

However, the seventh and final section, which includes God's object lesson, follows these parallel sections and stands out as the climax of the story.[5] In it, we see explicitly stated what we inferred from the rest of the book: God cares about people. Both the pagan sailors and the pagan inhabitants of Nineveh were worth enough in God's eyes to confront and to save. Rather than simply judging them, He looks for a way to turn their hearts.

God's actions in this book are an example of His extreme patience and long-suffering. We read about these qualities of God elsewhere in Scripture:

- "And the LORD passed before him and proclaimed, 'The LORD, the LORD God, merciful and gracious, longsuffering, and abounding in goodness and truth...'" (Exodus 34:6).
- "But You *are* God, Ready to pardon, gracious and merciful, slow to anger, abundant in kindness, and did not forsake them" (Nehemiah 9:17b).
- "But You, O Lord, *are* a God full of compassion, and gracious, longsuffering and abundant in mercy and truth" (Psalm 86:15).

Such passages echo what we find in Jonah, both in declaration (4:2) and in action. God's patience is adequately shown to people who don't deserve it. Sailors who never knew the Lord leave with a newfound faith and trust in Him. A city that never turned to God before discovers repentance and mercy.

God's patience is on full display in the book of Jonah, but it is not limited just to the pagans; it is poured out on Jonah himself. God endures Jonah's flight, Jonah's reluctance, Jonah's moping, Jonah's anger, and Jonah's failure to see His purpose. While Jonah does not feel like having faith, God demonstrates His own faithfulness. God refuses to allow the prophet to avoid carrying out the given assignment. God's patience trumps the prophet's hesitancy.

While Jonah did not initially feel like sharing God's heart in this matter, he eventually gave in and acted with obedience. Despite his own reservations, Jonah followed God. In the end, his choice of faith made a huge difference in Jonah's life and ministry.

*The dark sometimes made Jonah anxious. As night closed in around his home, an hour after sunset and with the moon still waiting to rise, the darkness outside brought memories of the stormy, sunless sea and the pitch-black interior of his fishy rescuer. But the floor beneath Jonah's feet was solid, and the oil lamps he had placed around the room kept it light and cozy. He knew that he should retire for the night, but just a few more minutes were needed.*

*Sitting at a table, Jonah squinted in concentration at the scroll before him. With a final few strokes of the pen, he smiled and looked over his work. The written account of his locally famous experience was a bit embarrassing. How could he have been so blind and foolish toward God? Still, the lessons were important for others to learn. God had not only used him to deliver a message to the people of Nineveh, but the truths about God's patience and mercy needed to be shared widely. It would be hard to reveal his own flaws in the story, but Jonah had learned it was always better to say "yes" to God no matter the cost.*

*With that knowledge, Jonah rolled up the scroll, tied it up, blew out most of the lamps, and laid down.*

## Jonah's Faith Lessons

Jonah's tale opens the door for us to learn from his reluctant faith. His attitudes and reactions are on full display, presented in a format which drives the point home. Having faith when you don't feel like it can be a difficult experience. Yet, Jonah's obedience and willingness to (eventually) put himself where God could use him shows us that a "yes" to God's call is always best no matter how hard it seems.

What can we learn from that attitude? Consider the following faith lessons.

## Lessons for Israel

Reading through the Bible, one can easily get myopia. God's special relationship with the nation of Israel is a central and defining aspect of Scripture. However, stories like Jonah's remind us that God has been and continues to be active in the lives of other peoples. He is the God of the Israelites as well as the Assyrians, Mayans, Prussians, Chinese, Navajo, and Arabs – not the god that their cultures worship, but the God who reigns nonetheless.

Israel has often faced persecution at the hands of other nations and cultures, but God's love for His people does not retaliate immediately against these enemies. Instead, God consistently shares the fact that He loves Gentiles, too. Jews should see that love in the Old Testament, and they should recognize the prophesied Messiah carries forward God's same love and desire to win over the nations.

Instead of having reluctance to share the goodness and grace of God with these foreigners, Jews should hear in Jonah the message that God's goodness and grace extend beyond the boundaries of Israel to the world. It is a message that is echoed in the New Testament:

> *"Now I say that Jesus Christ has become a servant to the circumcision for the truth of God, to confirm the promises made to the fathers, and that the Gentiles might glorify God for His mercy, as it is written: 'For this reason I will confess to You among the Gentiles, And sing to Your name.' And again he says: 'Rejoice, O Gentiles, with His people!' And again: 'Praise the LORD, all you Gentiles! Laud Him, all you peoples!' And again, Isaiah says: 'There shall be a root of Jesse; And He who shall rise to reign over the Gentiles, in Him the Gentiles shall hope.' Now may the God of hope fill you with all joy*

133

> *and peace in believing, that you may abound in*
> *hope by the power of the Holy Spirit" (Romans*
> *15:8–13).*

Instead of reluctance, let there be an enthusiastic "Yes!" to God's plans to rule over *all* people, first the Jews and then the Gentiles. Embrace the Messiah, Jesus Christ, who loves not just Nineveh, but all of mankind. Embrace those who are grafted in like a wild olive root to the tree of God's covenant. See God's plan of salvation from His perspective, and you will gain both a greater vision of how big His glory can be and a bigger faith.

## Lessons for the Nations

Nations are reluctant to act in a way that presents humility. Security seems to demand a projection of strength to convince others that any threat can be turned away and avenged. From the parades of chained and defeated captives in the ancient world to goose-stepping soldiers flanking missile trucks in the modern world, strength is paramount.

But God prescribes a different source of security.

When faced with a threat of attack, the king of Nineveh took action that was surely unpopular, or at least unwise according to conventional standards. Rather than rally an army, the king called for repentance. Leading by example, he set aside his own dignity and clothed himself in sackcloth and ashes, a symbolic demonstration of mourning and humility. He extended his actions by decree:

> *"And he caused it to be proclaimed and*
> *published throughout Nineveh by the decree of*
> *the king and his nobles, saying, 'Let neither man*
> *nor beast, herd nor flock, taste anything; do not*
> *let them eat, or drink water. But let man and*
> *beast be covered with sackcloth, and cry*

> *mightily to God; yes, let every one turn from his*
> *evil way and from the violence that is in his*
> *hands. Who can tell if God will turn and relent,*
> *and turn away from His fierce anger, so that we*
> *may not perish?"' (3:7-9).*

Can a nation really gain strength by adopting weakness? Such a move is hard to accept. It is difficult to say "yes" to an action that guarantees diminished respect by peers. Yet humility puts a nation on better terms with an almighty God. Nineveh went from certain destruction to safety simply as a result of this spiritual about-face.

Humility is hard to implement. It goes counter to our every impulse as a nation. But even though it is difficult to say "yes," our leaders should heed the warning of Nineveh's king and point people toward a relationship with Jesus in order to place their nation on solid ground.

## Lessons for the Church

Of any group that shouldn't have to worry about saying "yes" to Jesus, the Church should be it. Given the gift of the Holy Spirit, spending time each week gathered to discuss the Word of God, we would expect the Church to always be excited to follow God. Yet, individual churches have a difficult time living out the ideals of Christianity.

Sometimes the challenge comes as a result of personality, such as a church that gets caught up in a debate over matters of personal perspective. The gridlock makes it hard to quickly follow God's leading. Other times the challenge comes as a result of theology, such as a church that embraces social justice at the expense of the salvation of the soul, and finds itself turning aside the very people it presumably wants to help. Still other times the challenge is a matter of practicality, such as a church that hesitates to step out in faith and follow God's leading because they can't guarantee funding for a critical outreach project.

In most of these churches, Jonah provides the necessary course correction. We find it in an incident where Jesus responded to a crowd of Jewish leaders who asked for a sign.

> *"He answered and said to them, 'An evil and adulterous generation seeks after a sign, and no sign will be given to it except the sign of the prophet Jonah. For as Jonah was three days and three nights in the belly of the great fish, so will the Son of Man be three days and three nights in the heart of the earth'" (Matthew 12:39-40).*

The sign of Jonah that Jesus promised was a picture of Jesus' death, burial and resurrection. These primary doctrines of the faith are the central point of agreement that can help us overcome church difficulties.

We may not feel like agreeing in the face of doctrinal differences, but when we shift the focus to our risen Lord, we can agree to exhibit grace on the nonessentials and find unity on the essentials. We may not feel like showing love to those who are unlovely, but we need the reminder that Jesus died for the sins of mankind. Others are just as unworthy to receive salvation as we are. We may not feel confident about the provision of resources, but a look at the empty tomb and the rolled away stone melts our doubts that God can provide.

Jonah, serving as a signpost that points us to Jesus, gives us reason to say "yes" to God's call and God's commands. Our Lord's supremacy gives us the impetus to step out and follow even when we don't feel like having faith.

## Lessons for You

What has God called you to do? Perhaps, like Jonah, you heard the call and decided to pretend that God couldn't reach you where you are. Or, perhaps you fled to a spiritual Tarshish, like in a divorce, or with alcohol, or by self-loathing, or with pornography—just to "get away."

Jonah's book reminds us that we can't escape no matter where we go. If I don't feel like having faith, my feelings will not negate God's will. He will do whatever it takes to get my attention and accomplish His purposes. These situations don't have an exit strategy. They are circumstances that cannot be escaped.

The hesitant faith of Jonah reminds us that we face the same choices he did. We can respond by despising God's chastening and refusing to confess when we are wrong. We can respond by fainting and giving up. Or, we can respond by enduring God's chastening, confessing our sins, and trusting Him as we move forward.

Faith when you don't feel like it can be hard, but know that you aren't alone in facing these challenges. Look to the biblical example of those who have gone before. See how they trusted God, even when they didn't want to. Instead of fleeing in fear and anger, cling to the God whose plans are bigger than you can dream and whose purposes are mind-blowing in their scope and power.

Don't forfeit the mercy that could be yours. Like Jonah, learn to have faith when you don't feel like it.

## QUESTIONS FOR DISCUSSION

1. Share a time when you were reluctant to follow God's leading. Why were you hesitant?

2. What are the most common reasons people don't want to follow God's call?

3. How does our society discourage following God's call?

4. What counsel would you give to the residents of Nineveh as they engaged in repentance? What would help their newfound faith last in a culture that was not used to following God?

5. Jonah's example is mostly a negative one, full of attitudes and actions to avoid. Who are some positive examples of men or women who followed God's call even when they didn't feel like it?

6. What is the relationship between emotion and obedience?

# Faith Journey 6
# Micah: Faith When Government Has Failed

## God's Lawyer

"Please, Sire, please, I beg of you. Without our family lands, where will we live? We'll have nothing to grow. My family will starve!" The sobbing man pleaded on his knees before the king. His teary eyes gazing respectfully down upon the stone courtyard.

Ahaz, sovereign over all Jerusalem and Judah, scowled down from his lofty height upon the court's raised bench. With barely restrained patience, he sneered contemptuously, "What business is it of mine if your family doesn't have... What was it again? Ah, yes, food. Isn't it for the greater good of our nation that you do your part in keeping our Syrian enemies away?" Cocking an eye at the groveling man, Ahaz accused, "Do you not want us to be spared from their wrath?" The man's blubbering response was indiscernible. Rolling his eyes, the king shifted position on his dais in order to change tactics, then added with a feigned importance, "Take comfort! Your patriotic sacrifice will long be remembered."

At this remark a soft snort emanated from the jury benches of the twelve watching elders. A young prince in training, also observing the proceedings from his own spectator's chair, glanced timidly towards the softly snickering officials. These men made Prince Hezekiah feel even more uneasy than he'd already been feeling throughout the long day's proceedings. From this open courtroom situated just outside the Temple gate, he'd witnessed his *father the king and the governmental officials in case after case strip one poor farmer after another of their rights and land. The sacrifices, no, let's be honest—the thefts—were each couched in the flag of duty and patriotism. He shuddered inwardly at the sight, for the lofty counselors maintained the hungry look of a pack of starved wolves, and the peasant farmer was the rabbit!*

*Before the poor man could eke out one more plea, the king dismissed him with a bored wave of the hand. The bailiffs descended upon the weeping man with batons and dragged him harshly out of the king's presence. No sooner had the man's cries faded out of earshot than the king and his counselors erupted in uproarious laughter! Long moments later, when they'd finally gotten control of themselves, a fat official in silken blue robes commented, "Did you see the look on his face as he was being 'escorted' away, Sire? I believe that one wins the prize." The king wiped a tear from his eye and nodded a reply. "Oh, no, the prize is yours. Indenture the farmer to finish the season and then throw him out. I expect you to double my portion of the harvest, though." The official smiled wickedly and gave a slight bow. Hezekiah had watched queasily as this scenario play out again and again with each passing case, as Judah's officials reduced their own countrymen into destitution.*

*The king's head lolled over towards Hezekiah and fixed him with a disappointed glare. "No stomach for being a ruler, Hezekiah? You not man enough?" The disdain in his father's voice was evident. Hezekiah knew better than to disagree with his father, or end up just like his brothers, all of whom were now dead. Out of the sight of this court, the punishment for his mild temperament would be yet another harsh beating. Here at least he only had to endure public humiliation.*

*King Ahaz, disappointed at not getting a rise out his weakling son, rubbed his hands together and asked the court's scribe, "Okay, who's next on the docket?" The scribe read from his schedule. "Sire, it is a plea from the city of Moresheth near Gath. They are disputing the decree to turn their town over to Assyria as payment for their* aid." He studied the page for a second confused. "And, they're being represented by a man calling himself 'Micah, God's Lawyer'." At that strange pronouncement the court members yet again lost their composure and burst out in another round of laughter. Hezekiah merely attempted an awkward smile. After gaining back some control, the king challenged, "Scribe, are you joking?" Stricken, the secretary fell to the ground and promised emphatically that he was not.

The king scowled across the courtyard at the spectator priests. Hezekiah pitied them, somewhat. They had little to do since the king had closed up the Temple and stripped it of all its valuables. Now they just counted the king's money, rather than their own. "You, priests," demanded the king, "ever heard of this man Micah?" Their heads rocked back and forth negatively in unison like a bunch of cows grazing on grass. One of their number did step forward. He was dressed in the finest of robes, hair slicked back and beard braided. When he smiled it was like the sun exploded his teeth were so white. Hezekiah recognized him as one of the king's favorite prophets. "I know of him, Sire," the prophet stated in a voice as oily as the last press of olives. "He is Micah the Prophet. Known to the lowly people as the 'Prophet of the Poor'."

A hawk-nosed official snorted. "Prophet. Lawyer. Whatever! If he's a lawyer he's one of us, right? Sire, I recommend we just offer him a small bribe and send him on his way." The elders agreed this was a good plan. The king also nodded in agreement and had the bailiff call the lawyer in. While waiting, they descended into mocking speculation about what this small town "lawyer of God" must look like.

Somewhere between their taunts of "prissy little" and "muck covered," a terrifying howl interrupted their sport. Like a jackal baying at the moon combined with the mournful wail of an ostrich, Hezekiah observed, was this horrible sound clamoring up the white stone steps towards their court. First a bare, uncovered head topped the platform, followed by a totally bare, uncovered body. From *courtiers to priests to king, all recoiled in horror. Except for a burlap loincloth, the spindly man was totally naked! Without slowing his pace, the prophet Micah with one bony finger jabbing at the court exclaimed powerfully, "Hear now what the Lord says: 'Arise, hear the Lord's complaint, for the Lord has a complaint against His people, and He. Will. Contend. With Israel!'"*

## FLEEING INTO THE ARMS OF A BULLY

Did you know that right now nearly 200,000 people are suffering in the modern-day equivalent of Nazi concentration camps? These horrific work camps can be found in North Korea. This Asian country, officially and ironically named the Democratic People's Republic of Korea, is according to the United Nations Commission of Inquiry on Human Rights one of the worst offender of all the nations when it comes to their appalling human rights record, infringing on nearly all of their Universal Declaration of Human Rights such as the freedom to have an opinion and expression.[1] CNN News reports that murder, torture, slavery, sexual violence, mass starvation and other abuses are common methods employed by this authoritarian government for the purpose of terrorizing their population into submission.[2]

When the Korean Conflict unofficially ended in the early 1950s, the dictator of North Korea, Kim Il-Sung, declared himself "Eternal President" and closed his nation's borders in order to establish a totalitarian Communist government. This type of government controls every aspect of its people's lives. So controlled are the North Korean people that they have no access to the Internet or media outside State sponsored propaganda, and the basic freedoms of movement, expression and the right to assembly are nonexistent. To protect the power of the regime, the people are starved in order to fund the massive military engine stationed along the United States-protected South Korean border.

Since Kim died, his son and grandson have continued the con job of pretending they are gods deserving of worship. Therefore, to be a Christian is a crime in North Korea, with the automatic sentence of hard labor in the work camps. Conditions are horrific for those living in these labor camps. Voice of the Martyrs (VOM), a persecution watch ministry, estimates that some 30,000 Christians suffer daily in these death camps for the "crime" of not worshipping their "Dear Leader," and some never even make it there alive.[3]

VOM tells a true day-in-the-life story of Christian persecution in a little village there called GokSan.[4] A pastor and 26 of his underground church members were bound and taken before a screaming crowd of Communists. The soldiers demanded that the Christians "Deny Christ or die!" Not getting the answer they were looking for, the soldiers threatened to kill the children. The only response was a mother of a young girl who leaned down and whispered to her daughter, "Today, my Love, I will see you in Heaven." The Communists proceeded to hang all of the children. When the sobbing parents still refused to deny Christ, the soldiers brought out a huge steamroller and crushed the remaining church members who were singing "More Love, O Christ, to Thee, More Love to Thee."

Governments such as North Korea do not understand the purpose of government. What then is the purpose of government? United States Founding Father Thomas Paine, in his pamphlet *Common Sense* (1776), wrote that security is "the true design and end of government." Another Founding Father, John Adams, in his book, *Thoughts on Government* (1776), believed the purpose of government was to be found "in the goal of happiness through virtue." Thomas Jefferson, in his writing titled *Political Economy* (1816), declared "The most sacred of the duties of a government is to do equal and impartial justice to all its citizens."

Security instead of enslavement, justice instead of corruption, virtue instead of vice, and the preservation of the happiness of its people rather than the cause of their suffering—

those were the godly ideals these men founded a nation upon. These ideals correspond to what the Bible says is the purpose of government—namely, to provide an atmosphere in which believers can live as 1 Timothy 2:2 teaches, "a tranquil and quiet life in all godliness and dignity."

Are nations like North Korea merely bad apples, or do they demonstrate that government in and of itself is inherently evil? Because they were steeped in the Bible, the Founding Fathers thought very poorly of human government. Thomas Paine wrote that "government, even in its best state is but a necessary evil, in its worst state an intolerable one." The reason the Founding Fathers believed government was inherently evil was because they believed in the biblical teachings such as Romans 3:23 and 10:10-18 that mankind is inherently evil and in need of a Redeemer. In fact, the Bible says in Jeremiah 17:9 that there is nothing more corrupt than the human heart. The Bible therefore warns over and over not to trust in Man. One of the strongest of these warnings is found in Psalm 118:8-9: "It is better to take refuge in the LORD than to trust in man. It is better to take refuge in the LORD than to trust in princes [politicians]."

As another Founding Father, Alexander Hamilton, confirmed: "Men are inherently evil, governed by greed and lust and love of power and a host of even less endearing passions."[5] America's first President, George Washington, put it this way: "Government is not reason. Government is not eloquence. It is force. And, like fire, it is a dangerous servant and a fearful master."[6]

The authors of the United States Constitution knew that while government is a necessary evil, it remains prone to falling into villainy and corruption. Therefore, in their writings they wisely taught that government must be limited. Government must constantly be checked by the population so that it can only extract the least amount of taxes in order to perform the most limited of functions—providing security for its people.

A government that isn't constantly monitored will grow into a monster, one that in order to feed its endless thirst for power will consume its population's money and trample on their God-given inalienable rights. In other words, the Founding Fathers knew that government is composed of people, and people are inherently fallen and evil. And, the more corrupt and evil a government becomes, the greater the people will suffer. As the former president of Fuller Theological Seminary, Dr. David Allan Hubbard, once remarked:

> *When the lawless, vicious men are the government, where do the people go for help? They must feel like a little child who flees from a bully into the arms of his father, only to have his father hold him while the bully beats him.*[7]

Whom can we flee to when our own "father" is also a bully? How can we then, like those Christians from the little village of GokSan, maintain our faith in God when government has utterly failed us, even to the point of death? The answers can be found in a seven chapter book found in the Old Testament, inspired by God and authored by the Minor Prophet Micah.

## THE PROPHET OF THE POOR

## Time of the Prophet

"The word of the Lord that came to Micah of Moresheth in the days of Jotham, Ahaz, and Hezekiah, kings of Judah, which he saw concerning Samaria and Jerusalem." That's how Micah, the prophet of Yahweh God and author of the sixth book in the order of the Minor Prophets, humbly began his message. And that's about as low-key as the book gets, for the continuing verses are anything but quiet. If only Micah could have leapt across the centuries and quoted Charles Dickens' 1859 classic novel *A Tale of Two Cities*, how better suited to Micah's tenure as prophet would have been Dickens' opening paragraph:

> *It was the best of times, it was the worst of times, it was the age of wisdom, it was the age of foolishness, it was the epoch of belief, it was the epoch of incredulity, it was the season of Light, it was the season of Darkness, it was the spring of hope, it was the winter of despair, we had everything before us, we had nothing before us, we were all going direct to Heaven, we were all going direct the other way...*

Micah lived and ministered from 737-690 BC during the reign of three kings who ruled over the Southern Kingdom of Judah. Each of these kings were in personality and ability as totally different as possible.[8] Their stories can be found in 2 Kings 15-20 and 2 Chronicles 27-30, and it begins with Jotham. There's not much recorded about King Jotham, other than he was a mighty warrior king who served the Lord and Judah, yet neglected the spiritual condition of his people.

Jotham's son, Ahaz, was an immoral monster who showed nothing but contempt for God. He stripped the Temple of its valuables, set up the worship of the gods of his enemies, robbed his own people blind, and burned his own children in pagan child sacrifices. Corruption oozed out of every pore of the king, his officials, and the priests and prophets who catered to his rule. God caused Ahaz to suffer for these actions by granting Judah's enemies devastatingly successful victories. One such victory occurred when the Syrians killed 120,000 Hebrews in a battle and marched a great multitude of captives away. Ahaz was so hated that when his 16 year reign ended, he wasn't even given burial in the tombs of the kings of Judah.

Ahaz's remaining son, Hezekiah, then took up the crown. He demonstrated weakness and a lack of good judgment throughout his long 29 year rule. Nevertheless, due to the faithful teachings of Micah and his contemporary, the famous Major Prophet Isaiah,

Hezekiah took to heart God's messages through the prophets. His heartfelt love for God led Judah to witness some of the most mind-blowing miracles God had ever performed for His people. But first, Hezekiah had to survive Ahaz.

Like a rollercoaster soaring high and crashing low, some-times slowly and often times at breakneck speed, the people in Micah's time were tossed about by the opposing forces of kings and foreign enemies. Into this wild ride Micah came forth presenting his prophetic message like a lawyer bringing God's charges against the corrupt government of his day.

## Construction of a Prophet

The name Micah, which is short for Micaiah or Michael, means "who is like God." He tells us he was raised in the little town of Moresheth near Gath on the Philistine border some 20 miles southwest of Jerusalem. Along the great highway between Assyria and Egypt both traders and armies would pass through Moresheth. The town was batted about by different nations who claimed it as their own or used their possession of it to barter favor with an enemy. In Micah's writings, it is clear that he loved his land and its poor, downtrodden people, and by God's command sought to represent his hometown to the big city people of Jerusalem.

## Call of the Prophet

"But truly I am full of power by the Spirit of the Lord, and of justice and might, to declare to Jacob his transgression and to Israel his sin." Micah 3:8 is the prophet's business card, so to speak, authenticating his right and authority by Yahweh's divine name to accuse even the highest of officials of abusing their power.

In style, Micah is much like his predecessor Amos, unflinchingly using the power of words, fearlessly holding nothing back, as if his tongue were a whip. Like his contemporary, the big city prophet Isaiah, he also targeted the people of Judah as his audience. But, like his other contemporary, the prophet Hosea who ministered up in the north, Micah softened each thundercloud outburst of prophetic utterance with sweet drops of mercy, hope and love that brought "sweet refreshings on the parched and blasted land."[9] These four prophets formed a "mighty quartet in that troublous age" that has led theologians to label the last half of the Eighth Century BC as the "Golden Age of Old Testament Prophecy."[10]

For a small town attorney, Micah exhibited an uncanny skill at courtroom exposition as he represented Yahweh God. He was a very eloquent communicator who stated God's case using a wide array of puns and poetry. His clever use of wordplay in 1:10-15 can be lost in translation, but those who came from the towns he mentioned would have caught his insightful meanings. "The town of Aczib will prove deceptive to the kings of Israel," where Aczib means "deception." "I will bring a conqueror against you who live in Mareshah," where Mareshah sounds like the Hebrew word for conqueror. He also rattled his adversaries by showing up nearly naked and howling like a wild animal (1:8). So caught off guard by this unconventional prophet who utilized both words and acting so effortlessly that his hearers were stunned into silence. Micah could work a courtroom with the best of them!

At a time when "the judges were venal, the priests were immoral and corrupt, the prophets were hirelings, the nobles took peculiar delight in fleecing the poor, and the entire group had built up a wall of enmity, fear and hatred that made life miserable for all classes," Micah proved to be a champion of justice.[11] Micah's writings demonstrate that he had ethical integrity, was of no ordinary courage, exhibited an unflinching truthfulness in speaking the whole counsel of God, and maintained a rock solid faith in God that was unwavering under the strain of a failed government.

## THE HOUSE OF THE WICKED STANDS ACCUSED

Whether King Ahaz had officially called court into session or not, nobody there could recall. Ever since the Prophet Micah's unorthodox entrance, it was abundantly clear to everyone present that Ahaz had gone from judge to defendant, the jurors from counselors to the accused, and even the court's spectators were now on trial. God's Lawyer was the only one truly running the proceedings as prosecutor, with Yahweh God Himself serving as Plaintiff on behalf of His people, primary Witness, and ultimately Judge.

Micah trumpeted out the introduction of their Accuser in 1:2-4, "Hear, all you peoples! Listen, O earth, and all that is in it! Let the Lord God be a witness against you, the Lord from His holy temple." If there was going to be any objection to this upside-down switch in authority over who presided over this court, Micah crushed it with this terrifying imagery of the arrival of the Plaintiff:

> *"For behold, the Lord is coming out of His place;*
> *He will come down and tread on the high places*
> *of the earth. The mountains will melt under Him,*
> *and the valleys will split like wax before the fire,*
> *like waters poured down a steep place."*

Stunned into silence by Micah's oration, the cowed people of the courtroom listened, stomachs churning, as Micah presented five charges God had leveled against what He labeled the "House of the Wicked" (6:10).

## Charge #1 – Oppression of the Poor

"Hear now, O heads of Jacob, and you rulers of the house of Israel: Is it not for you to know justice? They covet fields and take them by violence, also houses, and seize them. So they oppress a man and his house, a man and his inheritance" (2:2; 3:1). Even the women and children were not safe. "The women of My people you cast out from their pleasant houses; from their children you have taken away My glory forever" (2:9). Micah compared the rulers to cannibals who "eat the flesh of My people, flay their skin from them, break their bones, and chop them in pieces like meat for the pot" (3:3). In doing so, the very government whom the people should have been able to entrust with their protection, God had revealed was in reality an enemy who plundered its own people as if they were men pillaging during wartime (2:8).

Judah's government wasn't just stealing the land from its own people, in truth it was attempting to steal it from its own God. Yahweh in the Old Testament had set up the Promised Land as a stewardship, whereby the Hebrew tribes and families were given an allotment, but the title deed always remained in God's hand. Ahaz's government was trying to rob God Himself!

## Charge #2 – The Unscrupulous Use of Power

The Prosecutor divulged the second of God's charges in 3:9-10. "Now hear this, you heads of the house of Jacob and rulers of the house of Israel, who abhor justice and pervert all equity, who build up Zion with bloodshed and Jerusalem with iniquity." In the patriarchal society which defined Micah's time, the king was revered, performing the role as spokesman, father and shepherd whom the people should have been able to trust for wise counsel and value judgments.[12] Instead of leading the people up the bright path of righteousness, Ahaz and his officials had led them down into the dark tunnel of wickedness. Micah placed the blame for Judah's failures entirely at the feet of Judah's unscrupulous, power-hungry government.

## Charge #3 – A Lack of Integrity

Because the highest levels of government had utterly failed at promoting and preserving the integrity of God's righteous law, the local levels were themselves starting to descend into corruption. The bad apple was spoiling the whole bunch. Micah in 7:2-6 read his third charge from a laundry list of crimes the people were committing. "The prince asks for gifts, the judge seeks a bribe, and the great man utters his evil desire; so they scheme together."

Who was the real victim of this lack of integrity? It was trust itself, which tragically left the people with no faith or trust in family, friends and their Sovereign Protector. Everyone had to watch their backs, for "every man hunts his brother with a net." Micah, sadly shaking his head with great deliberation, revealed "A man's enemies are the men of his own household."

## Charge #4 – Greed in the Name of God

The fourth charge God's Lawyer pronounced in chapter 3 and 5:12-14 was against the religious rulers, both priests and prophets. They committed a most terrible crime. They had committed great evil—all in the name of God!

It's easy to picture Micah grasping firmly the ceremonial robes of a plump priest with both hands, mouth set in a disgusted grimace, and accusing the entire priesthood of soothsaying, witchcraft, superstition and idolatry. The priests might have acted all religious, but their true motives were the love of money, a life of ease, cheap popularity and a craving after luxury. Instead of serving the people as mediators between God and Man, they served only themselves, thereby cutting the people off from their Heavenly Father. "Her priests teach for pay, and her prophets divine for money. Yet they lean on the Lord, and say, 'Is not the Lord among us? No harm can come upon us'" (3:11). As God's supposed representatives, the priests' nefarious behavior made Yahweh look just as terrible in the eyes of the people, and as a result the people were losing faith in Him. Micah released the priest with a push and a grunt of contempt.

## Charge #5 – Heeding False Prophets

The false prophet with the used donkey salesman smile oiled his way over to God's Lawyer, a prophecy about Micah's downfall ready on his lips. Before he could utter a false word, Micah launched in 2:6-11, "'Do not prattle,' you say to those who prophesy. So they shall not prophesy to you; they shall not return insult for insult." The snake was dismissed like a hostile witness with the turn of Micah's back. Micah then lofted up high a money sack that he'd ripped off the false prophet's belt and charged God's fifth accusation, "Jerusalem, her prophets divine for money. Who make My people stray; who chant 'Peace'... but who prepare war—against Him who puts nothing into their mouths!"

And the true crime—the leaders ate it all up; every empty word that came out of the false prophets' mouths. They had exchanged the truth of God for a lie. The people's faith in God struggled as one prophecy after another that these false prophets had uttered never came to pass. For once in his life, the slick false prophet was left speechless.

# THE CHARACTER OF GOD

## The Verdict

With the five charges laid at the feet of the king, officials, priests and false prophets, God's Lawyer rested his case. The hills, mountains and strong foundations of the earth were then called to bring forth judgment (6:1-2). God wasn't just the Plaintiff, He was also the sovereign Judge of the Universe, and His verdict was already in.

For the charges of oppression of the poor, the unscrupulous use of power, a lack of integrity, greed in the name of God, and heeding the false prophets: Guilty! Guilty! Guilty! Guilty! Guilty! With each pronouncement of "Guilty" that Micah boomed, the members of the court winced.

The sentence: "Exile!" Micah promised in 2:5 the rulers would as punishment lose their own land allotments. "You will have no one to determine boundaries by lot in the assembly of the Lord."

The Northern Kingdom of Israel led by Samaria would first go into exile. The Judge declared in 1:6-7, "I will make Samaria a heap of ruins... all her pay as a harlot shall be burned with the fire." By 722 BC, Samaria was destroyed and Judah's northern brethren were marched off in chains into exile in Assyria.

Then Judah, led by Jerusalem, would be next. The Judge declared, "Jerusalem shall become heaps of ruins, and the mountain of the Temple like the bare hills of the forest... the land shall be desolate because of those who dwell in it, and for the fruit of their deeds... to Babylon you shall go!" (3:12; 4:10; 7:13). By 586 BC, after countless second chances, God finally handed Jerusalem over to the Babylonians who marched Judah's leaders off into exile far, far away to Babylon.

With judgment pronounced, God's Lawyer had finished his duty. Micah turned, abruptly walked out of court, and headed back to Moresheth. Case closed.

## The Probation

If King Ahaz's administration learned anything from this stern sentencing that Yahweh had pronounced on his corrupt little kingdom, it was evidently lost on them. We can imagine that Ahaz and his courtiers in their pride and false sense of power merely looked skeptically at Micah, one eye squinted, one side of their mouths curled and heads shaking. That Yahweh is a just God who cannot tolerate corruption, or the oppression of the poor, or the slandering of His name, and who will inevitably and severely act as Judge; this revelation of God's character was totally lost on them. The book of the Chronicles of the Kings of Judah records that Ahaz's government expired unrepentant (2 Kings 16; 2 Chronicles 28).

But, where the seed of God's verdict pronounced through Micah had been sowed on the rocky soil of Ahaz, thereby producing no fruit, one lone seed did fall on fertile ground—Hezekiah. Micah's message greatly moved the young prince. And, when it finally came his day to rule Judah, Hezekiah found his backbone. With the support of God's true prophets like Micah and Isaiah, the young king "did what was right in the sight of the Lord, according to all that his ancestor King David had done" (2 Kings 18:3). To the godly Hezekiah, who reformed the government and the priesthood at every level to follow God's Law and care for its people, God presented the other side of His character—His mercy.

God's judgment was final. Judah would be exiled for their crimes, but now the execution of that sentence would be delayed another 140 plus years. Hezekiah's heartfelt repentance garnered God's mercy, and the Judge placed His people on probation. Micah would later pen in chapter 7:18-20 an exclamation of rejoicing over God's mercy.

> *"Who is a God like You, pardoning iniquity and passing over the transgression of the remnant of His heritage? He does not retain His anger forever, because He delights in mercy. He will again have compassion on us, and will subdue our iniquities. You will cast all our sins into the depths of the sea. You will give truth to Jacob and mercy to Abraham, which You have sworn to our fathers from days of old."*

## The Promise

King Hezekiah's rule may have been a godly one, but it lasted only 29 years. Good kings and bad kings following Micah's time would come and go, and the Jewish people would experience two exiles as judgment for their lack of faith in God. But, the unconditional promise God made in 2 Samuel 7 to the line of King David, Hezekiah's ancestor, that his house and kingdom and throne shall be established forever, would be solidified in a new king—the King of Kings. The Prophet Micah, with his job passing down of God's judgments complete, would now joyously prophesy God's promises of a new and everlasting government headed up by the Righteous King.

In Micah 5:2-5, the Prophet of the Poor foretold the humble birth of the Messiah King:

> *"But you, Bethlehem Ephrathah, though you are little among the thousands of Judah, yet out of you shall come forth to Me the One to be Ruler in Israel, whose goings forth are from of old, from everlasting."*

Centuries later, the Magi from the East would travel far to Jerusalem and quote this prophecy to King Herod before traveling on to the little town of Bethlehem. There they would present their gifts to the baby Jesus, the fulfillment of Micah's prophecy. The One to be Ruler in Israel had been born in the very town the Prophet Micah said he would be born in, and would go on to be "great to the ends of the earth" and "shall be peace" personified. Micah foretold Christmas.

Micah also prophesied in chapter four that the Messiah—the Son of God as the New Testament would reveal—would one day set up a divine government on this earth. This is when it will happen: "Now it shall come to pass in the latter days," is a prophetic shorthand meaning the end of human history. And, where this kingdom would be ruled from: "The mountain of the Lord's house shall be established on the top of the mountains, and shall be exalted above the hills." The Lord will rule "from out of Zion... from Jerusalem." Jerusalem, God promised, would one day be the exalted capital city over all the planet, and all the nations of the world will "go up to the mountain of the Lord" in order to be taught "His ways" and hear the "word of the Lord."

When Jesus the Messiah returns and sets up His kingdom on this earth, there will be no more corrupted human government. All the nations will be ruled by the divine and righteous King. The law of the land will be God's righteous, merciful and loving law, and "He shall judge between many peoples."

The Messiah's Kingdom, revealed in Micah 4 and Revelation 20:1-6, will bring about the long awaited era of world peace that war-torn people have been crying out to possess for millennia. "They shall beat their swords into plowshares, and their spears into pruning hooks; nation shall not lift up sword against nation, neither shall they learn war anymore."

God promises a new era of government under His Son that will finally bring peace, righteousness and justice to the world. And, for the people of the world who have long only known suffering under the wickedness and weaknesses of failed human governments, under God's perfect government "no one shall make them afraid."

## MICAH'S FAITH LESSONS

### Lessons for Israel

How can the nation of Israel maintain faith when government has failed them? The failings and shortcomings of a human-led government have long afflicted Israel, but this has not always been the case. The origin of the nation's problems with their own human-led government can be pinpointed to an event which occurred 300 years before Micah's time. Up to that point God alone was Israel's one true King. That is, until the tragic story of 1 Samuel 8, where we learn of a nation that rejected their divine King and demanded instead a human one.

The people of Israel cried out to the Judge Samuel, "We will have a king over us, that we also may be like all the nations." You can actually hear the pain in Yahweh's voice in His response: "Heed the voice of the people in all that they say to you; for they have not rejected you, but they have rejected Me, that I should not reign over them."

God added a warning about what a transfer from divinely led government to human led government would look like: "He [the king] will take your sons and appoint them for his own chariots... will set some to plow his ground and reap his harvest... he will take your daughters... he will take the best of your fields... and put them to his work." The oppression the people would experience under a human government would be so great that "you will cry out in that day because of your king whom you have chosen for yourselves." And, because the foolish people wouldn't heed His warning, "the Lord will not hear you in that day." Yet still the people cried out for human government: "Nevertheless the people refused to obey the voice of Samuel; and they said, 'No, but we will have a king over us'."

Israel traded their righteous, merciful and loving Heavenly Father for self-serving kings and bureaucrats. And ever since, the Jewish people, who have been in exile over generations and across the globe, have suffered under human governments. But, Micah prophesied the end times would bring a Righteous King who would return to reclaim His throne.

Israel can maintain their faith in God by living securely in the knowledge that Jesus Christ, the Messiah, is returning to establish a perfect government defined by justice and peace. With that faith lesson, Micah 7:20 concludes with God's sweetest promise to Israel: "You [Yahweh] will give truth to Jacob and mercy to Abraham, which You have sworn to our fathers from days of old."

## Lessons for the Nations

How do the rulers of the nations maintain faith when government has failed? The problem with human government is that power goes to a leader's head. The popularity that catapulted them into authority makes them feel entitled, and complacency and corruption quickly settle in. The public servant becomes the public oppressor, and the people they are sworn to protect instead suffer for their vanity. And then, no matter how noble the beginnings of a nation are, entropy and bureaucracy over time inevitably wear down the moral stamina of its leaders to the point that the nation limps into extinction. This is the pattern proven by history over and over again.

Micah 6:8 instead provides the blueprint for what God requires of human leadership. "He has shown you, O man, what is good; and what does the Lord require of you but to do justly, to love mercy, and to walk humbly with your God?" The wise rulers are those who walk under the perfect moral code of the Lord. They know just what that code is by reading God's Word—the Bible—and by obeying it.

As famed preacher G. Campbell Morgan once warned, "Rulers who recognize God's sovereignty succeed, those who don't become corrupted and fail."[13] Don't be a failed ruler! "The supreme authority in all the affairs of men is God. All human authority is subservient to the divine. The powers that be are ordained of God."[14] Know then from Whom the source of your power derives and your faith will not be worn away. And, humbly rule knowing that your stewardship will not last, for as Micah so gloriously foretold— the King is coming!

## Lessons for the Church

What advice does Micah have for the Church today concerning maintaining its faith in God during times of failed government? When government oppression is bearing down, inevitably two types of churches are created.

The first type of church seeks to appease their governmental leaders by weakening their doctrinal positions. This is the church that Micah accuses in 2:11 of being the "prattler of this people," always preaching health and wealth and the good that government provides, but never providing the saving biblical nourishment their souls need. They unofficially, and sometimes even officially, become the State Church which divides its loyalty and its worship between God and Government. Officially, this would be like the Reich Church under Nazi controlled Germany during World War II, who disjointedly merged Nazi nationalism and heinous bigotry with Christian ideals. Man cannot serve two masters, so Micah promises in 3:7 that when these compromised churches cry out to the Lord, "there is no answer from God." This first church is likely the one Jesus warns concerning final judgment in Matthew 7:23, "And then I will declare to them, 'I never knew you; depart from Me, you who practice lawlessness!'"

The second church is just like the little underground church from GokSan, North Korea. They do not compromise their faith in Jesus Christ or the Bible with the false religion of emperor worship. The price for maintaining their stalwart faith is very high though, resulting in hardship and sometimes even death. They maintain their faith, even under such extreme oppression, because they live by Micah's hope found in 7:7, "Therefore I will look to the Lord; I will wait for the God of my salvation; My God will hear me." These are the true Christians, who having lived under the brutal lashes of a failed human government, will one day know God did indeed hear their pleas for help. They will joyously be listening to the Lord speak these words of victory from Matthew 25:23, "Well done, good and faithful servant... enter into the joy of your lord."

Churches can maintain their faith in God when they embrace two vital facts. One, that victory everlasting is already ours, made possible through Jesus' victory over sin and death on the cross. And two, by looking with hope towards that glorious day when King Jesus rides triumphantly back with His saints to set up His earthly kingdom.

## Lessons for You

How can we have mighty, unflinching faith like those Christians from that little village in North Korea who were being slaughtered by the hands of an oppressive government? We can only marvel at how they could be so brave under the threat of death, and not just give in and deny Christ. After all, faith often flees in the face of fear. The answer is—they lived by Micah's example.

Well, wasn't Micah afraid of his government? It seems not, for after all, he walked right into the court of the most corrupt government of his time, laid down God's charges, and then just walked away. He should have been terrified, and likely he was. Micah was after all merely a man, and just because he made it into the Bible doesn't mean he was some kind of Super Saint. For God he served as both prophet and lawyer, both professions despised and maligned throughout history, and yet his faith persevered. His faith persevered because he was empowered with the necessary fear-smashing courage from living by two maxims:

1. **Always Walk with God**
   "He has shown you, O man, what is good; and what does the Lord require of you but to do justly, to love mercy, and to walk humbly with your God?" (6:8)
2. **Have Hope**
   "Therefore I will look to the Lord; I will wait for the God of my salvation; My God will hear me." (7:7)

As one commentator explained so perfectly concerning the first maxim: "When God is God of our lives, when Christ is Lord of our lives, no one can make us afraid."[15] Micah fled into the safe, strong arms of our Heavenly Father. He is the very Almighty One who is recorded in Psalm 2 as laughing and scoffing at frail human governments.

The perfect love of God is what cast away Micah's fear. As 2 Timothy 1:7 reveals, "For God has not given us a spirit of fear, but of power and of love and of a sound mind." When we have this personal relationship with Jesus Christ, God's justice governs our heart, His righteousness is what we'll live for, and by allowing Him to work through our very lives the Good News of Jesus Christ shall go forth. The perfect love of God then not only casts out fear, but it enables us to live by faith.

When we have our doubts and faith seems to wane, we can remember with great joy the second maxim—the glorious hope

Micah shared about the future. As 1 John 4:18 exposes, "There is no fear in love; but perfect love casts out fear, because fear involves torment." There is no torment planned beyond this life for the believer in Jesus Christ. Those who have accepted God's Son, Jesus Christ—the perfect sacrifice for their sins—will know only joy during His Millennial Kingdom and on into eternity. As Micah 4:4 so wondrously promises, "But everyone shall sit under his vine and under his fig tree, and no one shall make them afraid; for the mouth of the Lord of hosts has spoken."

As for failed human governments, take comfort in knowing that their days on this earth are soon coming to an end. Judgment is coming just around the corner for all those who have abused their power and position, for the Righteous Judge promises in Micah 5:15, "I will execute vengeance in anger and fury on the nations."

Come, Lord Jesus, come!

## QUESTIONS FOR DISCUSSION

1. What kind of government do you live under?

2. What is life like for those who live under an oppressive regime?

3. Do you fear that government is increasingly taking away your liberties?

4. What if you were to live under the same conditions as Christians in North Korea?

5. How do we keep our faith when government has failed?

6. How does suffering and oppression strengthen our faith?

7. What is the fate of all human government?

8. What are the wonders God has in store for the believer in Jesus Christ that bring hope?

9. Have you accepted the hope of Jesus Christ, the Coming King?

# FAITH JOURNEY 7
## NAHUM: FAITH IN CERTAIN VICTORY

## THE HECKLER

Nahum sat with his legs crossed, his foot twitching, with a pile of figs beside him. Popping one in his mouth, he leaned back and craned his neck to see the streets of the city below him. Were they coming yet? All he could see was the typical daily foot traffic of Jerusalem. Still nothing to notice.

Unable to stand it any longer, he stood and bounced on the balls of his feet. His dark curly hair bobbed up and down with nervous energy. Nahum had good intel that the ambassador and his associates would be coming this way any minute. An older cousin who worked in the palace bakery knew the routines and gave him the scoop. Last night during dinner, he told Nahum that the king's meal would be over at the sixth hour, and then the group of Assyrians would be dismissed. A few formalities, a few less-than-sincere farewells, and they would be on their way. But that should have been almost an hour ago, and still no sign.

He reached down and scooped up another fig as he waited, his eyes never leaving the road. In his haste his elbow knocked over a scroll that had been propped against the stone bricks of the wall on which he had parked. Nahum heard it fall, but didn't pick it up. Why bother? For the past three weeks he had been staring at that roll of paper. He could point out every crease and tear, every stroke of the pen. That paper had been his life ever since the night almost a month ago when God spoke to him. He didn't need to see it to remember the experience.

And, oh, what an experience! Nahum allowed himself to think back to that day as he chewed another fig. Words could hardly convey the mix of terror and awe he had felt. He had tried to share a little about it with his parents and his teenage brother in the days after. Nahum knew his family thought he was young and cocky (bold and confident, he liked to think) and normally never lacking for words. But words to articulate the shock of God delivering a message through him? He had stammered and stuttered, trying to find the right descriptions. Instead of awe-inspiring, the whole experience just sounded weird, like a crazy dream. His family had brushed it off, tried to change the conversation, and went back to their chores. No matter. They would hear the message eventually.

He had spent the following weeks working to find the words that would do the message justice. Nahum had written and scratched out dozens of versions on the scroll that now rolled in the breeze on the quarried stones under his feet, trying his best to capture God's message in a fitting arrangement. He spent hours crafting poetic phrases and days working on the structure. He made sure his words never softened or overstated the Author's intent. Finally, the piece seemed right. The message was ready to share.

He read it and reread it to himself, memorizing every syllable and testing out inflections, making sure his delivery would match the tone and intensity God had shown him. The piece was ready, the performance polished. Now, it was just a matter of getting the right audience, which led him here: a trip to Judah's capital, camping on top of the defensive outer wall that encircled the city, and waiting, waiting for that perfect opportunity.

Pacing now, he made yet another turn on his feet and stole another glance back at the road. This time, however, he almost lost his balance. There they were! He hastily wiped off his mouth with the sleeve of his tunic and threw the scroll and figs out of the way (nothing would ruin the effect more than tripping while he preached, he thought).

Nahum positioned himself up on a ledge so that he faced out from the city, and he quickly straightened and tucked his clothes. He made sure he was in the sun, quickly looking up and down to make sure the shadows didn't hit him in an awkward way. Then, he struck a pose that he hoped conveyed both strength and authority. Just a few more seconds and the Assyrian representatives would be passing through the gate below him.

He took a deep breath, and a grin started to spread across his face. This was going to be fun!

As the Assyrians approached, their blue robes and golden rings gleamed in the sunlight. They passed underneath the wall where Nahum stood, through the gate and out of the city. None of them bothered to look up. Some were in conversation; others were mindlessly scanning the hills. So, it was a bit of a surprise when they heard a clear shout ring down from above: "God is jealous, and the Lord avenges!"

"What drivel was this?" the ambassador's group thought as they looked around until they noticed the figure silhouetted on the wall, pointing down at them.

"The Lord avenges and is furious!" Nahum bellowed from above. Others who were walking in and out of the city slowed to listen, trading glances as they tried to figure out why the young man on the wall was making a scene.

Nahum continued with an intensity that belied his slight stature, the words rolling off his tongue with a riveting fierceness and passion. The youth emphatically began describing a city under siege, a battle that would lead to destruction. It took the Assyrians a few beats to realize that these weren't the antics of a street performer. This message was supposed to be serious—and it was directed at them! Threats to Assyria's capital, proclamations of doom, insults to their image. The man's words were harsh, but his cadence was enthralling. The Assyrians couldn't help but listen, though their reactions hovered between scoffing at him and wanting to flay him alive. Holding their reply, the entourage waited and listened to Nahum's inventive verse to see where it might go.

The speech was over in just a few minutes. With his voice rising in a final crescendo, Nahum reached the end of his performance and stood there, chest heaving, waiting.

The Assyrian ambassador took a deep breath and was about to yell back a retort when he was suddenly drowned out by a victorious cheer. Looking around, he saw the crowd was stunned into silence no more. Instead, they were rejoicing over the message. Assyria destroyed! Her capital city of Nineveh overthrown! Yahweh fighting for them! Individually, they wouldn't have dared to mock the superpower's representative, but suddenly it seemed safe for the masses to jeer and insult the ambassador together. Nahum's words had struck a nerve, and that nerve spelled danger for the Assyrians.

The ambassador's guards pressed back against the throng as it moved threateningly close. Parting the crowd just enough to slip out, the band of politicians quickly retreated down the road, away from this godforsaken outpost and the insolent riffraff who lived here. They would certainly report this to their king and then the Jews would learn the meaning of suffering!

The crowd didn't care. They simply rejoiced in the word from the Lord. Laughing and cheering at the Assyrians' withdrawal, they turned back to look at Nahum. He said nothing more. He simply raised a fist, turned his back, and hopped down from his step.

His smile had never been bigger.

## CERTAIN VICTORY

Every spring, a large portion of the United States catches "bracket fever." The annual NCAA basketball tournament—dubbed "March Madness"—pits the top teams in the country against one another in a showdown to determine the college champion. Teams are divided into a bracket of four regions, each with sixteen teams. Over a few short weeks, dozens of games leave fans either cheering or crying as the contests whittle the challengers down to a "Final Four" and eventually a winner.

Casual fans look at the teams when the tournament bracket is announced and make their predictions for the eventual champion, many picking based on geographic loyalty, favorite colors, or random mascot preference. Others spend hours poring over advanced metrics to tease out teams' strengths and weaknesses, using computer models to simulate the results and determine the most probable outcomes of games. Either way, both basketball novices and basketball geeks can agree on one thing: It's good to be #1.

To this day, no #1 seed has ever lost a game to a #16 seed in the first round of the tournament. Since 1985, when the number of teams playing in the tournament each season was expanded to sixty-four, the top seeds are 100-0 against their lesser opponents. There have been a couple of close calls, but in the end being #1 always pays off.[1]

Certainty of victory is a nice luxury for these top seeded teams. While it is possible (inevitable?) that an upset will happen in the future, being awarded the #1 seed for the first round is about as close to a sure thing as can happen in sports. But that certainty brings up an interesting problem for the coach: How do you motivate a team that knows it will win? What kind of attitude and response can you coax out of a group of college-age boys who are convinced that their talent and tactics will overwhelm the opponent?

For a #1-seeded powerhouse, the coach's main concern is not whether his team *can* win. Everybody knows they have the talent and ability, so winning is not just a possibility—it is an expectation. The real concern is how he can ensure a healthy and rested lineup that can win the *next* game. The coach must motivate his team to play in a way that prepares them for the next round of the tournament. He must guard against injury as well as overconfidence. He needs his team to focus less on their projected domination and more on the attitude in which they will win. In other words, he needs the team to have the right heart while they play.

For Christians, there is a parallel challenge.

Historically, believers in Christ are used to being the "underdog." We have gone through periods of persecution, dating back to the earliest days of the Church. In the book of Acts, we see the first Christians hunted down and martyred. Later accounts tell of faithful men and women burned at the stake, slaughtered in the Colosseum, and tormented for refusing to renounce Jesus. Though Christianity has now become the default religion of the West, in modern times we are under attack from secular groups that want to undermine and silence any talk of our Christ. Conditioned to feel like a minority, we patiently explain and defend our beliefs.

But deep down, we know that we won't be underdogs for long! Christians may feel like they are losing the battle temporarily, but we know eventually we will win the war. When Jesus returns, we have a promise of certain victory. Satan is overthrown; death is defeated. God's triumph is guaranteed, and Christians get to enjoy their place on the winning team. In the end times, we are the #1 seed.

But with that assurance of victory comes a dilemma: How do we handle being the victor? How do we conduct ourselves while anticipating a sure win? What is the attitude in which we will prevail? The answer is more complicated than it at first seems.

On the one hand, we have no qualms about cheering for the demise of Satan. For example, a popular song in our church's ministry for kids sets the words of Romans 16:19 to music.[2] The climax of the song is when the kids sing, "and the God of Peace will soon crush Satan underneath your feet!" With an emphatic "hunh!"

the crowd jumps and lands in unison, creating the obvious mental image of Satan being crushed in our collective revelry.

On the other hand, we are called to care for those who have followed Satan. These enemies of the cross are not faceless demons; they are sinful humans like us. They are the same people we are called to love and the same people we try to evangelize. We have lived among them and invested in them and shared with them. While it is acceptable to jump and crush Satan under our feet, what about my neighbors who have yet to know Jesus as Savior? Can I truly celebrate the destruction of Amy or Brian?

If we rejoice in the victory, we risk being too flippant about the lives that will be hurt. If we desire mercy for the defeated, we risk questioning God's motives or methods in judgment. This is where our struggle lies. As a spiritual #1 seed with a certain victory ahead, the challenge is for us to have the right heart—God's heart—in the present.

We need to discern the best way to feel and to live out our faith. When the desire to revel in our own victory collides with our desire to grieve over the defeated, we can have a tough time reconciling our emotions. Our reaction in victory is one we need to wrestle with. In our confidence we must not sin, therefore we would benefit greatly having guidance that shows us how to proceed.

Thankfully, we have a book of the Bible that highlights this tension. In it, we find an example that provides insight about how we might handle the difficult task of certain success. The prophet Nahum gives us a message of triumph that shows us how to have the right kind of faith in certain victory.

# THE PROPHET OF "COMFORT"

## Time of the Prophet

As with most of our prophets, little is given to us in specifics about this author. The book simply opens with the line: "The burden against Nineveh. The book of the vision of Nahum the Elkoshite" (1:1). Our author's name and hometown are the only clues we are given regarding Nahum's identity, but they are a good place to start.

Nahum's name simply means "compassion" or "comfort." Often, there is a connection between a prophet's name and his message, but here the name seems to be more of an ironic twist. Since Nahum's message against the Assyrian capital city of Nineveh is one of judgment and destruction, the effect of calling him "Comfort" is the same as giving a big man the nickname "Tiny." Nahum's message in the book is one of the least comforting messages of the Minor Prophets, at least for its intended audience in Assyria.

Nahum's hometown of Elkosh also reveals little about him or his background. The town itself is unknown today. It is speculated to have been located anywhere from southwest Judea to northern Galilee, or maybe just outside Nineveh itself. Some have tried to connect the village of Capernaum with the prophet, since its name literally means "village of Nahum." However, all such thoughts are pure conjecture. The best we can do is to assume that Nahum was from somewhere in Judah and leave it at that.

While his name and birthplace provide few clues to his experience, the one thing that does add to our understanding of Nahum's identity is a clear timeframe in which his message was written. We can say with certainty that Nahum's message was written between two events in the seventh century BC: the destruction of the Egyptian city of Thebes in 663 BC and the destruction of the Assyrian capital of Nineveh in 612 BC. Nahum references the destruction of the former as past history and the destruction of the latter as a future event. For the message to make any sense, Nahum must have written in the fifty-year window after Thebes was destroyed but before Nineveh fell.

By knowing the timeframe, we can better understand the mindset of the people who would have heard Nahum's message, as well as the attitude of Nahum himself.

For the audience in Nineveh, we know that their nation was in a position of power and triumph during the Seventh Century. The Assyrians were the superpower of the region, and their dominant military force kept their empire secure. In a previous faith journey with Jonah, we discussed Nineveh in Jonah's time and learned that the Assyrians who lived there had a reputation as a cruelly violent people. They were known for butchering, dismembering, and torturing those they conquered. In the century that followed, that reputation of Assyrian evil and power had grown. After a brief repentance at the message of Jonah, they returned to being cruel, and proud of it. Their power and might increased as they brutally overtook all their enemies.

Few could imagine a scenario in which Assyrian control would crumble, and few were brave enough to openly hope for such a downfall. Yet that is exactly what Nahum foretold. Any Assyrians who heard his unlikely message would have scoffed at the idea that Nineveh would fall, and they would have marveled that anyone was stupid enough to say so out loud.

For the audience in Nahum's home country of Judah, we know that their nation was in a position of relative weakness during this time. Judah's brothers in the neighboring Northern Kingdom of Israel had been destroyed and scattered by the Assyrians over sixty years ago in 722 BC. During that campaign the Assyrian armies had also marched on Judah. While a miraculous intervention by God had saved the Jews from complete and total collapse at that time (see 2 Kings 19), Judah never regained much power. Instead, they were left as a weakened state that had to look to others for security. Consequently, the Assyrians were hated by the Jews. Any Jews who heard Nahum's unlikely message would have rejoiced at the prospect of Nineveh's doom.

## Call of the Prophet

For Nahum, the idea of Nineveh and the Assyrians falling would have been exciting. As a Jew, he would have reveled in an enemy's downfall; as a prophet, he would have been thrilled to have a message from God regarding the future. There would have been elation and a rush to share the good news of victory.

However, Nahum also had to have known that his message to Assyria was not the first and only message they had received from Yahweh. Nahum would have known about Jonah's ministry to Nineveh in the previous century and known about the city's subsequent repentance. He would have heard God's declaration of care and concern for a city filled with people who "did not know their right from their left" (Jonah 4:11). He must have known God's love extended beyond Israel's border.

This knowledge would have led Nahum to feel a certain tension as he crafted the harsh content of his own prophecy. While he didn't shy away from proclaiming destruction, what attitude should he show as he communicated God's words? Should he react to this impending victory with celebration or with sorrow?

Many modern commentators fail to recognize that Nahum felt any such tension. They only hear the words of condemnation presented in his writing. These commentators praise Nahum's poetic style, but distance themselves from his message. They claim the book is "representative of the old, narrow and shallow prophetism of the 'false' prophets." It is "rather a disgrace" and an "unwelcomed part" in Scripture. Nahum's use of vivid imagery and quick shifts between speaker and perspective make for "literature... as good as the religion is bad," they say. They even surmise Nahum was writing in order to express his personal delight and satisfaction over the destruction of Israel's enemies.[3]

These commentators make two critical mistakes. First, the content of this prophecy may describe a harsh and violent future for the city of Nineveh, but it is still the revelation of God. Our burden is to come to terms with that revelation, not reject it because we are uncomfortable with the meaning. If we struggle to grasp how a good and loving God could act in wrath, the problem is due to our limited understanding, and not due to a flaw in God's character or in Nahum's writing. Rather than recoil at the wrath described, we must work to see how it fits within God's heart and how it relates to His love, grace, and mercy.

The second mistake these commentators make is to hear in Nahum a smirk behind the sentences. Certainly Nahum shows no tender feelings for the ones about to meet their doom. In his writing, he makes some scathing critiques of the Assyrians. Their behavior flew in the face of God's decrees and stood in stark opposition to His heart. Judgment was deserved. Yet, Nahum exposes this harsh truth without a personal vendetta. He pulls no punches, but he is not adding to the word of God. He is not inserting his own agenda in the prophecy to showcase his own delight and satisfaction. No, Nahum stays true to his call as a prophet: he presents God's message and shares this burden about Nineveh in a way that keeps the focus on the divine Author, not on himself.

Nahum highlights an attribute of God that is key to our comprehension of his call as a prophet—God's jealousy. Jealousy in relation to God is not the same as envy. It is nothing so petty. God's jealousy is a zeal to have us recognize what is best, to not allow us to settle for something lesser. Since He is the ultimate good, a jealous and zealous God won't let us settle for cheap knock-offs. This quality of God forms the basis for His wrath. When humans persist in rejecting our supremely good and loving God, choosing behaviors and beliefs that fly in the face of His glory and bringing pain and heartache to others, God jealously seeks to change their outlook. He may present an opportunity to repent, or even multiple opportunities. But while God is patient and "slow to anger," He will not wait forever. He may unleash His fury in a number of ways, simultaneously crushing the self-destructive actions of those in rebellion while at the same time providing a chance to repent.

Nahum was called to share this jealousy of God with his audience in Judah and in Assyria. God had patiently given Nineveh time to repent. He had warned them a century earlier through the prophet Jonah. Instead of continued repentance, though, Nineveh embraced more and more rebellion. Subsequent generations failed to learn their lesson, and so God gave Nahum the task of sharing the news that God would jealously work to ensure that Nineveh no longer continued on their path of evil. It was a call to prophesy God's certain victory.

## GOD, THE AVENGER

Nahum embraces this call, and he writes a short but effective piece that colorfully shows how God's wrath would unfold.

In the opening chapter of Nahum's writing, God's power is on full display. Nahum 1:3b-6 emphasizes His control over nature in its most impressive states.

- The clouds, including storms and tornados (an imposing display in the sky) are simply the dust of His feet, located beneath Him and treated as insignificant.
- The sea (a magnificent and endless supply of water), can dry up at His word.
- Bashan, Carmel, and Lebanon (the pinnacles of agricultural abundance in the region) wither before Him and lose their beauty and prosperity.
- Mountains (an unshakable foundation) quake and melt and the earth heaves, leaving no place for refuge.

God controls the storm, the sea, the mountains, and the world! Nahum creatively shows that each of these powerful natural elements is powerless when compared to God. And the corollary of that truth is important: If God's fury is like fire and the rocks are thrown down by Him (1:6), what chance can a city like Nineveh stand once God has set Himself against her?

174

The fury that we see unleashed here is not an uncontrollable rage, though. In verse 2, "furious" literally means "one who has mastered wrath." God is not out of control—He is fully in control of His power, and He uses it to accomplish His purposes.[4] Nahum makes clear that God is making the choice to avenge the wrongs committed against Him, and He cannot be stopped. It is a strong statement of God's sovereign authority.

Up to this point in Nahum's opening, he has focused on the qualities of God's power. Starting in verse 7, he shifts his focus and considers ways that a powerful God relates to us. For some, "The LORD is good, a stronghold in the day of trouble; and He knows those who trust in Him" (1:7). The picture of God as refuge in times of difficulty is comforting. Those with whom God has a relationship can fear less during displays of His wrath.

However, for those who don't have that relationship, God's wrath is a frightful thing. Nahum goes on to describe the relationship between God and his enemies. The enemies of God are ones who "plot against the Lord" and oppose Him actively (1:9). Against anyone else, such plots might have success, but not against God. All such schemes directed against Him are doomed. God brings a complete end to these conspiracies and the ones who create them. Using several quick pictures to emphasize this end, Nahum says they will be entangled among thorns, be drunk from their wine, and be consumed like dry stubble (1:10). This is what happens to anyone who plots against God, and unfortunately for Nineveh, one has come forth from her who has done just that!

In case anyone was not paying attention, Nahum then takes these general principles and applies them to the two groups who would listen to his message. For Nineveh and the Assyrians, "Though they are safe, and likewise many, yet in this manner they will be cut down when He passes through" (1:12a) In other words, the superpower of Assyria is about to face judgment for opposing God. For Judah, "Though I have afflicted you, I will afflict you no more" (1:12b). The nation of Judah had suffered under the threat of

Assyrian force for years, but that suffering would be abolished after God poured out his wrath on Nineveh. Judah would no longer be shackled or yoked by Assyria's power.

This good news for Judah invited celebration. Hearing about the complete and utter destruction of Assyria would spark rejoicing for the Jews. God expected a positive reaction, and He directed it. The Jews are told how to have faith in the coming triumph. Their role is not to mock the Assyrians or to gloat. Instead, they are to continue in their own faithfulness. In their trust of God, they should make plans to obey Him both now and in the future. "Keep your appointed feasts, perform your vows," God says (1:15). By telling people to make long-range plans, He promises to care for His people.

God's promise to Assyria, though, is cause for grieving: *You're done. Your gods are done. I'm putting you in the grave!* His statement is a definitive proclamation of doom for Nineveh.

## A Detailed Account

While the initial chapter of Nahum's message provides the basic blueprint of God's plans, Nahum moves on to share particulars. Chapters two and three provide details of Nineveh's downfall. They are harsh specifics of just what will happen to the city of Nineveh, and they leave no room for questioning the outcome.

Nahum starts off by telling Nineveh to prepare for battle. In any other case, this would be a positive statement. Telling Nineveh to prepare to fight is like telling Julia Child to prepare to cook, or like telling the Hulk to prepare to smash. The Assyrians lived to fight! Consider the following description of the Assyrian weapons of war:

> *The city had in fact been well equipped to withstand both siege... and invasion. [The Assyrian King] Sennacherib had spent no less than six years building his armory, which*

> *occupied a terraced area of forty acres. It was*
> *enlarged further by [King] Esarhaddon and*
> *contained all the weaponry required for the*
> *extension and maintenance of the Assyrian*
> *empire: bows, arrows, quivers, chariots, wagons,*
> *armor, horses, mules, and equipment.... The*
> *royal "road" had been enlarged by Sennacherib*
> *to a breadth of seventy-eight feet, facilitating*
> *the movement of troops.*[5]

As a city, Nineveh was as well-prepared for war as any place in the world. Yet the certainty of Nineveh's doom as proclaimed by God in chapter one makes us realize the Nahum's advice was pointless. Whether the Assyrians prepare or not, their attacker would advance and have success.

Who is this attacker mentioned in Nahum 2:1? History tells us that God eventually used the combined forces of the Babylonians and the Medes to conquer Assyria. In 612 BC, King Nabopolassar of Babylon breached the walls of Nineveh as part of a ten-week siege. A number of creative strategies had been employed by the Babylonian army.[6] The defeat was total!

Nahum describes this forthcoming battle in surprising clarity using quick snippets of information. The details are presented like scenes of battle in a movie—lots of rapid cuts from action to action, without lots of focus. You get glimpses of the fighting and the tactics.

- **The shields of his mighty men are made red; the valiant men are in scarlet (2:3).**
  Here the Babylonian attackers wear their traditional colors, as opposed to the Assyrians who typically wore blue and purple.[7]
- **The chariots come with flaming torches in the day of his preparation and the spears are brandished (2:3).**

The Babylonians advance with their charioteers' lances ready.

- **The chariots rage in the streets, they jostle one another in the broad roads... (2:4).**
  Here we have a scene of chaos within the city as the Assyrians prepare for battle. Already there are hints of defeat as the defenders seem chaotic, rushing and darting around in confusion.

- **He remembers his nobles; they stumble in their walk (2:5).**
  More trouble for the Assyrians is shown as their elite forces are tripping before they even fight.

- **They make haste to her walls, and the defense is prepared (2:5).**
  This may show the Babylonians rushing the wall and put up a "siege mantel," a protective shield against falling objects or arrows shot from the ramparts.

- **The gates of the rivers are opened, and the palace is dissolved (2:6).**
  Nineveh was located on the Tigris River, and water flowed around and through the city like a protective moat. The Babylonians apparently opened floodgates upstream and the resulting rush of water undermined the city wall as well as the palace, making it easier to breach the defenses.

The details of Nahum's predictions are amazing when we remember that they were made years before the Babylonian army actually attacked. His prophecies match the future reality of Babylon's battle with Nineveh exactly. This shows that God is fully aware of what is to come. He knows not only the certain victory that lies ahead, but He also knows the methods that will usher it in, as well as the reactions it will bring.

As chapter 2 continues, Nineveh is in shock. The inhabitants can't believe what is happening. Nahum paints a picture of grief and disbelief. Slave girls (perhaps temple prostitutes) moan in agony.

The glory of Nineveh drains like a pool (cleverly referencing the water around the city). Assyria's vast hordes of silver and gold, taken by plundering other nations in conquest, are now plundered themselves. The people have the body language and posture of a people struck by terror and disbelief as their "hearts melt and knees tremble" (2:10).

The message continues with no pity for those who are suffering. Nahum next heckles the Assyrians using the symbol of lions. The lion was one of the primary symbols of Assyria, like the eagle for the United States or the bear for Russia. Their palace was decorated with lion symbolism, and worship of one of their key goddesses (Ishtar) used lion imagery. While lions were typically used to project strength, here the image is turned against Assyria. "Where is the lion's den?" God asks mockingly (2:11). Nineveh had served as an impenetrable fortress that none dared disturb, but her reign was now over. Assyria's "young lions"—her troops—would be mercilessly annihilated (2:13).

## Woe and Shame

Nahum next moves from a description of the future to a description of his present time and the reason for Nineveh's forthcoming destruction. While Nahum 3:2-3 continue to show the devastation ahead, verses 1 and 4 show some of the reasons for God's judgment: Nineveh and the Assyrians had long abandoned their moral footings. Violence, lying, stealing and other sins were part of everyday life in this ancient metropolis.

Verse 4 picks up a double illustration—Nineveh is both a prostitute and a sorceress. The combination is intended to heap insult on the city. Nahum's harsh language and borderline vulgarity may surprise us in the Word of God, but the shocking words serve a purpose. Assyria is shown in a position of humiliation. God will lift her skirts (3:5), pelt her with filth (3:6), and call her troops women (3:13). These are not literal statements; they are statements meant to shame.

In Western culture, we typically view the world through the lens of *right/wrong*. However, Eastern cultures are more prone to view the world through the lens of *honor/shame*. In such cultures, the respect of the community is paramount.[8] While God could have emphasized the list of Nineveh's sins and argued Nineveh's guilt, instead he chooses to make Nineveh a spectacle—something that others would look at in horror because of the shame heaped upon her. With her honor removed, she would now face shame for her actions.

Nahum also presents a comparison between Nineveh and Thebes (called No Amon in some translations). In 664-663 BC, the city of Thebes, a great and powerful city in Egypt on the Nile, fell to the Assyrians. In the attack, the city was razed to the ground. Though possessing great defenses and allies (as described in 3:8-9), the city was conquered. Nahum asks, "If Thebes can fall, what makes Nineveh immune to attack?"

The combined weight of these messages shows that Nineveh is deserving of punishment and certainly not resistant to a great defeat. She would lose, and lose decisively.

Nahum wraps up his prophecy with another call for Nineveh to prepare the defense, but yet again he shows such action to be futile. The city's inhabitants will be cut down. Nahum uses the idea of grasshoppers (like a swarm of locusts) to show both the unstoppable power of the Babylonian army as well as the corruption and looting of Assyria's own merchants and leaders. From inside and out, Nineveh would be plundered.

The Assyrian king is last to be addressed. While implied in previous passages (e.g. Nahum 1:11—"one who plots evil against the Lord"), here is a direct statement to him. The nobles and leaders are dead; the population is scattered and killed. Nineveh has a fatal wound that cannot be fixed—and everyone around claps with approval!

## Total Victory

The future God showed to Nahum was one he would have found exciting. Judah's enemy obliterated! The idea would have been appealing to any citizen living in the Middle East at that time, especially to a Jew like Nahum. It was cause for celebration, even if it did sound unlikely.

To imagine the Assyrians' demise would be similar to imagining our world no longer being threatened by the likes of North Korea and Iran. At the time Nahum was standing on the wall and delivering his message, the Assyrians were the dominant power in that part of the globe. Their reach was broad, their military unstoppable. Nineveh, according to one of her most successful kings, was:

> *The noble metropolis, the city beloved of Ishtar, wherein are all the meeting-places of gods and goddesses; the everlasting substructure, the eternal foundation; whose plan had been designed from of old, and whose structure had been made beautiful along with the firmament of heaven.*[9]

Yet within a few years, the city and the nations under her control were gone.

Nineveh's total collapse is one of the wonders of ancient history. Not only was the city defeated, it was obliterated. The site of the city was deserted for at least three hundred years. It disappeared so completely under the sands of the Mideast that many believed its prior existence was a myth. Without the work of key archaeologists who eventually excavated it, we could not claim with confidence that the city ever existed.[10] When God promised Nineveh would have "no descendants to bear [her] name" (1:14), He wasn't kidding!

In the aftermath of Nahum's speech, we can imagine him coming down from the wall to a throng of excited Jews clapping him on the back and praising him for speaking out against the Assyrian tyrants. But we can also see Nahum rebuking them for being too giddy. Much to their surprise, Nahum wasn't wrapped up in personal satisfaction. He was excited to share God's message, glad that it was received well, and happy about the blessing that would come. He also wanted his fellow Jews to understand what this meant.

While certain victory would bring blessings to Judah, it was not to be taken lightly. Complete and total victory meant that an entire population would be decimated. It meant that men and women would have no more chances to repent. It meant that the weight of Nineveh's sins would come back upon her.

Nahum's message contains strongly worded rebukes, but its tone isn't flippant. There was a seriousness to Nahum's words of condemnation. In fact, an analysis of the book's structure shows us that it is arranged with patterns that reminds us of a funeral. One commentator observes, "The use of a 4+3 pattern (echoing the cadence of a Hebrew dirge) in the books' final four units reinforces the sense of a eulogy over Nineveh's demise."[11]

I believe that Nahum, in presenting the material with both harsh condemnation and solemn concern, helps find that elusive balance between rejoicing and grieving. Nahum gives us a message of success and shows us how to have the right kind of faith in certain victory. He helps us see God's heart in triumph.

First, we see that victory is rooted in God Himself. Judah could take no credit in Assyria's defeat. This was not a resurgence of national pride or military might to overthrow an oppressor. It was a divinely orchestrated event. In certain victory, we remember that only One is responsible for the outcome. We rejoice, but we rejoice over His agenda and on His terms.

Second, we see that victory has a moral component. Nineveh was rebuked for her immorality and other sins, and these were listed as the reason for her defeat. By listening to the crimes she committed, we are forced to consider how our own culture compares. The conclusion we are forced to reach is that if God could find fault with these people, certainly He could find fault with us. In certain victory, we rejoice while remembering that all of us have the potential to become God's enemies and face His wrath.

Third, we see that victory was not callous. God did not condemn Nineveh because He didn't value them. To the contrary! In the previous book of Jonah, we saw God exhibit concern for the people of Assyria. His love extended beyond the borders of Israel; He cared about other peoples. However, proper care meant that He would jealously steer anyone and everyone toward Himself and away from their own evil practices and worship. It is because God loved the people of Nineveh that He allowed them to fall from such heights. In certain victory, we rejoice while aligning ourselves with God's heart for the people He defeats.

Nahum had faith that understood these components of God's victory. His written version of God's message wasn't just a gloating mockery of a defeated enemy. It was a carefully crafted, powerfully written, honestly joyful view of God defending His name. In the same way, we rejoice over God's love and mercy. We should look at Nahum's message and rejoice in God's jealousy, His justly executed vengeance, and His intolerance of shameful attitudes and behaviors.

## NAHUM'S FAITH LESSONS

So how do we maintain joyful, confident, yet humble faith in the face of our own certain victories? How do we handle being the champion? How do we conduct ourselves while anticipating a sure win? Consider some of the following lessons that we can take from Nahum's message.

## Lessons for Israel

Promises of success can be difficult to trust. As a nation, Israel and the Jews have faced persecution on a number of fronts. They have been attacked by Lebanon, Syria, Iraq, Jordan, and Egypt. They survived wars against them when they became a nation in 1948 and then again in 1967. Waves of terrorists and salvos of missiles have threatened Israel every year of her existence. This has led many to have no hope of peace or victory.

Such an attitude of pessimism is understandable. Sometimes we miss out on hope because we can't see a way around an obstacle. The near-term trouble that we can't solve blinds us to the long-term blessings that we will have.

But God's promise of restoration and protection to the Jews in Nahum's days still continues to ring true: "The Lord is good, a stronghold in the day of trouble; and He knows those who trust in Him" (1:7).

Israel as a nation must remember that she has received countless promises and blessings from Yahweh. There is no doubt that Israel is the equivalent of a #1 seed in the college basketball tournament. Despite consistent and strong opposition, her long-term success and triumph are promised from the hand of God. So, to maintain the right kind of faith in certain victory, Israel must remember that victory comes from the Lord alone.

The nation has shown she can muster military might. However, Israel would do better to focus on religious revival. By trusting in the Lord, she can find in Him a stronghold better than any defense. Military tactics and defensive fortifications may be necessary for a season, but Nahum reminds us that it is the Lord who will be her refuge.

## Lessons for the Nations

Nations other than Israel face the same challenge from the opposite side of the coin. Certain victory is God's, and often nations find themselves on the losing side of a battle with Him.

Like Nahum, we should bear in mind the lessons of history. Just as Nahum challenged the Ninevites to look at history and compare themselves to the fallen city of Thebes, our nations should pause and consider their own guilt and susceptibility to defeat.

No city or nation is too big to avoid God's wrath once He feels it is necessary.

God had patience with Nineveh and Assyria, even as they participated in dark and dreadful activities. However, His patience did not last forever. God opposed Nineveh, and he took action against her. He took similar action against His own people when they turned away from Him. A mere 30 years after Nineveh's destruction in 612 BC, the same conquering doom came to Jerusalem in 582 BC. Certainly, if God wouldn't spare His own chosen nation, He would have no qualms about holding other nations accountable for their sin.

In faith, we need to humbly hear the condemnation of other nations and consider well whether we are just as guilty. We must ask ourselves, "Is our country on track for revival or ravaging?" In asking we must remember this truth: God is less interested in the historical, economic, or military importance of our nation than He is the spiritual status.

As such, let us conduct ourselves in a manner that prepares for God's certain victory. Let us advocate repentance on a national level. Let us stand against practices that blatantly oppose God's Word. We can do so with tact and with love, but we must align ourselves with God's priorities and strive in faith to match His heart.

## Lessons for the Church

How does the Church have faith in certain victory?

Our knowledge of the coming Day of the Lord means we possess a hope that millions of people do not know. Jesus' return means sure victory for Christians. We can either selfishly hoard this hope, or we can use it as a motivation to tell others about Jesus.

Some Church groups and even denominations have allowed their certainty of salvation to morph into exclusivity. "We are the only Christians," say people like the members of Topeka's Westboro Baptist Church who have protested and picketed their way to infamy. Rather than trying to build relationships to win the lost, they hold up signs celebrating the damnation of their opponents. Whether homosexuals or Hollywood stars, soldiers or secular organizations, the Westboro group and their late leader, Fred Phelps, have chosen to shun and condemn all opponents.

The Church as a whole has an opportunity to do better. We can and should stand firm on essential doctrines of the faith, and we should never shy away from proclaiming our beliefs. Doctrine and lifestyle issues require us to speak up.

However, our attitude towards those who are misinformed or unsaved should not be that of a gloating or hateful bigot. Our victory shouldn't come by rubbing our opponent's nose in their defeat. Rather than celebrate and mock the destruction to come, we should intentionally show God's love and holiness. Our faithful attitude should lead people to Jesus, rather than to death.

## Lessons for You

If God has promised a coming triumph, we should use that promise to give us joy.

Nahum's message provided comfort to the people of Judah. They were able to hear God's plans, to know His intent, and to celebrate what it would mean for their nation.

186

Do we allow God's promises to truly provide joy for us? Too often we see church members who read God's promises for the future spend their time agonizing over the meaning of certain passages. They stress over interpretations, or they worry that we are creeping one step closer to Armageddon.

But, if we trust God's promises, we can see those same signs and celebrate. Our joy is not in the destruction of others. Rather, it is an expectation of what God will do. It is the joy of knowing that the culmination of history is near. It is the excitement of knowing you'll soon have a tangible glimpse of God's glory.

Nahum pointed out a future in which God's people could rejoice in God's certain victory. Sure, there was tension in that victory. We know that punishment was deserved, and we are sad that men and women wasted their spiritual potential and suffered (even eternally) as a result. But, our hearts and the expressions of our faith should align with God's to know that He is jealously pursuing what is best for us as well as for Himself.

Certain victory is ahead. Let's embrace it and celebrate!

## QUESTIONS FOR DISCUSSION

1. What does it mean for God to be "jealous"? How does this impact His role in vengeance?

2. God is presented as powerful and dangerous, yet worthy of trust. How does this affect the way we feel in His presence? Is God "safe" or "good?"

3. Does the destruction of a city like Nineveh make you excited or sad? What does your reaction say about your faith in God?

4. How easy do you think it was for the Jews to believe God's promises about Nineveh? What factors might have weakened their faith? Is your faith in God's promises ever weakened in the same way?

5. Look at Nahum 3:1-4. What are some of the charges against Nineveh? What parallels do you see with your own city or nation? Do you think God would ever pour out wrath against your town?

6. Nahum utilizes shame in his message to the Ninevites. How does shame influence our behavior? The behavior of others? Why might God want to shame Nineveh instead of simply proclaiming her fate?

7.  What is your emotional view of the return of Jesus? What do you think about the coming triumph? How does it impact your faith or change the way you treat others, especially non-Christians?

# FAITH JOURNEY 8
# HABAKKUK: FAITH WHEN
# YOU'RE CONFUSED

## THE PATIENT MUSICIAN

*Music drifted down from the tower, softly plucked notes quietly joining the sounds of the night. The melody mixed with cricket chirps and harmonized with croaking frogs down below in a tune that was both familiar and new. The song was an improvisation by gifted fingers, like the type enjoyed around campfires when everyone settles in to relax before bedtime. Not a focused piece, just a mindless distraction while the musician's thoughts wandered elsewhere.*

*As the fire crackled and embers rode the waves of heat up from the stone wall toward the stars, Habakkuk breathed in deeply. Smoke from a fire was one of his favorite smells, and he allowed himself to enjoy it while the fire baked his ample front and the darkness cooled his back. But as he continued to play and think, his smile dissipated like the clouds of smoke travelling up and away on westerly winds.*

*Sitting on the ramparts, Habakkuk's attention turned to his God. For some time now, he had been plagued with concern for his city and his country. Every day he saw injustice played out on the faces of the worshipers who came to the Temple in Jerusalem. As he played for the choir in that holy place, he watched family after family offer their sacrifices with pain, knowing that the God they worshiped had not fixed pressing issues in their lives. They bore the weight of violence, some even trying to hide fresh cuts and bruises. He saw the ruthless effect of the thugs and cheats who ruled the city, some from a street corner and some from the palace. His heart broke every time he saw such sights, and his constant prayer had been for God to step in and take action.*

*"How long?" he asked. Each day passed with no answer, yet Habakkuk had persisted, believing that his supplications would do some small part in getting the Lord of Hosts to act.*

*It was with great surprise then that one night God answered. The response had been thrilling and shocking all at once, but it had been neither the answer Habakkuk wanted, expected, nor (if he was honest) understood. It had confused him. It made no sense! He had written the message, but reluctantly. Not that he doubted. God forbid! It was just that he could not wrap his curly-haired head around the plans God gave. His question changed from "How long?" to "How can this be?"*

*And so, the troubled musician had come up to an overlook above the city, asking even more of his Lord. Amidst the chords and runs of his music, he prayed long and sincere prayers. He ran his fingers through his beard as he asked His God for clarification. Feeling as bold as Moses or Job, he presented his questions to Yahweh, knowing that his boldness would be rewarded, or rebuked. The reward, though, would be worth the risk. Plucking the strings and pouring out his heart, Habakkuk watched and waited in the cool, clear night.*

*Suddenly, beyond the crackling fire, Habakkuk saw a strange glow on the horizon. It wasn't a gradual fade-in like the sunrise, a warming light that gives comfort. No, this one had a chilling intensity quite different from the heat of the sun or even his small blaze. Habakkuk's calloused fingertips slipped off the strings and his instrument rattled to the stone blocks below.*

*This was the vision he had waited for! Habakkuk watched the supernatural scene unfold on the hills around him, showing distant lands and nations as an inaudible Voice explained their meaning. It lasted only a few minutes, or was it a few hours? As the cool brightness faded, Habakkuk was left staring at only the orange flames and radiant embers of his fire once again.*

*He sat there, motionless and thinking. The breeze blew, but it could not take away his excitement and confidence that God had spoken. The crickets chirped, but they could not drown out the words of prophecy still ringing in his ear. As Habakkuk picked up his instrument and absent-mindedly tuned their strings, he felt an aching burden to share the message far and wide.*

*And yet, he thought as he stared at the stars with a wry smile, it still didn't make any sense.*

## WHATEVER MAY COME

Ian Rappaport went from an everyday guy to a marketing sensation overnight.

During the 2014 Super Bowl, the biggest stage for advertising in American culture, a beer company took a calculated risk and based their entire ad campaign around one man who didn't even know he would be in a commercial. The plan was simple: take this man and ask if he was "up for whatever happened next." If he said yes, he would be taken on a series of staged and improbable scenarios, all filmed with secretly placed cameras to catch his reactions. If he said no, the entire night would be an expensive and embarrassing mistake.

Luckily for the company, Ian responded in the affirmative and so ended up surprised all night by beautiful and famous people. They showed up in limos and elevators and secret rooms, with llamas and DJs and games of ping pong. Ian took each bizarre twist with a smile on his face and a readiness to jump into the craziness. In a situation that should have bred confusion, he had total ease and confidence.

Of course, these reactions weren't an accident. While Mr. Rappaport was truly unaware of the reason for his adventure, he had been carefully selected for that night. As part of a focus group, the advertisers had identified his personality and had a good sense of how he might react in unusual settings. He was chosen by the marketing gurus because they could safely predict the attitude he was sure to have. Ian would almost always be willing to do 'whatever' because of his temperament.

> *"I didn't know what was going on," he said. "Not the slightest clue. But I knew I just had to go with it. That's my personality and who I am. I live in the moment and have fun. I guess that's why I was picked to be this guy."*[1]

And a few beers probably didn't hurt, either!

However, life isn't like a beer commercial, and most of us aren't like Ian. We get hit with surprises, but our surprises aren't always fun and positive. A spouse serves divorce papers, a company makes unexpected job cuts, a doctor makes the prognosis of cancer, or a child brings home a fiancé who will surely doom their future together. Such predicaments seldom make us feel like "living in the moment" and going with it. Instead, we are hit with confusion. "Why God are you doing _____?" we cry out.

Scripture is filled with men who share our confusion in the midst of events and announcements. Job, a faithful man blessed immeasurably by God, was rocked to the core when his family and fortune were destroyed. The Old Testament records Job's and his friends' attempts to make sense of his tragedy as they engage in debates and questions. And what about Joshua, asked to attack a city armed with nothing but a power-walking crowd of immigrants with some trumpets? Or Abraham, who was encouraged to try to have a baby with his ninety-year old wife? Or Joseph, as he was sold into slavery by his brothers? No doubt each of these men and their families were lost in the moment, unsure of what to say or do.

"For My thoughts are not your thoughts, nor are your ways My ways," says the Lord in Isaiah 55:8. Intellectually, we have no problem with that statement, but emotions don't always listen to reason. Confusion is a natural human sentiment when faced with our God's sometimes-incomprehensible plans. So, when faced with plans or commands we don't understand, how do we carry on? How do we have faith when we are confused by God?

## THE PERPLEXED PROPHET

Habakkuk, the eighth minor prophet in Scripture, gives us a great case study to see how to handle our confusion with God. This prophet was called to share a message from the Lord, but he also had an honest reaction to that message—a message that he found difficult and puzzling. The result is a conversation where we see both the prophet's mind and the Divine Author's heart, and consequently we learn a thing or two about how we have faith when we're confused.

### Construction of a Prophet

With most of the Minor Prophets, our knowledge of their life situation is speculative. We have to stitch together a few bits of information, plus some inferences from the text, to produce a fuzzy image of who the writer might have been. Habakkuk is no different; the details of his background are vague and our concept of his story comes more from imagination than the text. However, we don't need facts of his life story to know certain things about the man, especially concerning his deep faith. Several indicators in the prophecy are enough to show us that Habakkuk was definitely a mature follower of God.

For example, in the book's opening verses, Habakkuk asks God "how long" before his prayers will receive an answer (1:2-4).

194

"How long" indicates a history of repeated and fervent prayer, so we know Habakkuk was a man of faith. The nature of his prayer is in regard to justice for others, wanting the wicked punished and injustices cured. This shows that Habakkuk loved people and was heartbroken by hurt. He was in tune to God's ideals, and he hated to see those ideals violated. From the very start of his book then, we witness a man who exhibited a committed and powerful faith.

Further passages also show evidence of a deep faith. He addresses God as *My* God, *My* Holy One, *My* Rock (1:12), showing a personal relationship with the Lord. In other places, he shows familiarity with God's works in history (chapter 3), and he rejoices in the God of his salvation (3:18). This is a man who knew the Lord, who trusted Him, and who had great faith. As one commentator summarizes:

> *Through this extended dialogue with Yahweh...*
> *we hear Habakkuk's vibrant faith and deep*
> *humanity, learning and growing in relation to*
> *God. He asks healthy questions (1:2-4) and is*
> *persistent in his questioning (1:12-2:1). He is*
> *historically grounded in the memory of Israel*
> *(3:1-15). He expresses a profound faith in song*
> *(3:16-19). His humanity and joy are a model and*
> *a challenge.*[2]

Such faith must have originated somewhere. Additional evidence in the text helps us make some educated guesses about this prophet's background that match up with what we already know about his character. The concluding chapter of the book offers perhaps our biggest clue. It is a poetic prayer that is also a song. Like the Psalms—the Old Testament's hymnbook—Habakkuk 3 includes technical musical terms such as "on shigionoth" (3:1) and "selah" (3:3, 9, 13). These terms indicate tunes, musical styles, and musical divisions. By treating his words as lyric, Habakkuk reveals himself to be a Scriptural singer/song-writer—the Old Testament's Chris Tomlin.

Habakkuk, though, isn't just an independent artist struggling to make ends meet. His ascription of the song to the "chief musician" in the final verse of the book (3:19) causes us to think he likely served as a Temple prophet-musician, one of the official positions of service at the Temple.[3] If this prophet's day job involved service at that holy location, then it is easy to draw some inferences about his daily focus and dedication to the Lord. The strong faith we see in his writing would be an extension of the faith he lived every day serving in God's presence.

## Call of the Prophet

While Habakkuk's occupation would have strengthened his faith, his life in Jerusalem (where the Temple was located) would have tested it. Habakkuk ministered during a dark time in the nation of Judah. Contextually, we can determine that Habakkuk served somewhere between 630 to 605 BC, overlapping the reign of King Jehoiakim, one of the last kings of Judah and one of the worst. Jehoiakim's actions and policies, which we've seen in relation to other prophets, led to an oppressive spiritual climate for those who sincerely tried to worship Yahweh.

> *He killed the innocent who opposed him and refused to pay poor laborers (Jeremiah 22:13-19). Under his administration the prophets and priesthood were corrupted in adultery and abuse of authority (Jeremiah 23:1-2,9-11). The king sent assassins who killed the prophet Uriah for prophesying (as Habakkuk and Jeremiah also did) that Jerusalem would fall (Jeremiah 26:20-23).[4]*

This difficult situation weighed heavily on Habakkuk. He struggled with the things he saw happening in the streets, the courts, and the palace. Injustice and immorality were the norm, and it led to a crisis of faith for him. How could this be happening? Like many of the other prophets, theodicy (the problem of why a good God permits evil) was at the forefront of his mind.

Habakkuk's prayers poured out his heart to God: "How long, O Lord, must I call for help, but you do not listen? Or cry out to you, 'Violence!' but you do not save? Why do you make me look at injustice? Why do you tolerate wrong?" (1:2-3). It is a cry echoed in many places throughout Scripture, from the desperate pleadings of the psalmists to the voice of the martyrs in Revelation 6:10. The difference is that Habakkuk's questions are not just the righteous struggle of a God-fearing man; they are the occasion for God to provide a direct answer. Habakkuk's questions seem to initiate his call, since God responds and gives an answer that must be shared.

Habakkuk's rare privilege of dialogue with his Creator, though, is not satisfying. Rather than answers, he stumbles into more questions. God's solutions are complicated and confusing, something "that you would not believe, even if you were told" (1:5). It is a message bittersweet and strange, worthy of the title "burden" used to describe it in the opening verse of the book.

God uses this back-and-forth conversation with the confused musician as an occasion to share something deep and meaningful.

## QUESTION AND ANSWER (PART 1)

### "How Long?"

The world around Habakkuk did not value the things that God values, and so Habakkuk begins this exchange as one who is offended. King Jehoiakim is not the only one who is abusing the system. The violations are widespread among the population, and they are not minor. Violence. Plundering. Strife. Contention. Habakkuk sees these, and he sees that the official remedies of law and justice are not working. "The law is powerless, and justice never goes forth. For the wicked surround the righteous; therefore perverse judgment proceeds" (1:4).

We may think of a number of modern parallels to this situation. For instance, many Southern courts failed to provide justice for African-Americans before the Civil Rights movement began making changes. Innocent blacks were beaten or lynched rather than be absolved through the legal system. Guilty whites were able to escape punishment as the law turned a blind eye to their hate. Ancient Judah was just as corrupt, and the corruption wasn't limited to racial issues. Civil and religious crime went unnoticed and unpunished.

Habakkuk plays the role of the distraught observer, knowing that change is beyond his power to effect. His sensitivities have not been dulled by this wickedness around him; instead they have been sharpened. He is more keenly aware of the abuses against God's Word than his countrymen are, and that knowledge is pure agony to him.

So he cries out, and his pleadings receive a divine response.

## "Be Utterly Astounded!"

Habakkuk's social commentary had been about Judah, but God answers by shifting his focus. "Look among the nations and watch—be utterly astonished! For I will work a work in your days which you would not believe, though it were told you" (1:5).

Instead of finding an internal remedy to social injustice, God points to an external solution. He reveals a plan to bring punishment upon the evildoers in Judean society by using an army of evildoers, the terrible and dreadful Chaldeans!

Anyone who is familiar with the history of the Bible immediately knows about the Chaldeans (a.k.a. the Babylonians). Their rise to power and their eventual conquest of the nation of Judah is a foregone conclusion. To us, that statement is no more shocking than a *Star Wars* aficionado hearing yet again that Darth Vader is Luke Skywalker's father. Yet Habakkuk is like a man who has never heard about or seen a *Star Wars* movie. He is blown away by this new piece of information. The news, as God says, is utterly astonishing.

Part of Habakkuk's shock was tied to the low level of influence the Babylonians held in his time. The Babylonians were a surprising choice because they were not yet a regional superpower. For years, the leading nation in the Middle East had not been the Chaldeans; it had been the Assyrian Empire. Their cruel dominance had been felt by every nation in the region, from what is now modern-day Iran through the land of Egypt. The Assyrians had been unstoppable for decades. They were the ones who devastated the Northern Kingdom of Israel, scattering Judah's cousins in every direction, including six feet under. Assyrian might had ruled this corner of the world with no substantial opposition. Yet, in a shockingly short amount of time, Assyria would fall to a new power. This fall had been revealed already in the prophetic book of Nahum, so a godly Levite like Habakkuk might not have been surprised to hear of their defeat. However, he would have been flabbergasted to think of the still-insignificant Babylon as the aggressor who would easily rise in power to chastise God's Chosen People.

The other part of Habakkuk's shock and astonishment came from God's surprising answer that He would punish the evil in Judah by using a nation that was even more evil. Rather than finding an internal remedy to social injustice, God planned the destruction of Judah's society. Instead of curing the patient by cutting out the cancer of evil, God was going to allow the patient to be killed and the eaten by a wild animal!

God's description of the evil Babylonian force is poetic yet terrifying. This "bitter and hasty nation" (1:6) would sweep across the region, taking control of lands they had never before possessed. They are compared to leopards in reference to their speed. Their fierceness is likened to an evening wolf. As a speeding eagle ready to eat, the Babylonian army would swoop in for the kill (1:8). The ease with which the Babylonians would conquer is reminiscent of a child playing in the sand at the beach. Captives are gathered like sand (1:9) and earthen mounds are heaped up (1:10) to seize cities. The cities and countries of the Middle East are sand castles being razed by a callous youth, and Judah is next to be flattened.

The Bible's progressive revelation regarding these world powers helps us remember that such changes do not happen by chance. It was by the hand of God that Assyria fell, and it would be by the hand of God that the Babylonians would rise to conquer. It was a work that God would work in the days of Habakkuk (1:5), not a coincidence or accident. These revelations made God's answer to Habakkuk's first question of "How long?" even more confusing.

## QUESTION AND ANSWER (PART 2)

### "Did I Hear You Correctly?"

As Habakkuk listens to this answer from God, he is awestruck and confused. The unanticipated response takes him by surprise. Certainly this doesn't seem to answer his initial question.

"How long until you fix the injustice in our country, God?" Habakkuk asks.

"I'll smash Judah with the Chaldeans!" God replies without explanation.

Our musician trusts God implicitly, yet he struggles to make sense of this answer. What does God mean in this response? Habakkuk must now ask "Why?" "Why do You look on those who deal treacherously, and hold Your tongue when the wicked devours a person more righteous than he?" he probes (1:13).

If any situation warrants confusion, certainly this one does. God had a special relationship with the nation of Israel. They were His people, promised to Abraham, rescued from slavery in Egypt by Moses, settled in the Promised Land under Joshua, and ruled by the anointed King David. God has done amazing things for his people, and now he seems to be siding with the enemy! Habakkuk feels as betrayed as Canada when Wayne Greztky crossed the border to play hockey in the United States. His people seem to be in danger of falling under the judgment of an evil, pagan society to which God seemingly has no positive ties. Searching for confidence, he feebly protests, "We shall not die" (1:12), but the musician's declaration rings a bit hollow.

He paints a picture of how he feels in the next few verses (1:14-17). Fishermen at sea, he says, use their hooks and nets to haul in and devour unsuspecting and defenseless fish. And now, Judah is the fish; Babylon is dragging in the nets of impending disaster; and God is the one who has granted a fishing license.

Of course, there is irony here. The same "pure and righteous" group that Habakkuk contrasts to Babylon is the Jewish nation whom he had just excoriated in chapter one for their faithless acts. As bad as Judah's population may be, they can't be *that* bad, Habakkuk reasons. His own nation's flaws are seemingly minor in comparison to the ever-growing evil of the Babylonians that God had just described. So, he stands there in his confusion and pours out his heart, honest and baffled.

Like Moses at the burning bush, the prophet has the boldness to say more than "Yes, Sir" when he can't comprehend God's answer. Instead, he decides to ask further. Like when Job questioned God, Habakkuk knows that the Lord may reply forcefully and with little or no explanation to his queries. But his desire to hear an answer to these questions is worth the risk. So Habakkuk takes his place on the city walls and waits hopefully for God to speak.

## "Make It Plain"

To His praise, God provides a response. He is not harsh with Habakkuk, just determined to continue on the course He has laid out. Judah will fall to the Babylonians. But, that is not all.

"Write the vision," God says, "and make it plain on tablets, that he may run who reads it." The message will be made plain, whether the running is from messengers delivering it to the people quickly, or whether it is running after hearing the prophecy's words.[5] Even though the fulfillment of this prophecy may take some time, "Don't worry" is what God in indicating, for "It will surely come" (2:3).

Habakkuk 2:4 contains the most important part of God's reply—probably the most important statement of the entire book—and we will come back to it shortly. But the rest of God's message answers some important points. Though they conquer, Babylon will not be left unpunished. There is no free pass, no playing favorites. God will justly punish the Babylonians for their evil and their insatiable appetite for conquest.

Beginning in verse 5, Babylon's fate is laid out. It is presented as a taunt. Structurally, the material is divided into two sets of ten lines each. Each half concludes with a significant theological statement. Verse 14 foretells, "The earth will be filled with the knowledge of the glory of the Lord." Verse 20 commands, "But the Lord is in His holy temple. Let all the earth keep silence before Him." Together they provide a set a five different woes proclaimed against the Chaldeans.[6] These woes bring to life a negative example of the Golden Rule, where the things Babylon has done unto others are now revisited upon her own people.

Such a declaration of woe against Judah's future oppressors would have helped Habakkuk feel a little better about the seeming injustice of this situation. At least God would hold the evil Babylonians accountable, even if His use of them to chastise Judah still seemed confusing.

Yet, the statement made immediately before this section of taunting and woe would have rung in Habakkuk's ears. Even as he heard Babylon's fate unfurl, the bigger point was God's statement about how to handle this entire message: "Behold the proud, His soul is not upright in him; *but the just shall live by his faith,"* says God (2:4, italicize added).

The just shall live by his faith. That quote is of particular theological importance in the Bible. No less than three New Testament letters mention this passage (Romans 1:17; Galatians 3:11; Hebrews 10:38). Commentator Warren Wiersbe notes, "The emphasis in Romans is on *the just,* in Galatians on how they should *live,* and in Hebrews on *'by faith.'* It takes three books to explain and apply this one verse!"[7]

Here, though, Habakkuk finds in this verse a way out of his confusion. While he had hoped for an explanation from God regarding the methods He chose or the timing He would use, instead God provides Habakkuk a path of action. Habakkuk doesn't have to understand or like God's plan, and he doesn't even need to question it, he just has to trust God and live by faith.

## A SONG OF FAITH

In response to this revelation, Habakkuk takes the path God gives him in 2:4 and responds like any good musician would—by putting his thoughts and feelings to song. Chapter 3 is a powerful and beautiful work that compiles and applies the truth of his messages from God. In it we see several things that Habakkuk learned.

First, Habakkuk looks for a revival of God's works. As with the beginning of the book, he wants God to act and move. While chapter one was full of questions such as "How long?," here there is confident expectation that the Lord will act and move. "O Lord, revive your work in the midst of the years!" (3:2).

Habakkuk is able to look back at history and see God's works spanning the centuries. He presents it in splendid terms, painting word pictures of God's glory and power and might. Rays flash from His hand (3:4), mountains see Him and tremble (3:10). All of nature—seas, rivers, hills, sky—are shown deferring to God. There is no question that the Lord has acted in the past, and Habakkuk trusts that He will do so again.

So, Habakkuk's first lesson is that even when we are confused, we should trust that God is at work.

Second, he sees God's heart. "You went forth for the salvation of Your people, for salvation with Your Anointed." God's purpose in these actions ultimately benefits His people. This is not God on a random warpath; it is a God the Warrior fighting for His chosen ones. The Anointed in this verse could either refer to Israel (see Exodus 19:6; Psalm 28:8), the king of Israel (as in God's choice of Saul and David), or the expected righteous King (the Messiah).[8] But, no matter the reference, the actions of the Anointed show that God is fighting for a people He loves.

Even when we are confused, Habakkuk discovers, we should trust that God cares for us.

Third, Habakkuk remembers God's victories against evil. He writes in terms that remind the reader of God's victory over Pharaoh during the Exodus, and he shares the language of victory found in places like Psalm 74. This remembrance helps give him confidence of God's power to overcome and victoriously establish justice and order.[9]

Even when we are confused, we should trust that God will achieve His purposes.

Habakkuk ends the song in chapter three no less confused than when he started. He knows God *could* act powerfully now, and He *could* solve Judah's problems without using the Babylonians. He also knows that God *won't*. God still intends to use what Habakkuk considers a strange course of action—a course that still doesn't make sense.

However, the path out of confusion presented in 2:4 gives Habakkuk opportunity to trust God anyway. He makes the conscious choice of faith despite not having all the answers he would like. And so, his song concludes with this poignant expression of trust:

> *"Though the fig tree may not blossom, nor fruit be on the vines; Though the labor of the olive may fail, and the fields yield no food; Though the flock may be cut off from the fold, and there be no heard in the stalls—yet I will rejoice in the Lord, I will joy in the God of my salvation. The Lord God is my strength; He will make my feet like deer's feet, and He will make me walk on my high hills" (3:17-19a).*

# HABAKKUK'S FAITH LESSONS

Habakkuk's display of faith despite confusion provides a powerful example for all of us to follow. His dialogue with God brings to light several faith lessons that can be applied when we are confused ourselves.

## Lessons for Israel

Israel, according to Scripture, plays an important role in the end times. In fact, her role is so prominent that almost every morsel of news involving the country is eagerly scrutinized, parsed, and analyzed to see if any connection to Bible prophecy exists. The nation's role in eschatology cannot be doubted, but for Israel and those who support her, the constant speculation can be confusing. Where do Egypt and Iraq and Syria and ISIS fit into the picture? Do current events point to an imminent return of the Messiah, or will Jesus tarry a bit longer?

Lost in the scramble to understand timelines, the nation of Israel and her supporters would do well to hear God's words in Habakkuk 2:3: "Though it tarries, wait for it; because it will surely come, it will not tarry." While current events may cause us some confusion and disagreements about the timing of God's ongoing, redemptive work with Israel, God's words remind us to simply trust Him. We should not doubt nor fret; we should not be concerned or indifferent. We should simply have expectant faith that God will carry out His promises.

For Israel, this means looking more closely at God's messages and being reminded of His great promises. We must be aware that the Lord's perspective on time and His use of words like "soon" are much different than our own. Despite our hurry, God remains true to His own pace and only asks that we believe His faithfulness. Accept that there will be some confusion, and don't let your faith be daunted by events that are now happening. Simply trust that God's plan will unfold in His own time.

## Lessons for the Nations

Countries across the globe struggle to explain their own rise to power or fall from it. The rise of the Babylonians was shocking, but it was just as inexplicable as the demise of the Mayan empire, baffling as the longevity of the Chinese, or implausible as the ascendance of the United States. Such changes are often attributed to economic, geographic, or military factors. Habakkuk reminds us that there is an unseen spiritual component to these national changes.

God is working in the rise and fall of countries in order to further His own purposes. His plans are more important than government policies, and He will use a nation's actions to accomplish His own will.

Knowing that our own political and national initiatives are secondary to God, we can relax a little. Voters may elect surprising choices, and lawmakers may back vexing programs, but God will use them all in ways we are not able to predict. You may be confused by national success or by national failure, but the true opportunity to have faith is grounded in the fact that God's Kingdom is always and ever advancing.

## Lessons for the Church

*"The righteous shall live by his faith."*

In every age and culture, the Church faces certain issues that seem more pressing than others. In one generation it is dancing and playing cards, in another it is braided hair, and in another it is gay marriage. Each wave of increasing sin and its subsequent challenges may cause us to join Habakkuk in crying out, "How long, O Lord?" We see the pain and loss that sin produces, and we ache for our culture to see the error of its ways and repent.

Habakkuk's words of faith, so important to the New Testament authors, provide a plan of action for us to navigate the onslaught of sin. Rather than aggressively fighting to cure a culture or passively assuming it is beyond repair, we need to trust that changes will happen when we live by faith. By keeping our focus on God rather than others' behaviors, we can avoid the over- and under-reactions typical in many congregations. Our churches need to remember that "faith is demonstrated *as faith* in *faithful living.*"[10] When we are confused by the sin of the world around us, we need to keep our focus on the One who remains above it by pursuing a lifestyle that brings glory to Christ's name and provides evidence that He is the one, true Savior.

## Lessons for You

It is ironic that emotional honesty is sometimes frowned upon by Christians. For the man or woman going through a difficult time due to marital struggles, the death of a child, or an impossible financial mistake, the questions of "Why?" and "How long?" are too often frowned upon. They are mistaken as signs of a weak relationship with God.

Habakkuk reminds us that it is perfectly fine to suffer and be confused. We need not pretend everything is fine and put on a mask of tranquility when we are in turmoil. While we search for answers, we need to remember that our God is bigger than our questions and problems. We need to trust that He is ultimately good even when we can't comprehend His plans. This faith is not blind. It simply puts more confidence in the truth of Scripture than the pain of our own experience.

Habakkuk was able to experience the confusion, yet still trust Yahweh God. Faced with injustice and plans to deal with it that made little sense to him, Habakkuk still calls God "my God... my Holy One... O Rock" (1:12). He is able to look beyond the murky present and live by faith.

We need to remember the lessons Habakkuk learned.

We should trust that God is at work. Jesus promises, "Behold, I am coming soon! My reward is with me, and I will give to everyone according to what he has done" (Revelation 22:12). There is a Divine plan in motion. We may not see how our confusing events lead there, but each step takes us closer to the return of Christ.

We should trust that God cares for us. Jesus reminds us that, "For God so loved the world that He gave His only begotten Son, that whoever believes in Him should not perish but have everlasting life" (John 3:16). No matter what we are confused about, we can trust that God loves us deeply.

Finally, we should trust that God will achieve His purposes. Jesus has achieved victory already:

> *"He forgave us all our sins, having canceled the written code, with its regulations, that was against us and that stood opposed to us; he took it away, nailing it to the cross. And having disarmed the powers and authorities, he made a public spectacle of them, triumphing over them by the cross" (Colossians 2:13-15).*

When we are confused, we need to remember that we are and will be victorious in Christ. So then, how do we have faith when confused? Embrace the confusion, and then trust anyway.

## QUESTIONS FOR DISCUSSION

1.  What injustices confuse you today? Describe your prayer life in response to those injustices. How does it compare to Habakkuk's?

2.  If you had heard God's plan to punish evil people with even more evil people, what would your reaction have been? Why are we surprised by God's actions, even though His ways are higher than our own?

3.  Consider Habakkuk's line of questioning in 1:12-17. When is it appropriate to question God's plans? What kind of heart do we need to have when presenting such questions to Him?

4.  How does the judgment on Babylon in chapter two help you better accept God's surprising actions?

5.  Who are some examples of Christians you know who "live by faith"? What behaviors of theirs are worth following? What preparation do they make to be able to live in that way?

6.  Is there a time when you have had to trust God despite evidence to the contrary? What gives you confidence in Him when your world fails?

# FAITH JOURNEY 9
## ZEPHANIAH: FAITH UNDER PEER PRESSURE

## THE NERVOUS NOBLEMAN

The palace guards stood before the grand doors to the king's throne room like two stone monoliths. Though military protocol dictated that their eyes remain focused forward, curiosity drew them to watch out of the corners of their eyes a young nobleman.

Just into manhood, the richly adorned aristocrat paced vigorously back and forth before the guards while biting his once perfectly manicured nails. Sometimes he'd stop to look longingly out of the window and survey the vista of his hometown of Jerusalem, as if desiring to escape out of the window to the portico below. More than once he'd rushed up to the doors as if ready to enter, only to spin around and resume his worried pacing. The guards nevertheless appeared quite unconcerned that there was a potential security threat, for the nobleman was a regular to the royal court. They remained calm, despite a combination of bemusement and bother at having to be needlessly readied to open the entryway.

Halting before the massive doors for the umpteenth time, the nobleman laid his hands upon the cedar wood and sighed out an, "Okay, I'm ready." And yet, he remained leaning against the doors, unmoving as if glued to the floor. Unsure if it was to the guards or to himself that he was addressing, the three remained in the limbo of a lengthy and uncomfortable silence. The sentries decided it was finally time to move things along, and sharing a knowing look, pushed the heavy panels swiftly aside. The young man tumbled into the room.

After quickly pulling himself upright, the nobleman's eyes darted hurriedly around the cavernous hall. The king's royal court remained as lavish as he'd always remembered it since childhood. Ornate wood paneling etched with gold bedecked the marbled walls. Thick tapestries hung around the perimeter depicting the great exploits of a dynasty that stretched back almost 400 years. The massive throne stood as the centerpiece of the room, graced by two ferocious lion sculptures and a bevy of live peacocks spreading their turquoise feathers along its stone stairway.

Bounding down those stairs two at a time, the teenage king ran to meet his boyhood friend who'd just stumbled through the entryway. "Cousin Zephaniah!" exclaimed the king. Using an embrace as cover, the boy king whispered conspiratorially into his relative's ear. "I'm so glad you're here. This meeting with the foreign ambassadors is soooo boring. Do you have any message from the Lord that can liven things up?" The question caused Zephaniah to break down into a choking fit. The king, never one for protocol, whacked him on the back. Once his coughing was under control, Zephaniah realized in alarm that the room was full of dignitaries, and remembering his place, bowed deeply before his sovereign. "King Josiah, I am as ever at your service." The king smiled impishly, tilted his crown back upright atop his head, and then almost hopped back up onto his throne.

Zephaniah took in his audience. At the center of the royal hall sat the young king who'd returned to his throne, surrounded by a half dozen or so advisors standing around the base. These old men had practically raised Josiah since the tender age of eight after the murder of his father, King Amon. They were the true power in the land and were as extremely corrupt as Amon had ever been. Zephaniah had spent much time behind the scenes countering their advice to Josiah. Besides the ever-present royal guard and military generals, various ambassadors from Philistia, Moab, Ammon,

*Ethiopia and even dreaded Assyria were there in full pomp and circumstance. They had been deep in a meeting to discuss a new threat from the distant north.*

*All eyes in the room now focused silently on Zephaniah, some revealing barely concealed impatience while others outright contempt at the intrusion. All were held only in check by the king's request that their attention be given to this gangly young interloper.*

*Zephaniah just stood there frozen, his insides shuddering from a mix of dread and adrenaline. His stomach felt queasy and his tongue stuck to the roof of his mouth. Only a prophet of Yahweh God for a brief time, he understood he wasn't just suffering from the inner turmoil that comes from being inexperienced. No, he was suffering from the terrible realization that if he gave the message God had sent him to give, this may very likely be the last time he ever enjoyed the privileges of the royal court and a special friendship with his king and kinsman. The worst case scenario, and the most likely one, he'd be killed right there on the spot. Zephaniah was facing the loss of everything he'd ever cherished.*

*With one last mental cry of desperation, Zephaniah begged God for strength and courage. And then, the young nobleman was jolted as if lightening had shot through his body. Peace like a blanket followed, wrapping around him to chase all his fears away. Now divinely assured of what he must do, consequences be accursed! Rising to full height, back straight and eyes steeled, the novice prophet spoke up with a voice so strong that inwardly it took him by surprise. "Thus says the Lord, 'I will utterly consume everything from the face of the land!'"*

# I'M NOT GOING TO DENY JESUS!

## Paying the Ultimate Price

"I'm not going to deny Jesus!" Those were the last words that Pastor Ghorban Tourani ever spoke in his life.

On November 22, 2005, Ghorban received a curious phone call at his home in Gonbad-e-Kavous, Iran. The caller had heard the pastor boldly sharing his testimony in the shops at the local bazaar earlier that day and seemed excited to know more about Ghorban's Christian faith. Because of Iran's hostility towards non-Islamic religions, the man was requesting a private meeting at a park.

Ghorban was instantly wary of the request. His time serving a murder sentence in a Turkmenistan prison had taught him to guard his back at all times. Now a Christian, thanks to the witness of a Russian cellmate, Ghorban had finished his prison sentence and had been freed to return to his native Iran, though not free to share his newfound faith there. The nasty cut across his face his very own brother had given him and the constant threats of assassination by Islamic clerics for having converted from Islam to Christianity were a continual reminder of just how careful Christians in Iran had to be when sharing Christ. Still, the seeker on the phone seemed to honestly want to know more about Jesus, and he believed no pastor could ever turn down an opportunity to lead a soul to Christ.

Lured out of his home, Ghorban made it only as far as his back alley before he was greeted by three men wielding wicked looking knives. "Why have you turned to Christianity?" the recognizable voice of the caller asked. "We are giving you one chance to deny your Christian faith and return to Islam."

Ghorban knew he had a choice to make, and to make it quickly. He could give into all the intense pressure from the town's religious authorities, family and peers and finally be safe from harm. All he had to do was declare the Shahada: "There is no god but Allah and Muhammad is the Messenger of Allah." Or, he could remain faithful to his Savior, Jesus Christ. In the time it took for his heart to skip a beat, Ghorban with absolute conviction chose to remain faithful to Jesus Christ. Upon telling the men his decision, three separate knives plunged into his body. The faithful pastor was sent home to be with his Savior.

The story of the Iranian pastor's faith didn't end there. Ghorban's wife, Afoul, soon after found his lifeless body bleeding out among a growing crowd of gawkers. With the same conviction her husband had shown, Afoul wailed out to the throng, "O people, remember that Ghorban is a Christian martyr who laid down his life for the sake of Christ!" Later that day, the Islamic secret police raided their home and carried her and her children off for interrogation. Ghorban's entire family took a stand for their faith in Jesus Christ and paid the ultimate price.[1]

## Weighing the Costs

As magnificent as Pastor Tourani and his family demon-strated their faith, such absolute devotion to Jesus Christ is tragically a rarity in this day and age. Just think about it. Living ensconced in the comfort of our Western cultural diversity and national Judeo-Christian roots, when have you ever been challenged to deny Christ or die? Probably never. And yet, Western Christians are leaving their faith in Christ at an alarming rate. According to a five-year study of young adults by the California-based spiritual research company, the Barna Group, by age 15 a whopping 59% of Christian teens have dropped out of the faith. Of those who identify as Christian into the ages of 18 to 25, a staggering 38% have significant doubts about their faith.[2]

Why the mass exodus of Christians from their faith in God and church families? According to the Barna study, the most prevalent reason reported by those surveyed was their feeling that biblical morals had become old fashioned and therefore totally obsolete in our modern hedonistic society. The Bible, the youth believe, couldn't possibly stand against the appeal of a society which tells its people that they should be free of the moral constraints the Bible has placed on them. Society woos us with the pretext that marriage is a dated and suffocating contract. It coerces us with the freedom that sex should be with whomever and whenever you want it. It consoles us that consequences can be avoided by a speedy abortion or STD vaccine. It lies to us that non-Christian religions are also truth. It swells us with pride when proclaiming we are the center of the universe and deserve all the best life has to offer, so go ahead and take it by any means. These are the falsehoods society rams down our throats through incessant advertising, marketing and the most effective tactic of all—peer pressure.

Who are the most susceptible to society's anti-biblical teachings? According to Dr. John T. Chirban, clinical instructor in psychology at Harvard Medical School, it's the children.[3] Dr. Chirban explains that, "individuals often find themselves conforming to the group's norms, behaviors, attitudes, speech patterns, and dress code to earn acceptance and approval." In other words, our self-worth is tied to being accepted by our peers and society. Conform and you're cool and accepted, do not conform and you are ridiculed and ostracized. That's why Christian parents are repeatedly confronted by these statements from their children: "My friends are all doing it. Why shouldn't I?" "I don't want to be left out." "What if they don't like me anymore?" When faced with choosing to be cool like their friends or being fuddy-duddy like their parents and their outdated Bibles, most children invariably choose society. And, when society is the choice, what naturally follows is the abandonment of the child's faith in God. Their easily disposable faith had never been truly internalized as their own, lasting only as long as it had been because it was riding on the coattails of their parent's faith.

Despite the hardships, Christians can maintain their faith in God against the unwavering onslaught of societal peer pressure. The solution can be found in a little three chapter book written by the Prophet Zephaniah.

## THE PRESSURED PROPHET

### Time of the Prophet

"The word of the Lord which came to Zephaniah... in the days of Josiah the son of Amon, king of Judah." This is how

Zephaniah 1:1 introduces the ninth Minor Prophet, a faithful messenger of Yahweh God who lived in one of the most dynamic and fascinating time periods in all of Judah's history.

In the dawning years of Zephaniah's life in the 640s BC, the Southern Kingdom of Judah was held in the grip of Manasseh, the most wicked king in all of its history. Manasseh's father, Hezekiah, whom both Zephaniah and Josiah shared as a great-grandfather, "did what was right in the sight of the Lord according to all that his father David had done" (2 Kings 18:3). But, Hezekiah's son, Manasseh, utterly rejected God and his father's teachings and "did evil in the sight of the Lord" (2 Kings 21:2,9). For 55 years, since becoming king at age 12, King Manasseh seduced Judah to do more evil than all the nations whom the Lord had destroyed, including the Northern Kingdom of Israel. He polluted God's temple with idols, turned the priests of Yahweh into astrologers, consulted witches, filled Jerusalem with the blood of the innocent, and even sacrificed his children to the demon Molech in Jerusalem's Valley of Ben Hinnom.

The one son who did survive his father's blood lust, Amon, took the throne at 22 years old. He also was evil, so much so that his own servants had him killed two years into his reign. Amon's son, little 8-year old Josiah, was forced onto the throne by a cadre of corrupt noblemen who wanted to use him as a puppet to serve their own selfish plans.

For 57 years, the people of Judah grew up knowing nothing about God or His moral law. This moral void left the people committing acts so heinous that they made the child-sacrificing Amorites look good by comparison. The evils committed by both Judah's kings and her people were so utterly contemptuous that they greatly angered God. And so, God cursed Manasseh's evil nation with a death sentence. God would "bring such calamity upon Jerusalem and Judah, that whoever hears of it, both his ears will tingle" (2 Kings 21:11-12).

By the time Josiah ascended to the throne in 640 BC, the few believers in Yahweh left took a hard look at God's promise to Manasseh that He would "forsake the remnant of My inheritance and deliver them into the hand of their enemies" (2 Kings 21:14). They wondered if this prophecy was about to come true with the invasion of the savage Scythian hordes. The ancient ancestors of the Russians, the bloodthirsty Scythians had left their homes in the far northern Caucasus and headed south on a rampage, attacking countries even as far south as Egypt. The marauders came so very close to Judah's border when they laid waste to the Philistine's Temple of the Celestial Venus in Askelon.[4] Then they helped the Medes and Babylonians overthrow the declining Assyrian Empire, the destroyer of the Northern Kingdom of Israel. [5] The ruthless Scythians went on to dominate the Middle East for a blistering 28 years. So, when Zephaniah came to the king's court to present God's message, Josiah and the nations surrounding Judah were frantically discussing if they would be the ones next targeted in the Scythians' crosshairs.

## Construction of a Prophet

The moral and political climate under Manasseh which Zephaniah had been born into was very dangerous to a believer in Yahweh. It could be that his parents gave him the name Zephaniah, or Sophonias as it's sometimes translated, because it means "hidden, or protected, by Yahweh."[6] It could be that the family's faith in God had to be hidden or they'd face King Manasseh's wrath. Because the family was of royal blood, they would have been well known to Manasseh. And, because Manasseh was also well known for sacrificing even his own sons, he'd have no problem offing mere relatives.

Whatever the case was, Zephaniah and his contemporaries, the prophets Jeremiah and Nahum, had to be very careful about revealing their love of God and true faith in Him. Zephaniah had to be a nobleman in the Jerusalem capital where he served, assailed by evil from every direction, and still not surrender to the peer pressure to become as corrupt as his fellow aristocratic brethren.

## Call of the Prophet

At home in the political arena and in distinguished court circles, with plenty of political clout, never wanting for food and wine or fine clothing, and finally having the ear of his young cousin the king, Zephaniah had it made. And yet, something was missing. Being a believer in God, the young nobleman must have felt that there was so much more to life than wealth and position. What he was looking for was what one commentator explained, "The call of a God of love is to higher and richer experiences than the soul could reach without them."[7] God's love abounded in Zephaniah, but like Pastor Tourani, Zephaniah couldn't freely share that love with his people.

When it came to having a relationship with the King of Judah, the novice prophet walked cautiously on eggshells due to the eavesdropping ears of Josiah's crooked courtiers. Likely he could only hint around with young Josiah to guide him in making the right moral choices. "Could Josiah truly be trusted with the messages I'm beginning to hear from God?" he had to have wondered. Manasseh ascended to the throne as a boy and wrought havoc on Judah for almost six whole decades. "Would the boy Josiah also turn out just as bad as his grandfather and father? And, if he was to share God's word with Josiah, and Josiah chose to follow the evil path of Manasseh and Amon, will I lose it all, including even my very own life?" Those questions must have weighed heavily on Zephaniah's mind as day after day he stood in the courts and pretended to be only a shadow of what he truly was becoming—a prophet of God.

The messages from God were coming more frequently and more urgently until the young prophet must have felt ready to explode from keeping them all bottled up inside. He likely tested the waters by venturing to share just a few of the tamer prophecies with King Josiah, and was relieved to have them accepted with interest.

Josiah's interest in Yahweh was promising. But, what if he shared farther and deeper? Zephaniah's whole livelihood and possibly his life even were hanging in the balance. What would he do?

## THE CONDEMNED NATIONS

Whatever inner turmoil, doubts and fears of loss that must have plagued Zephaniah earlier, once empowered by God, Zephaniah cast them all to the wind. Unburdened by his fears, the young prophet let loose with God's thunderstorm of prophetic pronouncements. The tension of a lifetime of biting his tongue over the corruption and immorality that encircled him, coupled with the red-hot vehemence of God's righteous anger, poured out of Zephaniah like a flood bursting through a dam. The power of the message was so terrifying that acclaimed preacher Dr. G. Campbell Morgan was quoted as saying:

> *As I read those searching awful things which he says, and see the way in which he tears the veil from the sin of the people and leaves sin in all its naked, awful horror, and then pronounces upon it the swift, fearful doom of God's vengeance, I am startled and afraid.*[8]

One could imagine that Zephaniah's announcement that God would utterly consume everything from the face of the land would have left the dignitaries of the royal court thunderstruck. Disgusted that enemies would masquerade as allies in a time of crisis, Zephaniah in chapter two, and probably with some personal satisfaction, launched into God's judgments on Judah's surrounding nations.

### Gaza

Giving no reason to spell out why God had finally had it with the Philistines of Gaza, for they were well known for centuries of warfare and persecution against His people, Zephaniah pointed to their ambassador and growled out God's verdict. "The word of the Lord is against you. 'I will destroy you so there shall be no inhabitant. Your coast shall be for the remnant of the house of Judah'" (2:4-7).

## Moab and Ammon

Leaving only enough time for the Gazan ambassador's mouth to drop open, Zephaniah launched into Moab and Ammon, the nations bordering Judah on the east side of the Jordan River. Because these distant cousins made arrogant threats against their borders and against the people of the Lord of hosts, God declared, "Moab shall be like Sodom and the people of Ammon like Gomorrah—overrun with weeds and salt pits and a perpetual desolation" (2:8-11). Like Gaza, God declared that the remnant of His people would plunder Moab and Ammon and take back Israel's land which they'd been occupying.

## Ethiopia

The next ambassador to receive a shock was the tall, dark Ethiopian from distant Africa. Yahweh wasted very few words on Judah's backstabbing trade partner, "You shall be slain by My sword" (2:12).

## Assyria

The crimes of Assyria were too numerous to count. They'd scattered 10 of the 12 tribes of Israel when they'd conquered the Northern Kingdom of Israel a century earlier. The arrogance of Assyria clearly galled Israel's Defender. Because this nation said in her prideful heart, "I am it, and there is none besides me," Yahweh promised He'd destroy Assyria and make its capital city of Nineveh a desolation, as dry as the wilderness (2:13-15). Shaking his fist and reeling back in mock terror, Zephaniah punctuated the pronouncement of God's judgment. Nothing would be left of Nineveh except as a lair for wild animals.

# Judah

While Zephaniah was inwardly hoping he'd not receive the death sentence for offending the king's guests, what he was about to declare against his own nation of Judah certainly would place his life in mortal jeopardy. Everything depended on how King Josiah took God's message. Freed from the fear of the consequences, Zephaniah forged on as God's great herald of judgment, letting loose the Almighty's accusations with all the burning severity of a Heavenly Father deeply wronged by the children He loved so much.

**Corrupt Leadership.** Long sickened by the corruption of his fellow aristocrats, Zephaniah tore into Josiah's advisors (3:3-4). He compared Jerusalem's princes to roaring lions and its judges to devouring wolves who consume everything in their greed. The false prophets plaguing the court were unmasked as insolent, treacherous people. The religious leaders—the priest of Yahweh Himself—instead of keeping the Temple pure, stood accused of polluting the Sanctuary with their profanity.

Altogether, the leadership of Jerusalem had committed violence to the very laws they were sworn to uphold. The corruption of Judah's leadership caused Jerusalem to be known throughout the world as the "Oppressing City." It was defined by rebelliousness towards God, moral pollution, fraud, violence, deceit, being too haughty to receive correction, lacking trust in the Lord, and keeping their own God at a distance (1:8-9; 3:1-2,4). As one commentator summarized, "In Zephaniah's indictment of Jerusalem he pictures the people as unteachable, the rulers as predatory, the courts as merciless, the prophets as traitors, and the priests as profane. It was a dark day in God's land."[9]

What had caused Judah's rulers to lead their people into the way of compromise, away from worshipping God in truth, for caring for each other in love, and in becoming utterly callous to the law and will of God, was no mystery. Dr. David Hubbard, former president of Fuller Theological Seminary, points to chapter one verses 8 and 9 for the reason: "They became fascinated with the cultures and customs of their rich neighbors like Egypt and Assyria, and imported their corrupt and selfish ways."[10] Judah's leadership had succumbed to the negative influence of their peer nations, clothing themselves in the foreign apparel of their neighbor's sinfulness.

**Religious Syncretism.** Next, Zephaniah opened up God's guns of judgment specifically on the Temple priests. "I will cut off every trace of Baal from this place, the names of the idolatrous priests with the pagan priests" (1:4). The Temple priests standing in Josiah's court looked stricken. They exploded into the argument that without the adoption of the Caananite fertility god, Baal, when the Children of Israel first came to the Promised Land all those centuries ago, their nomadic shepherd ancestors would have starved in their attempt at becoming farmers. Zephaniah knew better, for when the Israelite's adopted the Caananite's farming lessons, they were also pressured into embracing the magic and corruption of that licentious fertility cult. Baalism constituted serious competition in the people's hearts to the worship of the one true God, and Zephaniah would have no arguments. He cut them off!

Moving to the window to jab his finger at the starry night, Zephaniah proclaimed, "I will cut off those who worship the host of heaven on the housetops; those who worship and swear oaths by the Lord, but who also swear by Milcom." This was the real root of God's anger against the priests. Sure, they upheld the worship of Yahweh God in the Temple, but they'd denigrated themselves into becoming religious syncretists, meaning mixing heathenism with the worship of the one true God. These idolatrous priests worshipped Yahweh, but they also worshipped demons in the form of pagan deities such as the Caananites' Baalims and the Ammonites' Milcom. "You have turned back from following the Lord, and have not sought the Lord, nor inquired of Him" (1:4-6). God was sickened that His representatives had been pressured into also representing His satanic adversaries, and in His very own house—the Temple. The outrage!

**Absentee View of God.** Red faced from burning with consternation, Zephaniah barely got the final accusations out coherently. "I will search Jerusalem with lamps and punish the men who are settled on their lees, who say in their heart, 'The Lord will not do good, nor will He do evil'" (1:12). God was comparing the people to lees—the dregs of wine that settle to the bottom of the vat. Wine will not taste pure and sweet without successful decantation that removes the bitter taste of the lees. Just like those bitter people who "settle on their lees," Zephaniah was pointing out that they believed God would never deal with people's sin. Because they believed Yahweh had totally checked out, they could misbehave all they wanted without fear of repercussion.

Lees Men are essentially moral atheists who mistakenly believe God is powerless. As Pastor W. MacKintosh MacKay once warned, "There is no more fatal deity for any man to worship than an Absentee God."[11] God couldn't have been more insulted by these Lees Men, and was more than ready to show them just how omnipresent He really is.

## THE PENITENT KING

Zephaniah had maintained his faith in God against the unwavering onslaught of societal peer pressure. Despite his fears of loss and life, he had obeyed God and delivered all of His messages at great risk. Now it was all up to King Josiah. Zephaniah could only wonder nervously how the teenage king would react to God's poignant messages. He could ignore God, following in his grandfather and father's wicked footsteps, and have Zephaniah killed on the spot, or not. Those fearful moments as God's prophet waited for the king's reaction must have been nerve-racking.

One could imagine Josiah slowly raising himself off the elevated throne, eyes fixated on his cousin, his expression indiscernible.

The courtiers, accused and enraged, looked to the king's advisors, waiting for them to signal Josiah to have his captain of the guards cut Zephaniah down. Everyone was deeply surprised then when Josiah, who'd finally found his voice, order everyone but Zephaniah out. Under a torrent of protests, the palace guards firmly ushered everyone out through the massive doors.

Once the doors thudded to a close behind them, Josiah walked down to Zephaniah and stood before him face-to-face. After a weighty pause, the king collapsed onto the floor, weeping and tearing his clothes in an expression of heart-wrenching sorrow. Josiah wailed in anguish for Yahweh to forgive him and his people. With one hand gently on his cousin's shoulder, Zephaniah led the king into a night-long prayer of repentance.

What followed King Josiah's prayers is nothing short of one of the greatest attempts at bringing about a spiritual revival the world has ever known. Yahweh was indeed very present to Josiah, even in those tender years. The words from Zephaniah continually burned hot in his ears, "I will utterly consume everything from the face of the land" (1:2). Josiah didn't want to see his beloved country destroyed, and so without haste acted with tremendous zeal in righting the wrongs of his people.

Second Chronicles 34-35 and 2 Kings 22-23 record how this 16-year old king finally became his own man, discarding the advice of his corrupt advisors and courtiers. By 626 BC and in the twelfth year of his reign, now age 20, Josiah could still be found tearing through the countryside purging Judah of the heathen shrines, breaking down the altars of Baal, chopping up the wooden idols, and slaughtering the false priests and prophets atop their very own altars. He didn't just toss into the gutters the evils he encountered, Josiah in righteous fervor ground the idols to dust and the bones to powder. Josiah's righteous fervor to cleanse the land led him to travel as far north as the long-destroyed Samaria. There he toppled the remains of the North's founding king Jeroboam I's abominable altar, though not before digging up its dead pagan priests and burning their brittle bones upon it! Thus Josiah fulfilled a 300-year old prophecy from 1 Kings 13:1-3 which actually named him by name, "Behold, a child, Josiah by name... shall sacrifice the priests of the high places who burn incense on you, and men's bones shall be burned on you."

By 620 BC and in the eighteenth year of his reign, now age 26, Josiah ordered the repair of the Temple once the idolatrous elements had been cleaned out and syncretist priests killed. What followed reversed one of the saddest tragedies in God's people's history. The true worship of God had been abandoned for so long that there wasn't a Book of the Law to be found. The priests had been attempting to minister for decades, but without God's Word! Immediately upon finding a Torah hidden in the Temple, Hilkiah the High Priest and Shaphan the Scribe ran to King Josiah to read him God's freshly discovered Word.

Second Kings 22-23 describes Josiah's response to his first-time hearing of God's moral laws. Josiah tore his clothes once more in agony and wailed, "Great is the wrath of the Lord that is aroused against us, because our fathers have not obeyed the words of this book, to do according to all that is written concerning us." Josiah then ordered all the people out of their houses to gather together and listen to the reading of God's Law. The king stood by a pillar where he made a covenant before the Lord. He would follow the Lord and keep His commandments, testimonies and statutes with all his heart and soul, and perform the words of God's covenant that had been written in this book. All the people in the land also took a stand for the covenant and swore off the false influences of their peers.

The nation had finally given up their evil ways. Or, had they?

## CHARACTER OF GOD

## Messages

One can imagine King Josiah and the Prophet Zephaniah years later standing side by side, gazing out of the panoramic palace window overlooking the city of Jerusalem. The people down in the crowded streets were busy celebrating the Passover Feast, but something clearly was amiss.

Years earlier, after Josiah had the Book of the Law read publically, the public in response had surrendered in national repentance to reassert their covenant with God. Second Kings 23:22 and 2 Chronicles 35:18 record that Jerusalem followed the reading with the biggest Passover feast ever held since the old days of the Judges. But now, years later, this subsequent Passover Feast was a pale shadow of the glory of that revival feast. The excitement for the event had dried up. The passion for the purpose of the celebration—the worship of Yahweh God—had dulled to merely going through the motions. The people gathered to talk of politics and sports and fashion, but nothing was heard about the love of God. The spiritual apathy was palpable.

King Josiah, now in the thirtieth year of his reign and age 38, let out a long sigh. Since they were all alone except for the ever-present royal guard, Zephaniah felt it okay to place a reassuring hand on the king's shoulder. They continued to gaze down at the lethargic crowd.

The prophetic words of a another prophet of God, the Prophetess Huldah, had continued to burn in King Josiah's ears over the past decade since she'd spoke them at that first great Passover Feast. "Because they have forsaken Me, My wrath shall be aroused against this place and shall not be quenched" (2 Kings 22:17). Josiah broke his reverie and revealed to his cousin, "God through Huldah told me that because I'd humbled myself before the Lord when I heard what God spoke against our people, my eyes would not see all the calamity which He will bring on this place. When I go out to battle against Pharaoh Necho of Egypt tomorrow, maybe that prophecy will see its fulfilment" (2 Kings 22:18-20; 2 Chronicles 34:26-28). The king spat out an empty, bitter laugh. Despite his years battling against the evils of the land, Josiah's people were falling back under the immoral influences of their pagan neighbors. Because the king was sorely pained by the short-lived revival of his people, and with a heavy sadness knowing that even his own sons didn't share their father's love of Yahweh, Josiah's shoulders slumped in defeat.

Zephaniah wondered how he could comfort the king. Suddenly, his eyes opened wide, and filled with that old pang of fear mixed with excitement, spoke up. "My King, I have two final messages from the Lord." The prophet knew these messages would reveal a lot about the heart and purposes of their Heavenly Father, and he hoped they would bring some much needed encouragement to his sovereign.

**Tough Justice on the Day of the Lord.** Josiah braced himself, then Zephaniah began. "Be silent in the presence of the Lord God, for the day of the Lord is at hand." In almost a whisper, Zephaniah foretold, "I will punish the princes and the king's children, and all such as are clothed with foreign apparel." The king groaned over the inevitable loss of his wayward sons. Inwardly, Zephaniah must have winced and thought, "Ah, that's not too encouraging."

Still, he went on. "And there shall be on that day the sound of a mournful cry from the Fish Gate, a wailing from the Second Quarter, and a loud crashing from the hills. Wail, for all the merchant people are cut down" (1:7-11). So, the king now knew, invaders would enter through the northern walls—the merchant district—to destroy Jerusalem. Assyria had fallen to the Babylonians, so the Babylonians certainly would be God's hand of judgment. With the Scythians now out of the picture, it was clearly only a matter of time before Babylon would have conquered the known world anyway, bringing all of Zephaniah's prophecies about the destruction of Judah's neighbors into fulfilment.

Resigned, Josiah asked what the Day of the Lord would be like. As if in pain, Zephaniah described the coming days when God's wrath would be unleashed. Tough justice would descend upon the people of the land. "That day is a day of wrath, a day of trouble and distress, a day of devastation and desolation, a day of darkness and gloominess, a day of clouds and thick darkness, a day of trumpet and alarm" (1:15-16).

Zephaniah looked doubly troubled. "What is it?" questioned the king with genuine concern. With some difficulty, the prophet admitted he was confused. God's judgment was clearly coming on Judah and its neighbors, and yet God was describing how He was going to assemble not just the local nations against Jerusalem, but all the nations of the world, in order to pour out His righteous anger upon them. God kept saying the "whole earth" would be devoured by the fire of His wrath. Zephaniah remembered the writings of the Prophet Joel concerning this "Day of the Lord" and wondered what the huge scope of this all could mean. But, God remained silent, not answering his inquiries as to whether this prophecy had larger and more far-reaching implications concerning the distant future.

The two men could only marvel at God's passionate loyalty to His covenant with the Children of Israel. Yahweh might seem absent for a time, but that's only because His vast patience awaits true repentance, the kind of repentance from the heart that sticks.

God has no tolerance for Lees Men who believe Him absent and indifferent to the evils of sin. God will deal with sin after all possible chances for true repentance have run dry. God is committed to His covenants, both in the blessings and the curses. And, when men fall to the pressures of sin, God tries and tries again to restore a right relationship, even if the people are unwilling. One wise pastor summed God's character up best with, "God is present, powerful, and righteous, a beacon of righteousness in the midst of unrighteousness, a pillar of justice in the midst of injustice, the quiet voice of truth in the clamor of evil."[12] Both king and prophet could only utter a reserved "Amen."

**Tender Grace Through a Faithful Remnant.** Zephaniah broke his somber reverie with an excited, "But, there's more!" A sunny smile spread wide across his now middle-aged face. "O daughter of Jerusalem! The Lord has taken away your judgments, He has cast out your enemy. The King of Israel, the Lord, is in your midst; you shall see disaster no more" (3:15).

After just hearing about the destruction of all of Judah, the king could only shake his head in confusion. Stammering, he questioned, "When, when will this be?" Surprised that God would actually answer a question concerning timing, Zephaniah relayed that it'd happen when, "I will restore to the peoples a pure language, that they all may call on the name of the Lord to serve Him with one accord" (3:9). Josiah imagined a time when the twelve tribes would be reunited once more, no longer under the influence of the Gentiles and their idolatrous ways, and all speaking together with the same language in the worship of the Lord.

There was so much to God's message of the restoration of a faithful remnant that Zephaniah spent the next hour describing it. Judah like Israel would have to endure the punishment for their idolatry by being exiled throughout the world, but God would regather the captives once more back into the Promised Land. Now Zephaniah understood the prophecies he'd been given about how God would one day destroy Judah's enemies and then the Children of Israel would possess their land. God remained loyal to His covenant and would protect a believing remnant of Jews so He could restore them as a chosen people. They'd no longer be spiritually apathetic and chase after idols like Manasseh's people, but be true followers of Yahweh God in their desire to be in a covenant relationship with Him.

Josiah and Zephaniah, rebounded and refreshed, rejoiced together. "The Lord your God is in our midst, the Mighty One, He will save; He will rejoice over us with gladness, He will quiet us with His love, He will rejoice over us with singing!" (3:17).

## ZEPHANIAH'S FAITH LESSONS

### Lessons for Israel

What can Zephaniah teach the nation of Israel today about maintaining its faith in God against the unwavering onslaught of international peer pressure? Quite simply, learn from your history.

Josiah's reforms failed because the people refused to give up their evil ways and turn their hearts back totally to the Lord. And so, God followed through on His promise of justice against Judah's evil deeds, overwhelmingly proving He has never been absent. A gracious 34-year extension was granted after Josiah's reforms, but inevitably the Babylonian King Nebuchadnezzar in 582 BC swept over Judah, exiled her people, imprisoned and blinded one of Josiah's son, destroyed the First Temple, and left Jerusalem a memory for its survivors. Israel endured a Day of the Lord under God's unwavering sentence of wrath.

Scattered across Babylon, a remnant of Jews decades later were brought back to the Promised Land, but they too eventually fell into sin and remained a conquered people by various Gentile empires. By 70 AD, the Jews were once again scattered to the winds.

But, and this is an incredibly important point, the prophecies of Zephaniah are still awaiting final fulfilment. A modern-day remnant of Israel is back in the land, though not possessing her enemies' land. They've regained a common language by resurrecting the long-dead Hebrew, but they do not "call on the name of the Lord to serve Him with one accord." Israel does not exist in a time when "no one shall make them afraid," are "no longer haughty," Yahweh is king living "in your midst," and that through Israel all nations will worship God in offerings (3:9-17).

These promises of blessings to a believing remnant are still future, just as there will be a worldwide judgment called the Day of the Lord. That ultimate Day of the Lord will purify a remnant of Jews who will inherit these promised blessings.

If you're an Israeli then, will you give into international pressures and conform to your backstabbing enemies? Or, will you stand alone, yet victorious, in the one true God? He promises to "deal with all who afflict you; I will gather those who were driven out; I will appoint them for praise and fame in every land where they were put to shame" (3:19).

## Lessons for the Nations

**The People.** How can the "Christian" nations of the world maintain their faith in God against the unwavering onslaught of international peer pressure? Their people need to understand that the prophecies given by Zephaniah to the nations surrounding Israel came true. The once mighty Assyrian Empire fell to King Nabopolassar of Babylonian in 612 BC, with their capital Nineveh reduced to utter desolation and rendered a home for wild animals.[13] The surrounding nations fell shortly afterwards. Zephaniah revealed they fell because of their rejection of God and constant oppression of Israel.

The world's condemning attitude against Israel hasn't changed even to this day. Instead, the nations of the world must repent for straying from God's moral law. They must heed the stern warning Zephaniah pronounced against the nations concerning the coming Day of the Lord: "I have cut off nations, their fortresses are devastated; I have made their streets desolate with none passing by" (3:6). As God had promised Manasseh, so He's declared your nation's inevitable destruction as well. This will happen because God always follows through, though maybe He'll abstain for a time like He did for Josiah. So, repent to gain what little time is left!

**The Leaders.** For the leaders of nations founded on Judeo-Christian roots, will they lead like Hezekiah and Josiah, bringing blessing and abundance, or like Manasseh and Amon, causing their country to fall apart? As a leader put in position by God Almighty, they are called to follow King Josiah's godly example and lead their nation into a spiritual reformation. It all starts with the leader.

Leaders, respond by whole-heartedly, penitently seeking God. Make known to your constituents that God is their prime concern. Live by what is right. Be in a right relationship with Him through salvation. Rule and judge humbly instead of proudly, removing all self-sufficiency and arrogance.

Zephaniah revealed that a nation cannot be saved by armament or wealth, but only by God's grace through judgment. As Dr. David Hubbard prescribes as a formula for a bright future: "Not utopia but God's grace working among us, not idealism but His salvation, not our achievements but our repentance."[14] Through this formula, even if your people are not continually responsive like Josiah's people were, you will have fulfilled your duties to God and will receive your rewards in Heaven.

## Lessons for the Church

How can the Church maintain its faith in God against the unwavering onslaught of societal peer pressure? Remember that Israel in its time was the light-bearer for God's Word to the world. In this age, the Church now carries that duty and burden. We must then evaluate how our churches are doing at this task by asking, "Are we staying pure to biblical teachings, or conforming to the world?"

Israel fell because its love for the Lord had grown cold and conformed to the wickedness of its neighbors. If God was willing to wipe Israel out because they hid His majesty from their neighbors, then why do our churches believe they too can become worldly, failing as light-bearers, and not also have God wipe them out? Therefore, keep Israel's example in mind. Be a "meek and humble people" who "trust in the name of the Lord" and our churches will remain alive in God's will until He calls them home (3:12).

## Lessons for You

How can you as a Christian maintain your faith in God against the unwavering onslaught of peer pressure? The world will pressure you to become a spiritually complacent Lees Man who says in his heart, "The Lord will not do good, nor will He do evil" (1:12). Should you become one, you'll be consumed by bitterness and despair when God places challenges in your life for the purpose of restoring a right relationship with Him. God will inevitably rock your world as He did Judah's world.

Therefore, search your heart and be honest with what you find. Discern if you truly are a spiritually complacent Lees Man. This condition is easily recognized. When trouble comes in your life, you may run to the Lord for help, but only as a last resort. And, once that help is received, after a short time you will find yourself crawling back under the unspiritual blanket of apathy and sinful living. If this is your heart condition, and truly what a sad condition it is, then it's time to make a change.

You must make a stand and respond like Josiah, giving all of your life over to God, despite all the pressures to conform to society's immorality. In doing so, you will thereby gain the wisdom that brings true peace and an enduring faith in the Lord. Decide this day to, "seek the Lord, all you meek of the earth, who have upheld His justice" and "seek righteousness, seek humility" (2:3).

If you've never had that Christian faith to begin with, then surrender your life to Jesus Christ today by praying from your heart for His salvation: "Dear, Jesus, please forgive me of my sins and be my Savior." Place all your trust in God by growing in your newfound relationship with Him through daily Bible study and prayer. Build a wall of protection against falling into faithlessness through accountability with other believers in Christ by joining a church and in water baptism. You then can be assured that your newfound faith will be able to stand rock solid—just like the Prophet Zephaniah, King Josiah and Pastor Ghorban—against all of life's pressures.

> *"Yet indeed I also count all things loss for the excellence of the knowledge of Christ Jesus my Lord, for whom I have suffered the loss of all things, and count them as rubbish, that I may gain Christ" (Philippians 3:8).*

## QUESTIONS FOR DISCUSSION

1. What kind of negative pressures from friends and peers are you facing?

2. How do you respond to those pressures?

3. Do you really believe that God is distant and uncaring about the sin of the world?

4. Will God at some point deal in justice with the world's sin?

5. Will God at some point deal in justice with your sin?

6. How did Zephaniah overcome the pressures in his life and keep the faith?

7. How did Josiah overcome the negative influencers in his life?

8. Why did Josiah's reforms fail?

9. How can you take a faithful stand for God against the pressures in your life?

10. What will it cost you to make a faithful stand for God? And, what will you gain?

# FAITH JOURNEY 10
# HAGGAI: FAITH WHEN YOU'RE GUILTY

## A PROPHET'S JOURNAL

*Sixth Month, Day 1, 2nd Year of Darius*

*Daylight – Woke up to a partly cloudy sky and a pesky chicken next door that wanted an early start to the day. Back is sore from sleeping awkwardly. Note to self: get new material for my pallet. Another note to self: new material won't help the fact that my body is old. Spent normal prayer time before breakfast asking the Lord of Hosts to provide for the people in the midst of our current poverty.*

*Breakfast – Had a few scraps of bread left over from last night. Can't wait for the upcoming fruit harvest, though Tobiah says the crop is looking weak.*

*Mid-morning – Took a walk through the lower quarter of the city. Chatted with Peruda, Immer, Zakkai, and Hadid. Lots of construction has been going on in that area. Nebo wasn't home, but asked his son to have him come see me before the week is over. Concerned about him. He's seemed very discouraged lately.*

*Lunch – Grabbed a bit of food from the market. I love Bazluth's cheese. Not sure how he makes it, but it always has the best texture...*

*Mid-Afternoon – Got a message from God! (I'll never get used to those. Amazing and disconcerting at the same time). The Lord wants me to share something a little harsh, but the people need it. He's right, of course. My God is never wrong about anything, and*

*His eye is keen. He sees that our priorities here in Jerusalem have taken a wrong turn. Why weren't we aware enough to see it? No matter. The message must be delivered. Wish I could find my good sandals before meeting with the Governor and High Priest. Ah, there my sandals are under the...*

*Late Afternoon – DONE! Praise the Lord, I didn't have to wander the whole town to find the Governor and High Priest. They were observing some workers as they repaired the palace (how fitting—a perfect setting for the message I was about to deliver. Nothing like a built-in prop!). I got permission to speak to them in private, but since we were already outside where people could hear, I just belted it out! I love sharing God's messages. There is a certain thrill when you serve as His holy mouthpiece, but it sucks the energy out of me. If it weren't so late, I'd take a nap. Well, now that I think about it, maybe just a short one...*

*Evening – I've already started to hear the trickling of guilt turning into excitement after the word of prophecy began to spread throughout town. Sounds like people are already discussing where to get materials to rebuild the Temple. I praise you, Lord Almighty, for caring enough about us to intercede! Give us the strength and courage to follow your plans and to put You first in our lives. I'm praying You will allow me to see where this will lead.*

## UNFINISHED BUSINESS

My (Steve's) dad came home from the auction with a surprise. He had set out on a trip to a neighboring Kansas farm for an auction with a goal of purchasing camper jacks—tools you can use to maneuver a small portable camper into the bed of a pickup truck. The jacks came up for bid, and Dad jumped into the fray. After the bidding war was over and the auctioneer cried "Sold!" my dad was the victorious owner of the items he had set out to buy. But, when he went to claim his purchase at the auction's close, he discovered that the items weren't quite what he expected. Instead of just camper jacks, his bid had won the camper, too!

With his unexpected bonus, Dad returned home and made some plans. He placed the camper in our backyard, just east of the swing set. "A little work on the interior, a little paint on the exterior," my father had said, "and this will be a fantastic playhouse for you and your sister."

I was thrilled! What a great thought, to have the equivalent of a fancy treehouse on the prairie. My sister and I could spend a summer night outside on the farm, "roughing it" in our remodeled luxury accommodations. We could doze off in one of the two beds, grab a snack from the small refrigerator, and store all our essentials in the cabinets. It was a fantasy an eight-year-old boy could really get behind.

But, to this day, sadly, I never spent a night in that camper.

The plans started well. We had set to work that summer scraping the paint off the outer walls to prepare it for a fresh coat. We had removed some of the problem areas of the interior, tearing out stained carpet and loose cabinets. Dad was on pace to have it done before the nights started getting shorter. But then, other projects beckoned. A broken tractor stole a week of his time here, some sick cattle stole a week there. Summer turned to fall, fall to winter, and the promise of the camper was pushed back to the next season. Each new season brought its own issues and excuses for putting off the repairs. And so it waited for the next year, and the next, and the next.

Eventually, the dream of the backyard playhouse lost out to sports and cars and girls and college. I moved on, but the camper remained beside the swing set, a house in disrepair, a memorial to incomplete projects.

Looking back, I know that my dad wasn't a sinner for failing to build a playhouse, but I also know he felt a little guilty for not completing it. The stoic farmer hinted at it in conversations, and you could see it in his eyes as he stared at the wooden shell years later. He knew that he had missed an opportunity for his kids. His reasons were respectable, of course. Any delay in completing this side project was for the sake of putting food on the table and keeping a roof above our heads. Farm equipment absolutely needed to be repaired before he could even consider fixing the floor of a playhouse. However, he was still guilty—guilty of breaking a promise and of deflating a dream. In the grand scheme of things, these might not count as major violations, but they were upsetting nonetheless.

Imagine, then, a scenario in which the violation *is* significant. Imagine a situation when the project is more significant than a playhouse and the impact more acute than a disappointed dream. Rather than a failure to upgrade a camper, it might be a failure to make a marriage work. It might be guilt over a friend's suicide. It could come in the form of a grandchild on drugs, or a foreclosed house, or an ignored pain that turned out to be cancer.

Failure and guilt can elicit many different responses from us. We may respond by lying to ourselves, pretending not to know the truth. We may respond by sinking into depression, wallowing in our inadequacies. We may respond by seeking distractions, trying to find something to keep us from feeling the pain our guilt causes. We may even respond by trying to justify ourselves, explaining why our priorities outweigh God's.

Are these responses right, or is there a better way to face our faults? What is a godly way to handle blame? Specifically, how do you have faith when you're guilty of sin or failure?

Instead of allowing failure to escalate from a disap-pointment to a disaster, or from a minor regret to a major rebellion, we need to hear the words of Scripture and understand the heart of God. When facing a situation where you're guilty of sin, we need to remember the faith lessons His Word shows us. The Minor Prophet Haggai proves to be an ideal person to teach those lessons.

## THE PROPHET OF THE UNFULFILLED DREAM

Haggai's book of prophecy is located toward the end of the Minor Prophets, just before Zechariah and Malachi. It is a short book—only two chapters in length, just barely longer than the Bible's shortest book of Obadiah—but the message loomed large for the Jewish community where it was delivered.

## Time of the Prophet

To understand this prophetic book, not to mention its author and his faith, we need to understand its historical setting. While many of our Minor Prophets wrote in the time leading up to the fall of Judah to the Babylonians, this book moves us to a new period and addresses a time after the Jews' exile and subsequent return.

In 586 B.C., Jerusalem had been destroyed by the Babylonian siege, fulfilling a large library of prophetic material from men like Jeremiah and Habakkuk. God's temple had been demolished, the city decimated, and the people exiled to Babylon for a seventy-year period. God allowed them to remain in captivity during this time as a lesson to the nation, but He still remained faithful to His covenant promises. After the Babylonian empire was overtaken by the Persians, the new Persian king decreed that the Jews could return to their homeland and rebuild their temple (2 Chronicles 36:22-23).

By 538 B.C., a remnant of Jews returned. The Old Testament book of Ezra records their journey and their actions. They returned to Jerusalem under the leadership of Zerubbabel (the governor, a descendent of the former king of Judah) and Joshua (the high priest) and they began the rebuilding process. Reconstruction included not only their own homes, but also the temple of God. Things went well initially. The Jews quickly completed the foundation of the Temple. But then, opposition came from others who lived in that area. They began intimidating the Jews and frustrating their work. The Temple

241

rebuilding project was forcibly ceased, and God's house—Yahweh's temple—was left unfinished. The Temple's foundation sat in Jerusalem for years, a memorial to incomplete projects. It was a house in disrepair, a reminder of unfulfilled dreams.

## Construction of a Prophet

It is in this context that the prophet Haggai received a message from God to deliver to the people.

As a man, we know very little about Haggai. A hopeful reading of the text brings out potential clues of his background. Some infer that he was an older man who had seen the first Temple before it was destroyed. If this is the case, he would have been at least eighty years old at the time of this book. He may have been from a priestly family, based on his knowledge of the ceremonial law. However, he also mentions some items connected to government and agriculture, so we could speculate that he was a politician or a farmer just as easily.[1]

Most of what we know is based on his effect on others. Both his own book of prophecy and the historical book of Ezra testify to his role as a prophet in the post-exilic community. Ezra describes him, along with the young Zechariah, as a prophet who spurred the community to action. The two prophets were not just speaking passive messages; they were engaged and involved with the people. "And the prophets of God were with them, supporting them," says Ezra 5:1-2. To be *with* someone during a time of difficulty shows compassion and solidarity. To provide support shows empathy and a concern for the people's needs.

While Haggai's writing style is somewhat blunt and brief rather than flowery and poetic, his reputation shows that direct speech need not mean he was cold and callous. Instead, we can think of him as an educated man of God who happens to relate better to the blue collar construction workers of his day than to ivory tower elitists. He seems to be the perfect personality for this situation, able to directly point out a person's guilt and then matter-of-factly lead them to a godly response.

## Call of the Prophet

Eighteen years after the Jews' return from Babylon, Haggai is now in a position to deliver God's message to the remnant who had come home to Jerusalem. With laser focus, Haggai is given four messages to deliver in a four-month stretch of time. God called him to share the message with the people via the leadership pair of Zerubbabel and Joshua.

In our other books of prophecy, we have seen that God need not have a well-known source as His messenger. He chose relative unknowns like Amos or Obadiah at times to deliver messages of significance. In those cases, the obscurity of the individual lent credence to the message. The focus was on the prophetic word, not the one delivering it. At other times, though, God chose individuals such as Jonah who had a strong connection to Him and a reputation as a prophet. In these cases, the fame of the messenger added weight to the message. Since Haggai has already been known as a prophet to the Jews, the words he spoke are immediately identified as coming from God. "The Lord's messenger," as Haggai is called in 1:13, can relay truth and expect a swift response even from a guilty population.

## YOU MUST CONSTRUCT THIS HOUSE!

It was the end of August 520 BC, just before the start of the fig, grape, and pomegranate harvests.[2] While this should be a time of excited anticipation, it is looking more like a time of dread. The crops were suffering because of a severe drought. In Haggai 1:10-11, we hear a description from God of what the conditions were like. "Therefore the heavens above you withhold the dew, and the earth withholds its fruit. For I called for a drought on the land and the mountains, on the grain and the new wine and the oil, on whatever the ground brings forth, on men and livestock, and on all the labor of your hands."

This poor crop goes along with a general poverty that seems to have seized the people. They are underfed, unquenched, and unable to pay for adequate clothes or services (1:6). This seems to be in stark contrast to the blessings the exiles had on their return journey to Jerusalem. At that point, the king had commanded that the Jews be given supplies—animals, gold, and silver—to provide for the Temple sacrifices (Ezra 1:4). Now, it seems they could hardly scrape together enough to sustain, let alone prosper.

The people would have been wondering "Why?" and Haggai now gets to provide the answer.

## The Message

Punishments are preceded by warnings. That warning may be directly stated, or it may be assumed as general knowledge. The Jews of Haggai's time had a warning of the latter type. Rather than a fresh message from God telling them what might happen if they place God as a second-tier priority, God expected them to glean the warning from a trusted source: His Law.

"Haggai expects the people to notice that their experience parallels the kinds of curses outlined in the Torah when the covenant relationship between Yahweh and his people was strained,"[3] says one commentator. Passages like Deuteronomy 28-30 certainly seem to match what is happening in Haggai chapter one.

It is fitting, then, that Haggai's message is given to the leaders of the community—the governor, Zerubbabel, and the high priest, Joshua. These men would have been familiar with the Law and its blessings and curses. If anyone should be able to make the connection between the spiritual failings of the Jews and the physical failings of their economy, it was this pair.

So, on a New Moon Festival date, God's message comes and is delivered directly and simply. Haggai points out that the people had given up on the rebuilding project and were saying, "The time has not come, the time that the LORD's house should be built" (1:2). The Jews had rationalized their failure to finish the Temple and decided it could sit on the backburner. So, instead of focusing on God and making Him their priority, the people were instead building their own residences. The governor could live in a paneled house, yet God's house was in shambles. How far Israel had come compared to the priorities of Solomon and David, who recognized the irony in constructing their own home rather than focusing on God's!

Because of this backwards thinking, God had withheld blessings from his people as they placed their own desires above Him. Since they focused on their own priorities instead of His, God had made their lives harder. He used economic circumstances to challenge His people to focus on spiritual realities instead of physical realities.

"Consider your ways! Go up to the mountains and bring wood and build the Temple, that I may take pleasure in it and be glorified," God says through his servant (1:8). The command is reminiscent of the first Temple's construction, when Solomon brought in cedars from Lebanon (1 Kings 5:5-6). Now, their materials will be less opulent (likely from nearby forests, due to their current poverty), but at least the process can begin.[4]

## The Response

While many of people's negative responses to the other prophets' messages have conditioned us to expect more failure on the part of the people, the Jews here decided to respond positively. "Then Zerubbabel the son of Shealtiel, and Joshua the son of Jehozadak, the high priest, with all the remnant of the people, obeyed the voice of the LORD their God, and the words of Haggai the prophet, as the LORD their God had sent him; and the people feared the presence of the LORD" (1:12).

Amazing! Haggai's message was given on August 29, 520 B.C. By September 21 of that same year (23 days later), they had resumed construction of the Temple. The people, in a very short stretch of time, had assembled plans, agreed to an order of building, attained workers, and acquired materials. Though guilty, they did not wallow in despair. Instead, they took action. Their obedience did not go unnoticed, as God encourages the people. "I am with you," He says (1:13).

## Strength to Carry On

A little less than one month after the start of the project, on October 17, God's encouragement seems distant. Morale is down because clearly this Temple is not on par with its predecessor.

Can you imagine the disappointment? The Temple built by Solomon—the one destroyed by the Babylonians—was built from the finest materials around. It was a gleaming structure, an architectural wonder. This new incarnation, though, was a modest reconstruction. The current resources were scarce, and the construction was merely functional and not beautiful. This new temple was a shadow of its former self, like the Mona Lisa recreated in macaroni art, or the Eifel Tower made from Tinker Toys.

This poor imitation of former glory would have been on full display at this time, for the date of this message would place it on the final and climactic day of the Feast of Tabernacles.[5] Temple progress would have taken a backseat to the celebration of this festival. The slowing progress may have been discouraging, as would have been the celebration in an incomplete and second-class facility. On top of that, the Feast of Tabernacles was the feast celebrating the harvest, which this year was depressingly small due to the people's guilt. While they were working to remedy the situation, their guilt of sin must have been at the forefront of the Jews' minds.

Still, God tells all the leaders and the people to "be strong!" Three times He says it, first to Zerubbabel, then to Joshua, then to the people (2:4). "Work, for I am with you!"

God provides encouragement and motivation to the people during their time of despair. He reminds them that this temple, while less impressive structurally than its predecessor, is approved by God Himself. The following verses clearly show that the glory of the building comes from God's involvement, and not from the skills or the resources of the builders. While depression may have had them focused on their own failings and guilt, God readjusts their focus.

- "*My* spirit remains among you" (2:5, italics added)
- "*I* will shake heaven and earth" (2:6, italics added)
- "*I* will fill this house with glory" (2:7, italics added)
- "The silver is *mine*, and the gold is *mine*" (2:8, italics added)
- "*I* will give peace" (2:9, italics added)

God's perspective on the Temple is that its outward appearance is less important than the working of His own Spirit and the reality of His presence. God has plans to make this temple more glorious. In fact, history shows that resources poured in from the nations later to improve and upgrade the Temple, some under the Persians and most notably under the Romans, so that the Second Temple is viewed as even overshadowing the First Temple made by Solomon.[6] This new and upgraded Temple is also going to see a new and upgraded Presence, as Jesus himself will set foot there several centuries after its construction.

These promises are given to comfort the people, encouraging them not to be mired in the guilt of sin, but to press on and continue to obey.

## FUTURE HOPE

As work continues, Haggai comes to the final two messages God gives him to speak. Given on the 18th of December of the same year (520 BC), these two words from God follow the same basic pattern as Haggai's first two messages—one negative and one positive. However, the overall impact of these messages is to provide hope to the community.

Haggai starts with a reminder of the people's former guilt for failing to put Him first, beginning in 2:10. Using an object lesson from the Law, Haggai reminds the people that defilement is contagious (Leviticus 22:4-6). An unclean thing can cause other things to become unclean.[7]

The nation had suffered during its harvest because the attitude of selfishness had spread like uncleanliness. Haggai asks them to look back. They were afflicted with crop failures and poor harvests because of their own actions and attitudes. "The faint aroma of sanctity coming from their altar and sacrifices was too feeble to pervade the secular atmosphere of their life."[8]

God repeated the theme of chapter one: He was the One who caused agricultural and economic disaster, but it was a direct result of the people's choices. Now, however, things will be different. "From this day I will bless you," God says (2:19). Finding no more guilt, due to the people's obedient response to His messages, God would open up blessings upon them.

In addition to that message of encouragement, Haggai shares a special message of encouragement to Zerubbabel, the governor of Judah. As in 2:6, here in 2:21, God says He is about to "shake the heavens and the earth," to do something significant. While foreign armies and kingdoms would fall into disarray and disaster, Zerubbabel would be honored. "'I will take you, Zerubbabel My servant, the son of Shealtiel,' says the Lord, 'and will make you like a signet ring; for I have chosen you,' says the Lord of hosts" (2:23).

This statement had less to do with the governor himself and more to do with his descendants. Previously, God had likened one of Judah's faithless kings to a signet ring thrown away (Jeremiah 22:24). Now, Zerubbabel's faithfulness leads God to recover and restore that signet ring, leaving His promises to David intact.[9] The phrase "My servant" evokes thoughts of David and the Messiah and points toward the future fulfillment of this promise by Jesus, a descendant of Zerubbabel.[10]

The guilt of the people in this matter is finally pushed aside. Its impact on the people and the leadership gives way to forgiveness and blessing. Their positive response to the preaching of Haggai shows us that the best responses when you are guilty of sin are simple yet effective: repent and obey!

# HAGGAI'S FAITH LESSONS

The notion of guilt is not limited to the post-exilic Jews. Certainly we are all guilty of sin, individually as well as corporately. How, then, do we apply the lessons of Haggai?

## Lessons for Israel

Do a quick Google search of problems facing Israel, and you get many different results. Most of the top articles are focused on the military and political issues of the day, with the Palestinian conflict garnering the most press. Dig a little more and you'll also find discussions of issues ranging from economic and environmental challenges, to water usage and labor unions and refugees.

Like the drought in the days of Haggai, these issues seem pressing and paramount. Yet, like the ancient Jews, modern Jews have an underlying spiritual issue that needs to be fixed first. They are guilty of living in paneled houses while failing to recognize their true need for Jesus Christ.

Haggai's Jews were excited to return from exile and get to work rebuilding their lives. They recognized that Yahweh should be the priority, but they got distracted and discouraged. Modern Jews are also excited after a historic return from centuries of exile. The founding of the modern state of Israel is a miracle that continues to surprise the world. However, the building of something like a physical temple is not the spiritual solution the Jews need most. What is needed is recognition of the one true Messiah—Jesus.

We should be in prayer that the Jews would recognize their Savior, sharing with the hope Paul mentions in Romans 11:26-27. "And so all Israel will be saved, as it is written: 'The Deliverer will come out of Zion, and He will turn away ungodliness from Jacob; for this is My covenant with them, when I take away their sins.'"

May the Jews' guilt find redemption by putting their faith in Jesus Christ!

## Lessons for the Nations

Guilt is found not only in Israel, but also in every nation on the planet. The difference is that most other nations do not feel like they have the same kind of spiritual imperative that a nation like Israel does. Israel is a focal point of Judaism, Christianity, and Islam. The same cannot be said of El Salvador or New Zealand. The majority of nations see themselves as purely secular states that have little or no use for spiritual awakening.

They fail to see their own sin-induced guilt. God's message through Haggai was that prosperity was withheld because of the nation's failure to put Him first. That message certainly applies today.

The United States' economy, or Gross Domestic Product (GDP), is over $18 trillion dollars at the time of this writing, by far the largest in the world.[11] Yet, with all of that income and prosperity, God has poked some holes in our money bags. A national debt equal to our GDP constantly looms as a threat to our nation, a problem we cannot seem to solve.

A solution will not come in the form of tax policy or trade agreements. Our only solution is to return to God. We must repent of our sins and strive to obey God, not just as individuals, but as a nation. Perhaps if we consider and change our ways, reviving our national faith in Jesus Christ, God will say to us, "Be strong! I am with you."

## Lessons for the Church

Is the Church guilty of a failure to build? Certainly there is no shortage of church buildings in the United States. However, the Church itself is not a building.

Peter writes, "Come to Christ, who is the living cornerstone of God's temple. He was rejected by the people, but he is precious to God who chose Him. And now God is building you, as living stones, into His spiritual temple" (1 Peter 2:4-5a).

The church needs to focus on *being* the church instead of building new structures for the church. While church buildings continue to go up, overall church attendance continues to decline. Thankfully, there are signs that a shift may be underway. After a boom in construction during the turn of the century, 21st Century churches are now building less and thinking about their mission more.

"I don't want to sit at a table and worry about how to get the roof replaced," one pastor says. He would rather focus on "how to reach out to kids in the community." Another preacher echoes that thought. "We don't want to be about a building," he said. "We want to be about loving people and serving people, and sometimes buildings can actually be a barrier to that."[12]

The Church must continue to remember that its best construction material isn't steel—it is souls. Let us pray for congregations to recognize this truth, put our faith in the Holy Spirit to build our churches where it matters most, and glorify Jesus instead of hiring contractors.

## Lessons for You

*God's priorities must come before ours!* This is the main faith lesson we learn from the book of Haggai.

Like the Jews, we are also involved in building a temple. Ours is not a literal one, but a spiritual one. Our lives and our actions build upon the foundation of Christ Jesus. The Apostle Paul talks about Jesus Christ being our "foundation" (1 Corinthians 3:11). Christians "build" on this foundation, and together we are "the temple of God" (1 Corinthians 3:16). In Ephesians, we are called, "God's house, built on the foundation of the apostles and the prophets, and the cornerstone is Christ Jesus himself. We who believe are carefully joined together, becoming a holy temple for the Lord" (Ephesians 2:20-21).

The message from Haggai confronts us if we become guilty of focusing on ourselves rather than our responsibility to build spiritually.

When we accept Jesus as Lord, we accept a challenge to build for His Kingdom. We discover that God is not concerned with our 401(k) plans; He's concerned with our hearts. He is not concerned with our tackle boxes, our scrapbook pages, our lawns, our vehicles, our waistlines, or our shoes. No, God is concerned about our souls.

So, start building! If you said you'd grow in knowledge but didn't, get some metaphorical lumber and join a Bible study group. If you said you'd grow in service, but haven't, pick up a hammer and talk to someone about serving in your local children's ministry. If you said you'd grow in evangelism but have not, pour the cement and call your unsaved friend. In other words, get to work!

The command to build God's house is no less valid for us than it was for the Jews in the time of Haggai. The materials may be different, but God expects His priorities to come before our own. When facing a situation where you've done something wrong, remember the faith lesson Haggai shows us... Build God's House!

## QUESTIONS FOR DISCUSSION

1. Read the account of the Jews' return from exile in Ezra. What were the main forces that stopped them from focusing on God's Temple? Why do you think they feared those forces more than they trusted God?

2. How is Haggai's message harsh? How is it encouraging? What tone do you think he used to convey these messages to the people? Why?

3. In what ways does God keep our bags from having "holes in them" when we are following Him? (Consider the Israelites' clothes and sandals in Deuteronomy 29:5.)

4. What excuses do we use that prevent us from obeying God or putting Him first?

5. God planned to "shake the earth" and bring glory to a temple that the Jews viewed as inferior. What criteria should we use to evaluate someone or something's usefulness to God?

6. What made Zerubbabel worthy of God's honor (3:23)? What makes us worthy of God's honor?

7. What steps of faith should we take when we are guilty? How does our faith in Christ change the way we feel about our guilt?

# FAITH JOURNEY 11
# ZECHARIAH: FAITH WHEN THE FUTURE LOOKS BLEAK

## THE LITTLE BOY

*With a squeal of delight, the little boy raced in-between and around the wooden carts at dizzying speeds. His round, cherub-like face, was red tinged from playful exertion. He laughed out loud as he proudly evaded yet another oxen's pointy horn. The animal pulling the battered wagon on which his mother and grandfather rode replied with a loud snort through its drippy nose.*

*So caught up in his daredevil antics that the boy barely heard his mother calling out yet again for her son to, "Stop screaming around and just walk alongside the wagon like a normal boy." With an "Oh, Mom!" and a deep sigh of resignation, he resumed his place alongside the meandering cart. Quickly bored, for the billionth time on their journey he asked his mother, "Are we there yet?" He was expecting yet another grouchy, "No! And don't ask me again." But this time his mother's reply surprised him. "Yes, Zechariah, we're finally almost there." He just couldn't believe his ears. "Really? Really?!?" The only response was his grandfather's long beard waggling as he softly chuckled.*

*Zechariah, being an intuitive boy, realized the spirits of his family had risen a notch, together with all those others who were traveling along with them in the long, winding caravan. The travelers' eyes gleamed. They all sat up a little straighter, as if better posture could help them see over the next Judean hillside. Zechariah* had to pick up his own pace a little to keep up as the whole wagon train unconsciously accelerated. Taking a skeptical side glance at the one remaining ox still pulling his family wagon, the boy wondered if that bag of bones could keep up the speedier pace much longer. He'd half expected the poor animal to keel over, and that was well over a hundred miles ago!

Four months and nearly 900 miles hadn't just taken its toll on the animals, but on all of the weary travelers. Food stores had run low weeks back, and he'd cringed at just how thin and emaciated his friends had become. His sandals were worn frayed. Quite a number of wagons had fallen apart from the wear and tear. Beloved animals had been butchered into enough food to enable their owners to make it to the next trade caravan. His grandfather's money sack was about as empty as the boy had ever seen it, thanks to the constant raids by bandits. And, the never-ending, broken-down road was always empty and lonely when it wasn't dotted by the ever-hostile Samaritans watching from just above the ridgeline. They scared Zechariah the most with their angry faces.

And yet, despite the hardships of the road, the travelers had never complained. Well, other than that crotchety old prophet, Haggai, who was friends with his grandfather, but that was only now and then. Zechariah had long given up hoping his people would turn back, for they rode ever onward, driven by the high expectations of their ultimate destination. That magical place—that Jerusalem—his mother had said was what "put the smile" on all their gaunt faces.

His mother's imagery puzzled the boy only for a nanosecond, for having a child's hummingbird-like attention span, he'd already moved his sights onto something new. This time it was a donkey "hee-hawing" at the front of the pack, being ridden by the newly appointed governor. Grasping an official edict from the king, which Zechariah thought his leader carried protectively as if it was made of pure gold, the governor had led the people of Israel on what was to be a fantastic voyage. From Babylon on the plains of Shinar, up north along the Euphrates River, and then back south towards the city of Jerusalem, the remnant of Hebrew people were returning "home" after nearly 50 years.

Well, really, only some of the people had set out, Zechariah amended. He'd heard stories from his grandfather's time about how the old Babylonians had taken his people by force from a far off land called Judah to the only city he'd ever known all his short life— Babylon. The Hebrew people had tried their best to make a life there, but his grandfather had complained that they were merely second-class citizens, or something like that. He didn't quite understand what his family whispered about among themselves. Despite their troubles, though, most of the Hebrews didn't want to leave. Shoot! Zechariah hadn't wanted to leave. How was he going to visit his father's grave now?

But, finally, they were supposedly there! As the governor's donkey reared up over the crest of the final hill, it brayed hysterically and refused to go on. The ramshackle wagons began to pile up around the animal. Zechariah's own family in turn reached the pinnacle and also stopped. Men and women, young and even old, were leaping off and running ahead of their carts to get their first view of that famed city from what looked to potentially be a fantastic overlook. The excitement was palpable.

In just a heartbeat, their enthusiasm evaporated. The cheers of arrival were replaced by the sound of sharp intakes of air, then squelched to a murmuring of disbelief. Looking up at his grandfather's lined face, the boy was amazed to see tears running down his aged cheeks. Zechariah was just old enough to know the difference between tears of joy and tears of sorrow, and these were no tears of joy. Crying broke out among the elderly. Even that old prophet had gotten off his camel and began tearing at his clothes and wailing. "What's wrong with these grown-ups?" Zechariah wondered aloud. "Just what were they seeing?"

Zechariah dodged his way up to the front of the crowd in order to get his very own first look at the legendary Jerusalem. His *jaw dropped open. This was "legendary"?! A "rock pile" best described this dump, rough and heaped about and blackened by soot. Mountain goats jumped from crumbled walls to weed splattered, collapsed rooftops. Birds ducked in and out of nests perched in the charred remains of what could only once have been the mightiest building in all of Israel's history—the Temple. Human life was present, though barely, wearily dotting the rubble or hiding behind sheets pulled over makeshift entrances to tumbled-down dwellings. These ghosts stared up blankly at the swelling crowd of pilgrims. Zachariah's mood darkened, "This was what they'd traveled all this way for? This?!"*

*And then, from the opposite ridge, the Samaritans began descending.*

## TO HELL THROUGH HIGH WATER

This biblical story of a stalwart, faithful remnant who'd risked their lives making a perilous trek to a new land for the purpose of building a better life would many centuries later be reenacted by a different group of people. Their story began in the early 1600s AD, when a highly devout congregation of Christians decided they must separate from the Church of England. Just as the Jews feared being corrupted by Babylon, so too did this congregation fear their children would also become corrupted by bad theology. Their pious decision to separate from the State Church came at a terrible price, for by 1618 AD King James of England exiled them from his realm. These now homeless "Separatists" or "Puritans," as they were mockingly called, where hounded and bullied in every new European country they tried to settle. For years the Puritans remained strangers in strange lands, ever looking for a place to call home.

When all options seemed to have run out, news of a fresh and untamed world called America beckoned from across the Atlantic Ocean, and with it the hope of a new life. The Puritans prayed earnestly to God for direction, and in response they believed He had provided His answer. The Puritans were now set on becoming pilgrims to a brave New World. Little did they realize it would be a trip to hell through high water.

The hardships associated with venturing on a journey so few had ever made before immediately descended upon them. The Puritans turned Pilgrims gave up every scrap of money they owned to a financier named Thomas Weston who indentured them in exchange for passage expenses across the Atlantic. Their leader, William Bradford, secured two boats, but before they even set out the leaky *Speedwell* had to be left behind. Some 102 Pilgrims now had to "cram into a space equal to a volleyball court" on a little ship called the *Mayflower*.[1]

The never-ending Atlantic storms battered the little boat, even cracking the huge cross-beam that supported the main mast. For safety, the captain ordered the travelers to stay penned up below deck for the duration of their voyage. Down in the belly of the ship, the Pilgrims suffered from a lack of light and fresh air, gagging at the ever-present stench of the bilge. For 66 days the *Mayflower* battled headwinds that dragged the voyage out a whole month longer than it should have lasted. The food stores of dried goods were running dangerously low, and the lack of vitamins caused quite a number to come down with scurvy. Historians described the living conditions as, "It added up to seven weeks of the hell of an ill-lighted, rolling, pitching, stinking inferno."[2]

On November 9, 1620, to everyone's joy the watchmen finally yelled, "Land Ho!" But, the Pilgrims' problems were still far from over. It wasn't long before the navigator realized they'd been blown 100 miles north off course, far from Virginia where they were supposed to have settled. Weather conditions prevented the ship from traversing south, so the Pilgrims had little choice but to disembark in the sandy and untamed wilderness of what today is Cape Cod, Massachusetts.

A harsh winter had set in, causing food to become scarce. Starvation and sickness followed. Consumption and pneumonia killed off the Pilgrims at a rate of 2-3 people per day as what they called the General Sickness took their lives. "They were falling like casualties on a battlefield," where at one point only five people were well enough to take care of everybody else and still keep a watch out for more Indian raids.[3] By the time the General Sickness had run its course, 47 Pilgrims had died, leaving only a scant three families unbroken.

More than half of the Pilgrims had given their lives that winter in the pursuit of building better lives for themselves. The hardships and miseries were so severe that what remained of the sickly crew of the *Mayflower* begged the Pilgrims to return with them back to Europe. The captain was sure if the Pilgrims stayed any longer they would all be doomed. No supply ships would be coming. The last link to their old lives would be severed as the *Mayflower* pulled out of harbor on April 21, 1621. And yet, even though the future looked nothing but bleak and deadly, the Pilgrims remained faithful to God's calling and stayed.

How do we then, like the Pilgrims, maintain faith in God when the future looks bleak? The answer can be found in what is considered the "major" of the Minor Prophets—the 14 chapter Old Testament book written by the Prophet Zechariah.

# THE PROPHET OF FUTURE HOPE

## Time of the Prophet

The year is 586 BC. The mighty Nebuchadnezzar, king of the Babylonian Empire, had laid siege to Jerusalem. His armies succeeded in devastating both the city and the Temple before he marched off most of the inhabitants of Judah weeping and wailing far, far east to Babylon. God's stern promise foretold by the prophets to exile the people of Judah over their unceasing rebelliousness and unrepentant wickedness had finally been fulfilled. The land of Israel was left to the remaining poorest of the poor, and it fell into a decades-long slumber.

The years passed until the time of 538 BC. Some 50 years had elapsed since Jerusalem's demise. The Jewish people in exile had tried to thrive and survive under their captor's rule, but they had been relegated to second class citizenship, and were always a politician's scheming plot away from total annihilation. And then the conquerors had become the conquered when the Babylonian Empire fell to the Medo-Persian Empire. A new regime was installed with a new king—Cyrus the Great—known as the mighty Prince of Persia.

As the historian and priest, Ezra, would record decades later in his own book, in Cyrus' very first year as king, God moved on his heart to favor the Jewish people. Cyrus wrote a proclamation, called an edict, which would allow the Jewish captives to return to Jerusalem. They were to rebuild the temple to Yahweh, and with money generously granted from the king's own treasury.

Cyrus' Edict was a profound declaration, for it fulfilled a prophecy given through the Prophet Isaiah over 150 years earlier. Isaiah prophesied that one day a "shepherd" of God—and amazingly he even foretold Cyrus' name—would grant permission to the Jewish people to return from their exile and rebuild (Isaiah 44:24-28; 45:1-13). The Prophet Jeremiah also had decades earlier foretold the same homecoming of the Jewish people (Jeremiah 25:11-12; 29:10-14). While the Jews were ecstatic over this long awaited permission, their minds must have truly been blown over being the actual generation of people foretold in prophecy. Or, so they thought.

The day of departure had finally arrived, but surprisingly very few Jews were willing to leave Babylon. Making the long 900 mile trek over four months to Jerusalem seemed just too taxing, and starting a new life all over again outside of the riches of what was then the capital of the known world seemed unappealing. Where once the people of the Southern Kingdom of Judah numbered in the millions, Ezra 2 records only a scant (by comparison) 200,000 people put their faith in God and signed up to make the journey to return to their native home. Like the sifting of Gideon's men, those faithful and willing few believed they were the embodiment of God's promise to restore the fortunes of Israel.

The leader of this First Return expedition was Zerubbabel. A descendent of King David and legitimate heir to his throne, Zerubbabel was granted governorship over what was once known as Judah. Judah under the Persian Empire had become an administrative district, or satrapy, called Abar Naharah which means "Beyond the River".[4] To provide spiritual guidance and direction in rebuilding the Temple, the High Priest Joshua, or Jeshua as he was sometimes called, and the Prophet Haggai would join the leadership team.

As difficult as the journey to Jerusalem was for these Post-Exilic Pilgrims, once they reached their destination, life living in the ruins of Jerusalem became far, far more challenging. The Samaritans, those descendants of the Jews who had been left behind and then intermarried with Gentile squatters, did not want to give up their scraps of control over to a newly restored Jerusalem. They interfered with the reconstruction of the Temple and made life miserable in every possible way. Ezra 3-4 records that no sooner had the Jews managed to get the foundation laid and restart the Levitical sacrifices did the Samaritans succeed in halting their work. They'd sent a slanderous letter to a new Persian king accusing the Jews of trying to rebel, and he believed them. Only two years in and the work was ordered stopped. The elderly who remembered the glory of Solomon's Temple could only weep at the pitiful, unfinished foundation.

## Construction of a Prophet

Life growing up in Jerusalem for these Jewish pilgrims and for our young Zechariah would have been terribly difficult.

Whatever wind that blew their sails optimistically forward had died away at the command to halt construction. Every day that the people walked by the pitiful foundation of the unfinished Temple was a perceived slight that God must have abandoned them. The catcalling by the Samaritans was relentless. The city was in shambles. If it wasn't for the initial funds from King Cyrus, starvation would have claimed all their lives. The Jewish people had to move on and begin building their own homes, farms and vineyards, or go hungry. And yet, the resulting crops produced very little food. No matter how hard they tried to grow food, barely enough to eat was squeezed out of that parched land.

Greatly discouraged and depressed beyond measure, with the future looking ever so bleak, the Jewish returnees were losing their faith and zeal for God. Too young to make a difference, the adolescent Zechariah could only look on powerless as his people's faith ebbed away.

## Call of the Prophet

God, though, had certainly not given up on His people. He saw how by faith the Post-Exilic Jews had left everything far behind in order to rebuild His Temple and resettle His Promised Land. God remembered, and He was now ready to call on a new prophet to join Haggai in presenting His messages to His people.

The time is now August of 520 BC. Sixteen years had passed since the Temple project was shut down. Young Zechariah had grown into manhood. God was to remember by choosing this young man, whose name ironically meant "whom Yahweh remembers," to be his messenger. Zechariah was the son of Berechiah, meaning "Yahweh blesses," and the grandson of Iddo, the head of their priestly family, whose name meant "the appointed time." Zechariah's priestly lineage of names would become the living embodiment of God's new message: "God remembers and blesses at the appointed time" (1:1). The appointed time had finally come.

Even if the Persian Empire wasn't ready to allow the Jews to finish the reconstruction of God's Temple, God certainly was ready. Zechariah was called to assist the aged prophet Haggai in rallying the people to reaffirm their faith in Yahweh by the act of restarting the construction of the Temple, apparently even without permission from their Persian overlords.

For two whole months Haggai ripped into the people for putting their own needs above the building of God's house. He chastised, "Is it time for you yourselves to dwell in your paneled houses, and this temple to lie in ruins? Consider your ways!" (Haggai 1:4). Zechariah, emulating his mentor's stern style, reminded the people, "The Lord has been very angry with your fathers" (1:2). Haggai rocked his listeners with the cold, hard fact that God was causing the drought as long as His house remained in ruins. "You looked for much, but indeed it came to little; and when you brought it home, I blew it away" (Haggai 1:9). Zechariah punctuated God's tongue-lashing with His final ultimatum: "'Return to Me,' says the Lord of hosts, 'and I will return to you'" (1:3).

How did the people respond to these stern messages? Haggai recorded that "the people feared the presence of the Lord" (Haggai 1:12). And, Zechariah recorded their conciliatory response, "Just as the Lord of Hosts determined to do to us, according to our ways and according to our deeds, so He has dealt with us" (1:6). Zerubbabel and Joshua responded in obedience to the command to begin reconstruction of the Temple and led their people back to work. But, something was clearly wrong. Enthusiasm was still at an all-time low. Great fear chilled the air over what would happen if their Persian overlords found out construction had restarted without their permission. Those infuriating Samaritans were ever watching and sending their lawyers to the king. Food was still sparse, leaving them weak. As one commentator described this sad and defeated remnant, "Their strength was sapped; their zest for life had ebbed; their hope of future glory was dimmed."[5]

Though the people were dutifully working, they remained desperate for any real hope that would rekindle the fiery enthusiasm they'd once possessed when they'd first set out from Babylon. They needed to see a real victory. They needed to know that when God said, "I am with you," that He really meant it (Haggai 1:13). Their faith had ebbed because the future looked so bleak. What they needed was real hope for the future. Zechariah's call was to give them that future hope.

# THE GOD OF HOPE

The people's priorities had been straightened out by Zechariah and Haggai. God first! They now embraced the reminder of the right order of things, something Jesus Christ centuries later would teach, "But seek first the kingdom of God and His righteousness, and all these things shall be added to you" (Matthew 6:33). They knew through God's messengers that He had indeed not forgotten them. But now these crushed and defeated people needed proof to jumpstart their faith. They needed a miracle born out of love, not wrath. God was about to knock their socks off!

## A Call to King Darius

Ezra 5-6 records the Samaritan's tattletale attempt to bring the wrath of another new Persian king, Darius Hystaspes, down upon the Jews for restarting the Temple reconstruction without permission. All their previous efforts to halt Governor Zerubbabel had failed because, "the eye of their God was upon the elders of the Jews, so that they could not make them cease till a report could go to Darius." Yahweh desired a confrontation.

The Samaritans actually challenged Darius to prove that King Cyrus had once written an edict promising the Jews they could rebuild the Temple. Maybe they thought the edict was long forgotten, or the document was buried in some dark, backroom archive, never to be found. Either way, they seemed to believe that

Darius would inevitably fail, so they schemed, "and let the king send us his pleasure concerning this matter."

The favorable response the Samaritans were hoping for from King Darius and what they were about to get were two different things though. Darius actually took on their conniving request and issued a search of his archives. His librarians were relentless in their quest, and the sought-after scroll was found and dusted off in Palace of Achmetha, far off in the Media province. It was rushed to the king, and after reading it over and over, he issued a crafty response to the Samaritans. One can almost picture a gleam in Darius' eyes and a smirk on his face as his scribe recorded a letter back to the busybody Samaritans.

After confirming Cyrus' command to rebuild the Temple out of the royal treasury, Darius ordered the Samaritans and any Persians to "keep yourselves far from there." He ordered, "Let the work of this house of God alone; let the governor of the Jews and the elders of the Jews build this house of God on its site." To rub salt on the Samaritan's wounds, Darius ordered the troublemakers themselves to fund the reconstruction out of their own tax revenues, and to even provide the animals that would be sacrificed "day by day without fail." And, to make sure he was clear and absolutely obeyed, King Darius ordered anyone who dared interfere with the reconstruction of God's Temple be hung from a timber ripped off their own house, just before it was demolished into a refuse heap. "May the God who causes His name to dwell there destroy any king or people who put their hand to alter it, or to destroy this house of God which is in Jerusalem." The new edict was signed, "I, Darius, issue a decree; let it be done diligently."

Once the Samaritans received the king's letter, one could almost hear the deafening sound of the combined slapping of Samaritan foreheads along with the grinding of teeth echoing across the Judean hillsides. The Jews celebrated wildly at this permission given amazingly by a Gentile king. The fear of a dreadful punishment by the Persians, like a weighted vest, had been lifted off their shoulders. God had moved the heart of Darius, just as he had with Cyrus almost two decades earlier. The hand of God was indisputably with His people. They were finally fired up!

# 8 Visions Given

To keep that fire fanned, Ezra 6:14 records that while the Jews rebuilt, "they prospered through the prophesying of Haggai the prophet and Zechariah." The whole tone of Zechariah's messages also seemed to change, as if coaching was more to his own personal style of ministering than the harshness he'd earlier had to show. Words like inspirational, hopeful, encouraging, comforting, and visionary best describe how this young prophet now guided God's once disillusioned people forward. Zechariah knew the pains of his people first-hand. He was there with them from the beginning. He was on the scaffolding with his peers, getting his hands dirty as he built alongside them. With graphic vividness and skill and pluck, Zechariah was truly in his groove when encouraging God's people onward towards completion.

Standing out from the other Minor Prophets, Zechariah earned his claim to fame by being the sharer of prophetic passages that would surpass in detail and clarity those of many of his Old Testament peers.[6] God continued to provide faith-boosting hope by granting Zechariah amazing and far-reaching visions that once shared would energize His people. These would be no garden-variety visions from God, but significant glimpses into a great and glorious future for His People Israel. That far, far distant future would revolve around one key event—the coming of the Messiah. When the Savior came, "the Lord shall be King over all the earth" (14:9).

So, in the dark night hours of February 15, 519 BC, Zechariah sleeplessly tossed and turned in his bed as the word of the Lord came to him.[7] God would show His prophet eight visions, one right after another, as if Zechariah was a spectator at some surreal indie film fest. He was then supposed to share these visions with His people, and through these God would give the Jewish people hope for the present and for the future.

**Vision #1: The Horses (1:7-17).** "I saw by night, and behold, a man riding on a red horse, and it stood among the myrtle trees in the hollow; and behind him were horses: red, sorrel, and white." The Angel of the Lord, the title for Jesus Christ Himself in the Old Testament, explained what these horses were doing. "We have walked to and fro throughout the earth, and behold, all the earth is resting quietly." The Lord then proclaimed His zealousness for Zion. God was returning to Jerusalem with mercy to build His house. A time of peace and rebuilding had come to Israel.

**Vision #2: The Horns (1:18-21).** "Then I raised my eyes and looked, and there were four horns." These animal "horns" had scattered the Jewish people into exile, but "four craftsmen" had arrived "to terrify them" and "to cast out the horns of the nations." The strong nations such as Egypt, Assyria, Babylon and Persia had scattered the Jewish people, but God would send avengers to beat them back. A time of regathering and safety had come to Israel.

**Vision #3: The Man with a Measuring Line (2:1-13).** Zechariah encounters a man who is measuring the city of Jerusalem in preparation for the return of its King. An angel tells the Measuring Man to inform Zechariah that, "'Jerusalem shall be inhabited as towns without walls, for I,' says the Lord, 'will be a wall of fire all around her, and I will be the glory in her midst.'" Yahweh warns any nation that tries to mess with His "Holy Land" that, "he who touches you [Israel] touches the apple of His eye." The Messiah promises that eventually, "Many nations shall be joined to the Lord in that day, and they shall become My people. And I will dwell in your midst." A time when the King of the world would rule gloriously from Jerusalem was coming.

**Vision #4: The High Priest (3:1-10).** This vision was prepared directly for Joshua, the High Priest. Zechariah witnessed Joshua standing in filthy rags before the Angel of the Lord while Satan performed his vile work of accusing him and the saints. Jesus the Messiah is the "Branch" who will rescue Joshua and His people from their sins, cleansing them so that they are pure before the Father. His saving works declared, "See, I have removed your iniquity from you, and I will clothe you with rich robes." A time for cleansing God's people from their sins was coming.

**Vision #5: The Lampstand and Olive Trees (4:1-14).** This vision was prepared for Zerubbabel, the governor. Zechariah is shown a seven branched menorah flanked by two olive trees which fueled the flames. To the discouraged governor, Yahweh reminds, "Not by might nor by power, but by My Spirit." The power to rebuild the Temple came from God, and no man can stand against the Almighty. God promises Zerubbabel that the project would indeed be finished, powered by "the two anointed ones, who stand beside the Lord of the whole earth." A time when God's plans would march unstoppably forward had arrived.

**Vision #6: The Flying Scroll (5:1-4).** Zechariah is shown something most strange—a flying scroll some thirty feet long and fifteen feet wide. Noticing his curiosity, an angel explains to the prophet that the scroll is in truth, "the curse that goes out over the face of the whole earth." All thieves and those who take the Lord's name in vain will face a fiery finish. A time when the wicked will be judged for their rebelliousness against God was coming.

**Vision #7: The Woman in a Basket (5:5-11).** This next vision must have truly perplexed Zechariah. He was shown a woman stuffed into a large basket. She is the personification of wickedness. Two female angels, a rarity in the Bible, carry the basket to the "land of Shinar," which is Babylon. To the land where Mankind rebelled against God at the Tower of Babel, to the epicenter of all evil, she will go. There she will wait for her time to strike. A time was coming when evil will be forever removed from the Holy Land and be defeated in one final battle.

**Vision #8: The Four Chariots (6:1-15).** The final vision portrayed four chariots, each pulled by a different colored horse, and each traveling to the four points of the compass. The one that traveled to the north country found the Holy Spirit at rest. Joshua the High Priest was then given an elaborate crown as if he were king. He shall build the Temple. But, Joshua is only an example, a symbol, a type of Christ. The Messiah would be the true Priest and King who would unite the two roles into one. Not only will the Messiah build the Eternal Temple, but He will also "bear the glory, and shall sit and rule on His throne; so He shall be a priest on His throne, and the counsel of peace shall be between them both." A time was coming when the offices of priest and king would be united in the One who will rule the earth forever.

# One Epiphany of the Holy City of the Future

These eight astounding visions did their job of firing up the workers. Construction on the Temple was now progressing at breakneck speed. The Returnees were psyched up with hope in the unstoppable power of Yahweh God combined with the lesser blessing of the Persian king. But, the city of Jerusalem—that shining jewel of God's kingdom on earth—was still as black and sooty as a lump of coal. Zechariah could only have looked around at the tumbled down ruins of Jerusalem which surrounded him and wondered when that man with the measuring line would be arriving to prepare Jerusalem for its restoration to its former glory. But, God wasn't interested in the city's former glory, for He was instead about to share with Zechariah an epiphany about its future glory. This epiphany that follows is recorded by Zechariah in chapters 7 and 8.

On December 7, 518 BC, Zechariah was about his family's priestly duties when a delegation from Bethel arrived to inquire if keeping the four non-Law fasts commemorating past calamities were still worth practicing.[8] Zechariah answered by shooting right at the heart of the matter with this question: "When you eat and when you drink, do you not eat and drink for yourselves?" (7:6) He reminded the people that their ancestors had abused commemorative festivals for their own selfish pleasure, a wickedness that in part was the cause for the suffering of their exile.

God didn't want fasting, but obedience. What He wanted was for the people to "execute true justice" and "to show mercy and compassion, everyone to his brother" (7:9). If Jerusalem was to be that great and shining capital city over the world, its inhabitance must not make the same awful mistakes that their ancestors had committed. A heart of obedience towards God must be the defining characteristic of its population. When the people had the right kind of heart, God would then unleash His splendor upon His city and its people.

The Prophet Zechariah gazed past the ruins of a failed city to behold a distant future when Jerusalem would be shining in full glory. Yahweh Himself would in person return with great zeal to His city. Jerusalem would be renamed "The City of Truth" and "The Holy Mountain." Not a tiny remnant, but a great throng of people both young and old who'd been regathered from around the world would play in its streets. Truth and righteousness would define its peoples. Peace would be its eternal condition. "Many peoples and strong nations shall come to seek the Lord of hosts in Jerusalem and to pray before the Lord" (8:22). The once despised and defeated Jew would become the new global celebrity as, "In those days ten men from every language of the nations shall grasp the sleeve of a Jewish man, saying, 'Let us go with you, for we have heard that God is with you'" (8:23).

## Two Oracles Concerning the Messiah

The power of hope was driving the Jewish returnees forward in rebuilding the Temple. The promise of God's love focused His people towards the day when that glorious chapter in Jerusalem's future would finally be realized. Now what the people needed was the blessing of faith in the One who would make all of this possible— the Messiah. Zechariah in chapters 9-11 would prophesy the story of the rejection of the Messiah. And then, in chapters 12-14, he would prophesy the victorious reception of the Messiah. These two oracles would puzzle readers for many generations to come, because they foretold not just one advent of the coming of the Savior, as everyone had expected, but two advents.

**Oracle #1: The Rejection of the Lamb (9-11).** The first coming of the Messiah would come as a shock, for He would enter Jerusalem, not as a king would riding high upon a white steed, but "lowly and riding on a colt, the foal of a donkey" (9:9). Nearly 550 years later, on what is now called Palm Sunday, Jesus Christ would fulfill this prophecy by making His triumphal entry into Jerusalem riding a young colt (Matthew 21:1-11; John 12:15). The Lord their God had come to "save them in that day." If His people would only accept Him in faith as Savior, the Messiah would pour down salvation like the latter rains and empower the people like mighty men. "'So I will strengthen them in the Lord, and they shall walk up and down in His name,' says the Lord" (10:12).

Alas! The people rejected the Messiah. Their hails of "Hosanna in the highest!" one week later turned into the harsh cries of "Crucify him! Crucify him!" Zechariah in chapter 11 prophesied this tragic turn of events. Stricken by His people's eventual rejection, the Messiah would lament, "My soul loathed them, and their soul also abhorred me" (11:8). With the imagery of breaking staffs, so Yahweh declared that He might "break the covenant which I had made with all the peoples" (11:10).

Zechariah even prophesied the exact amount of money over which the King would be betrayed. "So they weighed out for my wages thirty pieces of silver... so I took the thirty pieces of silver and threw them into the house of the Lord for the potter" (11:12-13). Again, nearly 550 years later, Judas Iscariot, who was one of Jesus' 12 Apostles, would accept 30 pieces of silver from the Jewish leaders to betray Jesus. Eventually feeling guilty, Judas would cast the money in the Temple, which as blood money would be used to buy a potter's field (Matthew 26:14-16; 27:3-10).

Rejected by His people as King and sacrificed on the cross for mankind's sins as an offering lamb, the Messiah leaves the treacherous people in the care of the "Worthless Shepherd." These Gentile rulers, culminating in the Beast King of Revelation 13, "will not care for those who are cut off, nor seek the young, nor heal those that are broken, nor feed those that still stand" (11:15-17).

**Oracle #2: The Acceptance of the Lion (12-14).** Left to this Worthless Shepherd, the Jewish people would suffer under the tyranny of Satan for many generations to come. The Jews would be expelled out of their land a second time, this time by the Roman Empire in 70 AD. They would wander the world for centuries as a people without a home in this their second exile. Everywhere they went they would be despised and rejected and persecuted. That is, until one day when a holocaust of such horrific proportions carried out by the Nazis would soften the hearts of the nations' denizens just enough to allow the Jewish people to reclaim a small portion of their ancestral land. Zechariah, not even in his wildest speculations, could have imagined the date for the reestablishment of the nation of Israel would occur so many centuries later on May 14, 1948. But, Zechariah was told another holocaust would be coming some time afterwards, one God revealed would come when Satan's Beast King—the Antichrist—would one dark and distant day unleash all of his master's rage upon the tiny nation of Israel.

Because of Zechariah's spectacularly detailed description of the time surrounding the Second Coming of the Messiah, commentators have come to label chapters 12-14 as the "Apocalypse of the Old Testament."[9] This Apocalypse, this "unveiling" or "removal of something that hides," is so detailed that Zechariah's prophetic writings have been elevated among theologians to those of the great prophets such as Daniel in the Old Testament and the Apostle John with the book of Revelation.[10] This Tribulation coming to the world is known throughout the prophets as "The Day of the Lord." The following is how Zechariah explains it will play out.

For the Messiah to return a second time in order to claim His throne in Jerusalem as prophesied, the city of Jerusalem must be back in the control of the Jewish people. Israel is indeed a nation once again, but the control of Jerusalem is victim of an ongoing tug-of-war by the nations of the world, all of which struggle for control over that city for their own selfish ends. In response, God promises He will at that time, "make Jerusalem a cup of drunkenness to all the surrounding peoples" and "a very heavy stone for all peoples." For all the nations of the world who are gathered against Jerusalem and vie for its control, the Lord promises that "all who would heave it away will surely be cut in pieces" (12:2-3).

When the nations that comprise the Antichrist's empire descend upon Jerusalem to force control over it, Zechariah in chapter 14 explains how this one-world ruler will at first be successful. The city will be initially taken and many Jewish men will be captured and the women raped. And yet, God still empowers its fighters, for "in that day the Lord will defend the inhabitants of Jerusalem" by making each of its people as mighty in battle as King David once was (12:8).

Then the daylight oddly will grow eerily dark. The Messiah declares, "It shall be in that day that I will seek to destroy all the nations that come against Jerusalem" (12:9). And so He does! The Savior will descend out of Heaven like a roaring lion, with His armies following like a flood behind Him. Jesus will land on the Mount of Olives across from Jerusalem with such force that the mountain will split in two. The Lord will then strike the armies attacking the city so that "their flesh shall dissolve while they stand on their feet" (14:12). With just His spoken word, the Savior melts the armies away as if He were a nuclear furnace! Revelation 19 adds more details to Christ's glorious return, as Jesus throws the Antichrist and his False Prophet into the Lake of Fire and casts Satan into a deep pit.

While the inhabitants of Jerusalem are being crushed by the onslaught of the combined armies of the nations of the world and are staring down their utter annihilation, its people grieve and mourn. The grieving isn't because they think they're all about to die, but because when they see the Messiah coming to defend them, they'll realize just who He is. "They will look on Me whom they pierced. Yes, they will mourn for Him as one mourns for his only son" (12:10). Every family still standing against the onslaught will recognize the Messiah to be Jesus Christ, the One who was "pierced" by nails on the cross outside the walls of Jerusalem some 2,000 years earlier. If only they had accepted Jesus as King then, two millennia of terrible suffering would have been avoided. And so the people will weep and mourn, even with their salvation at hand.

By the time this new holocaust of the Jew by Satan and his Antichrist is stopped due to the Second Coming of the Messiah, Zechariah reveals in chapter 13 that two-thirds of the Jewish people will have been slaughtered. But, God promised that, "I will bring the one-third through the fire... They will call on My name, and I will answer them. I will say, 'This is My people'; and each one will say, 'The Lord is my God'" (13:9).

Finally, the Jewish people as a nation will have accepted their Messiah. All adultery to false gods through idolatry and the following of deceitful prophets will be eliminated. A people saved by God's grace through faith in Jesus Christ will become pure and holy, thereby gaining entrance into the Messiah's Kingdom. Zechariah describes that glorious Kingdom as the time of peace, safety, holiness, and heartfelt celebration of its King. The longed for Messianic Age will have arrived!

## One Temple Stands

The Prophet Zechariah probably had the best assignment of all the Minor Prophets. His compatriots mostly saw sin and judgment and defeat. Subsequently, they also experienced much of the resulting sorrow and persecution as the result of their faithful delivery of God's messages. Zechariah, on the other hand, while reciting God's given visions and oracles, got to witness repentance and rising hope and future victory. He took a people who'd fallen into the depths of defeat, with their faith barely hanging on by a thread, and infused into them an ocean-sized measure of God's unfailing love.

Ezra 6:13-22 contains the jubilant report that the construction of the Temple was completed in four years. It was finished in 516 BC, exactly 70 years from when the Jews were exiled from Jerusalem, as prophesied. "Then the children of Israel, the priests and the Levites and the rest of the descendants of the captivity, celebrated the dedication of this house of God with joy." The people held a great celebration, "for the Lord made them joyful... to strengthen their hands in the work of the house of God, the God of Israel." With a newly supercharged faith and a bright hope for the future, the enlivened Post-Exilic Pilgrims finally knew success. Their success would inspire two more great waves of Jewish returnees from Babylon who would join them in the purpose of rebuilding a nation.

## ZECHARIAH'S FAITH LESSONS

### Lessons for Israel

How does the Israel of today maintain faith in God when the future looks bleak? Bleak may be too mild a word, for the nation of Israel is surrounded by over 350 million hostile Arabs who wish to "wipe them off the map." They also remain accosted by incessant condemnation from the United Nations. The whole world has gathered against Israel, as Zechariah foretold, and the pressure is only going to worsen.

The message Yahweh gave Israel's ancestors continues to apply to their current life-and-death struggles. Thus says the Lord of hosts: "Do not be like your fathers, to whom the former prophets preached, saying, 'Turn now from your evil ways and your evil deeds.' But they did not hear nor heed Me." You, instead, heed the call of God to put your trust in Him. "'Return to Me,' says the Lord of hosts, 'and I will return to you.'" (1:2-3).

Israel can accept Jesus the Messiah in faith now, or "mourn for Him" later at His Second Coming after the next holocaust has killed so many (12:10). Jesus desires to restore His covenant with the Jewish people, if only they would embrace the glorious future God has promised. If only Israel would do that, their faith would grow from the size of a mustard seed into a mountain. And, just as the first Post-Exilic people did, they will become inheritors of that glorious future God has so lovingly described through the Prophet Zechariah.

## Lessons for the Nations

How can the nations maintain faith in God when the future looks bleak? The future does indeed look very bleak for the nations. Zechariah's prophecies tell of a day coming when all the nations will gather in rebellion against Jesus Christ for the futile purpose of preventing Him from becoming King. And yet, they will fail miserably.

Though the sands of human government have all but slipped through the neck of the hourglass, there are still a few national leaders today who have kept their faith in Jesus Christ. They do so by placing their allegiance squarely for God over human government. They keep their faith aflame by looking forward to the day when the world's true King will return. They yearn for the age God has promised through Zechariah 14:9 when, "The Lord shall be King over all the earth." They rule with the comforting knowledge that, because they are faithful followers of Jesus Christ, they will also hold authority in Christ's Kingdom, serving in roles such as governors and mayors and teachers. They rejoice in a future when they will lead the peoples God will one day entrust to them to a great annual celebration, which as Zechariah 14:16 describes so wonderfully, "And it shall come to pass that everyone who is left of all the nations which came against Jerusalem shall go up from year to year to worship the King, the Lord of hosts, and to keep the Feast of Tabernacles."

The future of government will go to those who have accepted Jesus as Savior. But, in the meantime, for those in power, they need to embrace the "deepest truth" of national greatness as revealed by famed preacher Dr. G. Campbell Morgan: "A nation is only great as it sees God behind events, and finds the way He is going, and moves along in step with Him."[11]

## Lessons for the Church

How can the Church maintain faith in God when the future looks bleak? With terrible persecution on one side, and spiritual apathy and apostasy emanating on the other, the future at this time does indeed look terribly bleak for the Body of Christ. To rectify these challenges to the faith, the Church needs to recapture what the Jewish people of Zechariah's time learned to embrace when building their "City on a Hill." As Pastor D. Stuart Briscoe describes, "A sense of divine majesty and power, righteousness, and justice needs to be recaptured in the modern church so that we can take God seriously."[12]

No people group has embraced this truth as well as the Puritan Pilgrims did back in American history. Taking God seriously was so evidently afire in their hearts and souls that it led them to take an unpopular stand against unbiblical teachings, leave all they knew behind, and travel to a vast unknown. Even with sickness decimating their numbers daily, and enduring hardships beyond measure, the Pilgrims were defined by their sensing of God's divine power. It drove them on against seemingly unbeatable odds to build their own "City on a Hill." And, the Lord rewarded the Pilgrims for their stalwart faith, for these seemingly defeated people went on in victory to birth a new nation. This new nation, christened the United States of America, because it was founded on the tenants of God's moral law, would grow to become the new apex of world evangelism.

The Church can maintain its faith when it remains in awe of God, and through faithful obedience allows Him to work miracles.

"And this shall come to pass if you diligently obey the voice of the Lord your God" (6:15).

## Lessons for You

How then can you maintain faith in God when your future looks bleak? Well, after reading the book of Zechariah, does the future really look so bleak? Didn't Zechariah "prepare the road along which the celestial King was to ride in solemn grandeur" when he painted in spectrum colors the absolute majesty of the Messiah's coming victory?[13] Sure, there are difficulties today which must be endured, but they wax quite pale in the light of God's glory and grace. Today's trials will soon be forgotten when the King returns. For the believer in Christ, the future is all about hope.

So, in the meantime, says the Lord of Hosts, live "not by might nor by power, but by My Spirit" (4:6). Take the lessons from the Vision of the Lampstand and Olive Trees and keep the channels of your life lamp clean from sin and unbelief. Don't choke out your faith with spiritual decadence and backsliding. Remain in purity and prayer, and the light of God's glorious future will shine through your life, restore your faith to a blinding brightness, and help kindle that fire in others.

## QUESTIONS FOR DISCUSSION

1. What were the causes for why the Jewish people were living in exile?

2. What events did God have to orchestrate so that the Jewish people would be allowed to go back to Jerusalem?

3. What difficulties did the Post-Exilic Jews have to endure to travel to the Promised Land?

4. How did the Post-Exilic Jews feel once they reached their destination?

5. Have you ever been so excited to reach a goal, only to be terribly disappointed once you got there?

6. What difficulties did the Post-Exilic Jews have to endure once they began resettling the land?

7. Why did the people fail so miserably in their efforts to build homes and grow food?

8. What events did God have to orchestrate in order to clear the obstacles away so that the Jews could return to rebuilding the Temple?

9.  Does your own future at this point look bleak? If so, what promises has God made that fire up your faith and give you hope for a better tomorrow?

# FAITH JOURNEY 12
# MALACHI: FAITH WHEN YOU'RE QUESTIONED

## THE MENAGERIE

*"That's some animal you've got there," he said. Malachi's comment hung in the air as he gazed at the emaciated brown bull lazily chewing its cud. A slack rope held the creature that showed no intention of moving anytime soon. The man holding the other end of the woven cord reached up to scratch his own nose, weighing a response.*

*"Yep," he finally said. "And you care because...?"*

*Malachi shuffled his feet and glanced around. The line of Jews waiting for their turn at the Temple was backed up at least fifty feet. Families were patiently standing with their offerings and sacrifices, waiting their turn, brushing off flies and making small talk in the shade. No one seemed to be paying attention to this conversation, but Malachi suspected that would change soon.*

*He absent-mindedly kicked a loose stone in the street that skittered next to the bull's obviously lame right hoof. "Well, I was just noticing that... um... well, the thing is," Malachi stammered, "that... OK. I'll just say it. Your bull looks terrible. And it shouldn't. I mean, you shouldn't be here with it if it's blemished."*

*The afternoon shadows made the man's scowl even more pronounced. He tensed up a little, then seemed to pause and reconsider. Rather than make a move to intimidate the slight man in front of him, he simply adjusted his robes and then gestured to the others in line. "You think mine's any worse than theirs?"*

*Waiting to respond, Malachi's eyes moved down the line, taking in the various and sundry livestock. Goats with broken horns, lambs with obvious eye infections, rams with patchy hair. The man had a point; the bull wasn't unusual.*

*Bleating and lowing mingled with the sound of conversations and a bit of laughter as the line shuffled forward a few steps, one family closer to the altar. The man he had confronted took Malachi's silence as a sign that his point hit home, and he pressed the advantage. "Look, friend, it is bad enough that I have to give up the bull at all. Livestock ain't exactly a booming industry right now. The herd at home is small, and times are tough. I know I've got a better bull at my house, but... I mean, I could sacrifice that one, but then what? It's money out of my pocket. My neighbor just made an offer to buy him... for DOUBLE what they'd pay for this loser here. No one wants this one, and since it's all getting burned up anyway... ya know?"*

*This was it. Malachi knew it. He knew that this was just the right opportunity to share. He wasn't being silent out of weakness; he was mulling over the words from the Lord he knew he must speak. The man's casual indifference to the Law was like a magnet drawing the words out of him. Despite his disdain for public speaking, words poured forth.*

*"Listen, guys," he called out. No longer conversing just with the sickly bull's owner, Malachi's voice carried down the line and caught the attention of everyone waiting. His voiced cracked as he continued emphatically. "God spoke to me the other day, and here's what He says to tell you. 'Children honor their parents, and servants honor their masters. I am your Father—why don't you honor Me? I am your Master—why don't you respect me? You despise Me!'"*

*Malachi paused, waiting for a penitent response or laments from the crowd as they immediately saw the error of their ways. He hopefully searched for the signs of remorse on the people's faces, but instead saw blank stares turn to smirks and ridicule. Laughter started to trickle towards him, and a few goats punctuated the air with cries that suddenly sounded mocking. Men gestured toward him, and the crowd seemed more surprised that he had broken Temple etiquette by shouting at them than struck by the seriousness of the accusation he had made.*

*The man with the bull looked around for backup and received it quickly from the next family in line. A burly husband shifted his malnourished lamb to his wife's arms and stepped closer to the anxious Malachi.*

*"Hey, pal... we're all standin' here givin' up our time to kill off a perfectly good animal. It's for God, you moron. The priests ain't turnin' us down. How have we 'despised' the Lord if we're in line to sacrifice to Him?" Heads nodded in agreement, daring Malachi to argue.*

*Looking up and down the line, seeing their ridicule and disdain for the words he spoke, Malachi's optimism quickly faded. Feeling the weight of their questions, the prophet suddenly realized one thing: this was going to be harder than he thought!*

## THE PRICE OF CONFRONTATION

In the "before" picture, he is robust and strapping. In the "after" picture, he is worn and frazzled.

Few jobs take such an emotional toll on those who step in and report for duty as that of President of the United States. After four years, or eight if the voters so choose, a president has made thousands of decisions that have impacted millions of citizens in the U.S.A. and influenced billions around the globe. He has been involved with negotiations that shaped the future of our country, and he has been exposed to classified information few will ever know or appreciate. Every word he has spoken carried weight, and even off-the-cuff remarks like "I do not like broccoli"[1] have riled entire industries.

Photographs of these men from Lincoln to Obama show the impact of such a high level of responsibility. Side-by-side comparisons of presidents' before and after photos show that these "Leaders of the Free World" seem to age much faster than calendar years should indicate. Where their eyes were once bright and hopeful, they now seem heavy and burdened. Hair goes from dark to gray, sometimes in a matter of a few months. Stress lines and wrinkles multiply quickly. And while there is still a winning politician's smile, it seems a bit forced and even weary.

To make decisions that have wide-reaching impact can be hard for anyone in a position of leadership, but American presidents experience the full weight of decision-making. Every choice they make—whether declaring war or signing executive orders or even choosing to play a round of golf—is scrutinized and questioned with rhetorical abandon by the press, the voters, and the political opposition.

No matter the position he takes, a president has no safe place to turn. He will be grilled on every issue in every place at every waking moment. Denied the relief of a true vacation or day off, the Commander in Chief's stress builds and builds until it comes out his pores and follicles, aging the man prematurely.

"Before" and "after" photographs allow the public to see the effects of that weight in a way words can never tell.

Thankfully, most people will never know that same degree of criticism or examination. John Q. Public has the luxury of going relatively unnoticed in most situations, but that doesn't mean he can avoid questions or the pressure those questions bring.

All of us face questions over the course of daily life. A teenage daughter scoffs at her father's choice of clothing. A disapproving wife questions her husband's navigational skills on a road trip. A supervisor demands changes to a presentation his employee spent hours perfecting. While we may have previously been confident in our choice or position, others' uncertainties force us to pause and reconsider. Their doubts replace our assurance and make us wonder just how right we actually were.

If questions can cause us a crisis of confidence when targeting things like our work or our parenting, questions can be absolutely devastating when aimed at matters of faith. Inquiries aimed at our convictions have the power to expose us, so that rather than feeling sheltered under the wings of the Almighty, we feel helpless and afraid. Instead of feeling secure in the refuge of a Strong Tower, we feel uncertain and in danger of losing everything.

The pressure of spiritual questioning leads people to react in different ways. Some individuals fight back in opposition. Thinking the best defense is a good offense, they quickly defend the Lord and verbally pummel their enemies into submission. Other individuals cower at the thought of arguing. Rather than engaging their accusers, they choose to avoid all types of conflict and leave the Lord to defend Himself.

The middle ground, though, is where many Christians find themselves. When challenged, they obediently give a reason for the hope that they have. But when they share that hope, it is met with an onslaught of doubt and criticism. Their faith is undermined as questions are levied at everything from credibility to creeds. Rather than coming out of such a conversation victorious, these Christians grapple with the discovery that their faith was not as rock solid as it once appeared.

When questions come, we need an example of faith that can provide answers. We need to see believers who faced difficult questions, but handled them with grace and wisdom. We need to see followers who had the courage to look their doubters in the eye and confidently state their trust in God. We need to see disciples that believed in God's promises without wavering.

When we've been questioned, we need faith we can imitate. We need faith like that of the prophet Malachi.

# THE PROPHET BEFORE THE LONG SILENCE

Malachi is probably the most read of all the Minor Prophets. This is due, of course, more to its location than its contents. As the twelfth and final book of the Minor Prophets, Malachi sits as the last volume of the Old Testament. Those who search for the beginning chapters of the New Testament are bound to flip a few pages too far in front of Matthew and stumble upon this prophetic gem. While they might stay for a verse or two, it's a shame that more don't stick around to read the entire book.

As with most of the other books of prophecy in this section of Scripture, a full reading would take just a few short minutes; Malachi is only four chapters long. However, in those four chapters we are treated to the words of a prophet who is both bold and patient. He calmly but firmly addresses his audience with the words of God, showing us in his message how he faithfully handled the burden of being questioned.

## Time of the Prophet

Like Joel and Obadiah, Malachi is a prophet without a time. The opening phrase, "The burden of the word of the Lord to Israel by Malachi" (1:1), is a standard opener in prophetic literature, but it tells us nothing biographical about the man. We are given no family names, no tribal information, no place of origin, and no date or kings by which we may assign a date. The content is vague enough to preclude a firm guess on the date of writing, so we have to make some educated assumptions.

Judah's national situation as described in this book seems to match many of the same social and religious concerns that faced the province during the years after Haggai and Zechariah. A corrupt priesthood, interfaith marriages, and social injustice top the list of

Malachi's concerns. These problems plagued the Jews from the time of their return from Babylonian exile in 538 BC up until the ministries of Ezra and Nehemiah some 80 years later. The language connects it to the reign of Persian King Darius I (522-486 BC), and if this is the case, Malachi would be chronologically the last book written in the Old Testament.[2] It would be over 400 years before God chooses to inspire further writers to put pen to parchment in recording the Gospels of the New Testament.

## Construction of a Prophet

With a name meaning "My Messenger," Malachi's identity has been viewed as a bit of a mystery by scholars. Some have taken the name to be a description rather than as a proper name. That is certainly possible, but the possibility remains just a guess and not a fact.[3] The main reason to lean toward Malachi being a proper name is simply precedent. All the other books of prophecy begin by identifying the author in the opening verses. If this book follows tradition, then we can assume that an actual man named Malachi served as God's prophetic messenger and wrote this book.

Based on details within the text, we pick up a few clues about this Messenger's personality. One clue relates to the style of writing. While most of the other prophets crafted Hebrew poetry to communicate their messages, Malachi sticks to basic prose. In straightforward verbiage, he writes as a teacher instructing the uninformed, using language they would grasp easily. The style is not lofty, but it is effective.[4]

Another clue about Malachi's personality comes from the tone of the book. Some commentators have described his tone as "argumentative."[5] It's true that there are back-and-forth moments in the text, but many of these arguments are initiated by his audience rather than by Malachi himself. While the prophet doesn't shy away from engaging their opinions, he shows patience while he responds to the numerous questions raised. His positive example of faith during these exchanges is encouraging for readers to see.

Additionally, Malachi shows the heart of a pastor. He seems to have the pulse of the community and knows their spiritual condition. He shows that he is aware of religious duties and activities, but he doesn't come across as a stuffy insider. He is equally informed about the financial and marital practices of the people, as well as the worship habits of those coming to the Temple. God gives him the eyes and ears to truly understand his community, and that understanding helps Malachi present his message about the ways in which these Jews failed to honor God.

## Call of the Prophet

The occasion for our prophet's service is simply God's displeasure with the state of His people. No details on Malachi's call to prophetic service are given. The author's concern is not himself. Instead, his concern is the Jews with which he lives. So, immediately after identifying himself and declaring the fact that this was God's message, Malachi makes a beeline to sharing the Lord's main point.

## A SERIES OF QUESTIONS

"I have loved you," God says (1:2).

In those few short words, God's heart is displayed for all to see. Though He will have harsh rebukes for the audience, this opening verse sets the tone for all that is to come.

While we usually assume such a declaration would be taken at face value, the people of Jerusalem are in no mood to believe it. Immediately they question God's statement of affection. "In what way have You loved us?" (1:3).

Thus begins the debate we find throughout this book. Malachi engages in what scholars call "literary disputations."[6] Reminiscent of the courtroom, the author and audience trade points. These statement-question pairings continue throughout subsequent chapters, and they pave the way for Malachi to elaborate on his God-given message. While arguing and defending every point could become wearisome, Malachi has a decisive answer for all of the challenges. His faith remains rock-solid despite the endless exchanges.

## Question #1: Love

God's declaration of love in 1:2 sets the tone for the entire book. However, the people doubt God's love and throw it back at Him like moody teenagers questioning their parents.

No one familiar with the history of Israel could seriously question God's love for His people. The God of Abraham, Isaac, and Jacob had done miraculous things for Israel. The books of Law and History in the Bible carried His fingerprints in events both big and small; the books of Poetry and Prophecy showed the ways in which God provided for and cared for His people. Yet the people adopted a "what have you done for me lately" mentality. In their immediate experience, God did not seem to be showing much love.

Malachi patiently defends God and His love. The prophet points out the favor the Lord showed the descendants of Jacob compared to the descendants of Esau. While God declared love for Jacob's side of the family, Esau's side—the Edomites—faced a far worse fate (see Obadiah for Edom's destruction). If the Jews would just open their eyes, they would recognize God's special care for their nation out of all the countries of the world, and they would be able to praise Him saying, "The Lord is magnified beyond the border of Israel" (1:5).

## Question #2: Purity

Though God loved the people of Israel, they didn't seem to return the favor. The priests, who should be closest to the Lord and most in tune to His holiness, instead showed contempt for Him. Malachi relays God's charge that the priests "despise [God's] name" (1:6).

"In what way have we despised Your name?" the priests shoot back. And later, "In what way have we defiled You?" (1:6-7).

Both questions would be laughable if they weren't so obviously rebellious.

Malachi had only to point to the animals standing in line at the Temple, animals that should have been immediately rejected as unworthy offerings. Rather than flawless, perfect specimens, these were blind, lame, sick, and even stolen! Like offering leftover cake from a dumpster to your wife on her birthday, these "gifts" were displeasing to God. He would not accept them, nor would He show favor to those who offered them. The Lord even goes as far as hoping someone would shut the doors to the Temple and stop these ridiculous sacrifices rather than continue them as a mockery. The majestic King would not allow such insults to slander His reputation. "For my name shall be great among the nations," He says (1:11).

The people may have been the ones bringing such pitiful gifts, but the priests were ultimately responsible. Rather than hold the givers accountable, the priests instead lowered their standards. Malachi stood up to these Levites and bravely faced their questions.

God's prophet presents the divine command to give glory to God's name (2:1). The command comes with the condition that failure to follow will bring curses. If the priests don't take that command to heart, God warns, "Behold, I will rebuke your descendants and spread refuse on your faces, the refuse of your solemn feasts" (2:3). The language of shame is used to threaten the priests, but it is really a backhanded presentation of grace.[7] The threat from God reminds the Jews of the covenant and its promise of life and peace they should already have, and that could still be theirs in the future. By contrasting the covenant ideals with the priests' current sinful reality, God gives these spiritual leaders a chance to repent.

## Question #3: Faithfulness

In the next dispute, Malachi stands shoulder to shoulder with the husbands of Judah and pleads with them to act faithfully to their spouses. Based on the truth of God's paternal care, he asks

"Why do we deal treacherously with one another by profaning the covenant of the fathers?" (2:10).

God loves marriage as a holy institution, but the people were introducing unholy elements into it, specifically intermarriage with women who worshiped other deities. While such a mixed marriage seems rather mundane in our modern climate, Malachi calls it an abomination (2:11). It was a direct violation of God's principles of holiness (see Ezra 9:1-2 for a related discussion).

In addition, the holy institution of marriage was being treated with casual contempt as divorce rates skyrocketed. The people "dealt treacherously" with their wives (2:16). That phrase is used throughout surrounding verses and can also have the sense of "being faithless" or "betraying." It is a harsh term but it fits; the people are betraying the spiritual union God created in marriage. Divorce has horrific consequences, as any victim of it—spouse or child—can attest.

As a result of these faithless marital interactions, God rejected the people's offerings, even the ones that weren't blemished sacrifices in the first place. The Jews weep and cry over this rejection, but they fail to understand that it is tied to their own behaviors (2:13).

As the people question Malachi about God's reasons for rejecting them, Malachi doesn't shy away from answering. Though he does not personally participate in this treachery, he stands as a member of a community in which its effects cannot be escaped. "God's Messenger" tries to help them see the source of their heartbreak—it isn't God's fault for ignoring their offerings and worship, but it is their faithless marriages that broke the spiritual relationship.

## Question #4: Judgment

God's patience begins to wear thin. He is wearied by the people's questions, yet more keep coming. "In what way have we wearied Him?" the Jews ask (2:17). Not content to stop with just one question, they increase their insolent attitude and question God even more! Accusing God of delighting in evil, they disdainfully inquire, "Where is the God of justice?" (2:17).

This may be one of the most infuriating questions Malachi has had to face so far. It was one thing for the people to question the Lord's claims; it was quite another for them to question the Lord's character and leadership. God was being treated like an absentee parent and the citizens of Judah held Him in contempt.

But, as one commentator points out, "The God of judgment was nearer than any of the skeptics imagined."[10] He provided an answer to the critics by announcing words of promise. Though His presence was under question, God revealed plans to make Himself known in a personal way. Malachi shared God's intentions to visit the Temple Himself, a plan that is presented with references to the coming Messiah and the events surrounding His incarnation.[11]

This coming Messiah would purify His people. Like a fire that helps burn away the impurities in metal, or a powerful chemical that removes stains, God's arrival will purge the flaws in His people (3:2). Despite their current criticisms and failure to trust God's character, the people are promised a bold display of justice. God and His current messenger, Malachi, can handle the questions because they know He has plans to act.

## Question #5: Repentance

The doubters and scoffers peppering Malachi with questions were no different than their ancestors. In this next section, God reminds the people of His faithful love despite the Jews' rebellion and lawlessness.

The Lord tells them simply, "Return to me, and I will return to you" (3:7). It is a magnanimous proposal. Despite the Jews' flaws and failures, God offers His glorious grace and His boundless love. For a nation mired in sin and rebellion, this is a fantastic offer! One can even picture Malachi making this proposition and expecting immediate repentance from the nation.

But, no. "How shall we return?" is their stubborn reply. Despite the grace He offered, the Jews continue to question God.

## Question #6: Trust

God wastes no time replying. He gives them a tangible practice to begin showing their devotion.

Up to this point, the Jews' questions have been verbal. However, God points out another way they've shown doubts. Rather than trusting God with their money and resources, they have been withholding tithes. This amounted to robbery, God says, and the consequences have been severe for the entire nation.

The people doubt this accusation and ask for explanation. "In what way have we robbed You?" they ask yet again (3:8).

The answer is familiar to anyone who has attended church. It is a passage that has been quoted in almost every stewardship sermon given and in every committee meeting about church finances. "Bring all the tithes into the storehouse... and see if I will not throw open the floodgates of heaven and pour out so much blessing that you will not have enough room for it" (3:10). Thus God responds with encouragement. The people are to take a step of faith by meeting their financial obligations. While the blessings God promises in response may be seen as motivation for giving, they are really just a demonstration of God's statement on repentance He made in the section above: if they would restore their devotion to God, God would reciprocate.

## Question #7: Reality

The back and forth discussion in this book has been emotional, even for God. "Your words have been harsh against Me," the Lord says in 3:13. But even in this statement the people question. "What have we spoken against You?" (3:13).

293

The multitude of complaints is magnified here for God to hear every word and every grumble. The people complain that serving God is useless, and that following His ways accomplishes nothing. It is an embarrassing display of ignorance on the part of the Jews. They show just how little insight they truly have. Instead of seeing the reality of their sin and the problems it caused, they naively turn the tables and blame God.

While the reader may have hoped for progress—seeing God's people *en masse* trusting and accepting His claims—this section near the end of Malachi's book reminds us of the majority's failure to trust. They end just as accusatory and doubtful as they started.

## AN ENCOURAGING ANSWER

One can imagine the criticism and mockery Malachi received from these wayward people as a result of his message. With each point and counter-point, he probably felt more and more alone. Yet, there were some listeners who heard and then responded positively to God's word.

In 3:16, those who truly "feared the Lord" discussed Malachi's words from God. Their response was praised by God and contrasted to their opponents' foolishness. They wrote a scroll to remember the words from the Lord and the ones who honored His name.

In response, God shares several points about the future and how He would deal with people. Commentator James Smith divides God's response into four coming days:[8]

- **A glorious day** (3:17-18)—a day when God would acknowledge His own. They would become a prized possession, like jewels.
- **A terrible day** (4:1)—a day for the wicked to face punishment. They would be burned up like stubble.

- **A healing day** (4:2)—a future day where those who worship and revere God will enjoy healing. The healing is connected with the Messiah, here called the "Sun of Righteousness."
- **A victorious day** (4:3)—a day when the oppressed would be victorious over the oppressor.

In preparation for the coming of the Messiah, God also promises the coming of another Elijah (4:5). This "Elijah" would play a role in preparing the people's hearts for God's actions. As we read in the New Testament, this prophecy finds partial fulfillment in the ministry of John the Baptist at the First Coming of Jesus Christ and ultimate fulfillment before His Second Coming (Matthew 11:1-19; Revelation 11:1-14). Presenting forerunners to announce the coming of the Messiah confirms Yahweh's faithfulness.

By choosing to believe God, this remnant of faithful Jews got a glimpse of His bigger plan. Rather than proceed with questions and doubts, their response ends the book on a note of trust and faith. Regardless of questions, they saw a God who plans and acts.

God is not swayed by doubts. And His Messenger, Malachi, was not swayed, either.

## MALACHI'S FAITH LESSONS

As we've read through the Minor Prophets, there have been two groups of prophets: those who fight through the trenches of faith *with* us, and those who shine as an example of mastered faith *for* us. The first group gives us encouragement to persevere while the second gives us motivation to succeed. Malachi, in relation to faith when we're questioned, has proven himself to be a master to follow. We can see his faith and be inspired to attain it.

When you face questions for your belief in God and your trust in Jesus, consider Malachi's example of faith and some of these possible ways to reproduce it.

## Lessons for Israel

As a cultural subset of Judaism, Messianic Jews face significant questions from their ethnic counterparts because of a failure to hold to traditionally Jewish beliefs. The questions are not minor. One rabbi even said, "Belief in Jesus as Messiah is not simply a heretical belief, as it may have been in the First Century; it has become the equivalent to an act of ethno-cultural suicide."[9]

Orthodox Jews question Messianic Jews' identity as Jews. Mainstream Jews question Messianic Jews' affiliation with places and businesses designed for Jews. The Supreme Court of Israel even had to wrestle with the impact that their belief in Jesus had on Messianic immigrants' desire to be citizens of the country.[12]

How do you answer the questions of identity, loyalty, ethics, or inclusion? Messianic Jews need to have the same confidence displayed by Malachi as he was questioned by his countrymen. Just as he refused to back down when facing intense pressure, Messianic Jews need to stand firm and know that their position is right, even if it isn't popular. They should unswervingly hold to Jesus, the true Messiah.

While Jews had been branches broken off the metaphorical olive tree because of unbelief, Messianic Jews can be branches that are grafted back in (Romans 11:17-24). Instead of allowing questions and doubts to shake their confidence, Jews who trust Jesus Christ as their Savior must find their assurance in Him and know that spiritual history will validate their faith.

## Lessons for the Nations

As we discussed earlier in this chapter, Presidents of the United States discover that, no matter their decisions, questions follow. Whether the questions come from expected political opponents or whether they come from people previously considered allies, doubt and uncertainty are thrown at national leaders at every turn. This truth applies at every level of government, from emperors to mayors, and in every country from Albania to Zimbabwe.

National leaders must learn from Malachi that questions are ever-present, and like Malachi they should learn which side to listen to. Malachi never caved to the skepticism thrown his way, whether it came from priests or commoners. Instead he chose to listen only to God.

While it would never be popular, leaders should have their first responsibility be to God instead of the voters. They should study Scripture instead of polling data. Rather than focus groups, they should have focused prayer.

Politically, this would seem to be suicide. The conventional wisdom says that politicians should follow the party line or the popular vote. Never does it recommend following what comes from the pulpit and the pews. But, if you are going to be questioned for everything anyway, isn't it better to have the doubts come from men rather than from man's Maker?

Follow Malachi's lead and listen to the right voice amidst the chatter. "My sheep hear My voice, and I know them, and they follow me," Jesus said (John 10:27).

## Lessons for the Church

The Church is slowly losing its place of relevance in our society. According to a recent Pew Research survey, the number of professing Christians in the United States shrunk noticeably in the past decade, from 78% to 70%.[13] The drop is in people who identify as Christian, meaning that those who are firmly committed to Christ make up an even smaller subset of that number. This decrease comes in conjunction with societal changes, such as homosexual marriage, which places the Church and her historical teachings on the backburner in favor of "progress."

These changes have left the Western Church in a position that it has largely ignored, which is as an increasing minority rather than as the dominant worldview. Teachings on subjects from Creation to the Resurrection are seen as quaint at best, ignorant at worst. Christian ministries and ministers are questioned and ridiculed. Experts in the faith are no longer viewed as experts, but instead challenged by armchair theologians with smartphones and Wikipedia.

The Church could learn something from Malachi.

When faced with questions from cultural and religious forces, Malachi was able to remain patient and accessible. He spoke plainly rather than poetically, making his points connect to the listeners' world rather than using "churchy" language. He didn't flinch at the difficult queries, nor did he shy away from addressing what needed to be said.

Too often, the Church tries to sugarcoat its answers by ignoring its own challenging doctrines, or it hides behind a politically correct version of the truth. Malachi simply spoke God's words. He didn't worry about how they would be taken, and he didn't get ruffled when God's points were thrown back at him. He simply spoke the truth.

Churches need to adopt the same attitude. We should be willing to state the reason for the hope we have and not worry that our stance will offend. Our attitude of gentleness and respect should shame those who question us when they see our good conduct and clear consciences (1 Peter 3:15-16).

## Lessons for You

Malachi's example of faith when he was questioned can help us on a daily basis, too. We all face questions from friends or co-workers or family. Their questions may related to minor decisions like meal choices or clothing selections, or they may relate to major issues like matters of Heaven and Hell. Such questions can be handled with confidence, patience, and hope, just like Malachi displayed.

However, there is one additional source of questions we must also address: ourselves. Our daily internal dialogue can be filled with exponentially more questions than we hear from others. Our inner thought life can provide a running dialogue that causes us to question almost everything. From decisions we make to words that we speak, our minds can create an ongoing backdrop of hesitations and doubts. Like Paul's internal debate in Romans 7, these questions can cause us to do the things we don't want to do and fail to do the things we really should be doing.

Malachi reminds us that our internal questions are just a type of distraction. When we ask ourselves a version of "How have we despised Your name?" or "In what way have You loved us?" we can drown out the Holy Spirit. Rather than listening to the Counselor's words, our questions tempt us to go the way of Malachi's opponents.

We must resist that temptation.

While inner questions will always be present, we should replace them with promises from God's words. We must turn up the volume on His answers so that our faith can drown out our doubts. By studying and reflecting on Scripture, we can build trust and confidence to patiently move past our questions.

The questions from within and the questions from others can be tough to face. We may face cracks in our spiritual armor or in our courage to find answers, but the faith of the prophet Malachi can be an inspiration for us. His experiences show us the grace and wisdom we can exhibit. His courage can strengthen us to facing a barrage of questions. His trust in God pushes us to match his assurance.

Like Malachi, we can confidently have faith even when we're questioned.

## QUESTIONS FOR DISCUSSION

1.  Who is the source of most of your doubts and questions? What types of uncertainty do they cause in your relationship with God?

2.  Why do you think Malachi and the Lord were able to have patience with the questions of the people? Are you surprised by either's tolerance of the questions?

3.  How does Malachi's faith inspire you to give confident answers?

4.  God's declaration of love provided the foundation for His works. If we question His love, how does that undermine His other actions and attitudes?

5.  Which question seemed most valid? Why? How satisfying is God's answer to that question?

6.  Which question seemed most ludicrous? Why? How can we avoid stooping to such lows?

7.  What questions does the Church encounter most today? What steps can we take to ensure that we respond well to those questions?

# IN CLOSING

Once there was a tiny waif of a child who wanted nothing more than to own her own pet cat. She asked her father hopefully, "Daddy, may I have a cat?" With an evasive smile he answered, "Sure, Honey, you may, but not until we move into a larger home." She excitedly asked again, "With all that room, may I then have two cats, Daddy?" He responded, feeling assured they'd never move out of their apartment, "Yes, you can then have two, three, or even four cats if you wish." The kindergartener skipped away, pig-tails bobbing up and down, feeling lighter than air.

Eventually the inevitable happened and the family moved out of their apartment and into the country, into a spacious house with a big yard and an old barn. Though Daddy had tried to forget his promise to his little girl, she had not forgotten, and she asked day and night when they were going to get those cats. While her father exhausted his list of excuses as to why they still couldn't get a cat (or two, or three, or four), the little girl remained hopeful that one day her father's promise would come true. And so, she appealed in her daily prayers for Jesus to provide just the right feline. As her confidence grew, her prayers transformed from "Jesus, please give me a cat" to "Thank you, Jesus, for sending me a cat."

A week passed by. While the little girl was playing in her new back yard, she heard a strange mewing coming out of the old barn. She chanced to peek through the big double doors. What she discovered lay in a pile of hay—a mother cat with her newborn litter of baby kittens! Nobody in the family knew the mother cat had made her home in the barn, but God knew. The girl knew that God knew, and she trusted that He would always provide according to His will. Both the little girl and the mama cat smiled proudly down at their new family of four baby kittens.

## THE FAITH OF THE PROPHETS

This little girl's purity of faith, a trust in God so absolute and confident, wonderfully exemplifies Jesus' teaching that for those who have such faith, the kingdom of God belongs to them (Mark 10:13-16). For a child, faith seems to come so easily. Maybe they trust because life has yet to wear them down with disappointments. Maybe they hope because they dream so big that anything seems possible. Maybe they remain confident because their relationship with God is so uncomplicated. The faith of a child fully encompasses its definition found in Hebrews 11:1, "Now faith is the substance of things hoped for, the evidence of things not seen."

As we grow up, such purity of faith is assaulted by many challenges. The Minor Prophets also had to endure such testing. Their faith was challenged when their hearts were shattered. Their lives was scarred from enduring devastating losses. Their confidence in God was diminished when they had to endure the fires of injustice. Their trust in God wavered when it seemed like He had forgotten.

Daily living wore down these messengers' enthusiasm, at times to the point where they just didn't feel like it anymore. Their hope faded as government failed them. Their attention was sidetracked when victory seemed certain. Their understanding of who God is became confused at times. Living out their faith was difficult under the pressure from peers. Their confidence in themselves was rocked when they stumbled and were found guilty. They despaired when the future looked bleak. And, they began to have doubts when their beliefs were questioned.

The Minor Prophets were clearly human, and therefore so very much just like us. But, what made these men great at maintaining their faith in God resided in how they approached these challenges.

For comparison, take the old story of the two frogs that fell into a tub of cream. One looked up at the high sides of the tub, and believing them an obstacle that could not be overcome, cried out, "It is hopeless!" He sank disheartened to the bottom and embraced death. The second frog remained determined to keep swimming, thinking, "Something might happen if I just don't give up." And it did! Due to all of his kicking, the cream was eventually churned, and the frog finally found himself sitting squarely atop a solid platform of butter. He jumped out to safety.

The first frog gave up. Likewise, as soon as trouble comes, some people simply give up on God and life. They lose faith. They give up because, as Hosea pointed out, they trusted in their own way (Hosea 10:13). Their own strength wasn't enough to keep them going. Time and again throughout the Minor Prophets, God's messengers warned how futile it was for Israel and Judah to look to their own strength, or the strength of their allies or idols, to get them through the tough times. How misplaced their faith was! If only they didn't rely on their own strength, but took Nahum's message to heart: "The Lord is good, a stronghold in the day of trouble" (Nahum 1:7).

The second frog persevered. Some people, such as the Minor Prophets, never give up, even if they want to. They don't lose their faith. They persevere because their strength abounds from another source—our Heavenly Father. They trust in God because they've experienced God's own faithfulness to them firsthand. As Joel proclaimed, "Rejoice in the Lord your God; for He has given you the former rain faithfully, and He will cause the rain to come down for you—the former rain, and the latter rain" (Joel 2:23). The prophets may have had their doubts, but they set them aside and just trusted in the goodness and power of Yahweh God. When these men made that "leap of faith," as some call it, God provided the strength to carry on, which opened doors to a deeper relationship with Him. As God promises when we simply trust, "I will betroth you to Me in faithfulness, and you shall know the Lord" (Hosea 2:20).

## I WANT THAT KIND OF FAITH

All the faith and trust that the Minor Prophets demonstrated in the Old Testament found fulfillment in the New Testament with Jesus Christ. Their faithful delivery of God's prophecies point readers to the coming Messiah and His Kingdom. So, if we wish to build off of their faith, we need to make Jesus the very object of our faith.

Maybe you, the reader, have already placed your faith in God and His Son, Jesus Christ. We hope this book on the faith journeys of the Minor Prophets has blessed you by bolstering your faith in your Heavenly Father and deepening your relationship with Him. Remember that, as one anonymous writer once explained, "Religious faith is not a final goal to be reached, but a highway to be traveled."[1] You are on your own faith journey. Keep on growing!

Or, maybe you haven't placed your trust in God yet. You have still to embrace the Christian faith. We hope that by reading these faith journeys of the Minor Prophets you will have finally concluded that your own strength will ultimately fail you. Living a life without faith is like a dark night's drive down a foggy highway, which will leave you apprehensive and scared. Realizing these truths, surrender your life to Jesus Christ as your Savior. Place your faith solely in God. Hebrews 11:6 tells us that, "without faith it is impossible to please Him, for he who comes to God must believe that He is, and that He is a rewarder of those who diligently seek Him." When it comes to trusting God, sure, you may have doubts. It's only human. But, as famed missionary to China, J. Hudson Taylor, once reminded us, "Not a great faith we need, but faith in a great God."[2]

The Minor Prophets demonstrated the might, power, strength, love, and determination of God. They have proved through their faith journeys that God always, always keeps His promises, and He promises that, "Whoever believes in the Son has eternal life, but whoever rejects the Son will not see life, for God's wrath remains on him" (John 3:36). Therefore, "Repent, then, and turn to God, so that your sins may be wiped out, that times of refreshing may come from the Lord" (Acts 3:19). Embrace God's promise to you, "Yet to all who received him, to those who believed in his name, He gave the right to become children of God" (John 1:12).

Pray from your heart right now something like, "Dear, Jesus, I confess that I am a sinner. I repent of my sins, and I ask you to forgive me of them and be my Savior." Jesus promises that He will indeed forgive your rebellion. He will remove the guilt caused by your sin. He will give you a new life and that bright future the Minor Prophets foretold, both here on earth and eternally with God.

Once you've placed your faith in Jesus Christ, you will have become a loved and cherished child of God. You will now be able to overcome the challenges to your newfound faith because God is your strength, for "Who is it that overcomes the world? Only he who believes that Jesus is the Son of God" (1 John 5:5). Be baptized as a public declaration of your new life in Jesus Christ. And, to bolster that faith, find a solid, biblically preaching church for Christian fellowship and accountability. We're all stronger when we carry the load together.

> *Faith, mighty faith, the promise sees,*
> *And looks to that alone;*
> *Laughs at life's impossibilities,*
> *And cries, 'It shall be done!'[3]*
> *- Charles Wesley*

# NOTES

## FAITH JOURNEY 1 – HOSEA: FAITH WHEN YOUR HEART IS SHATTERED

1. Kyle M. Yates, *Preaching From the Prophets* (Nashville, TN: Broadman Press, 1942), p. 54.
2. Irving L. Jensen, *Minor Prophets of Israel* (Chicago, IL: Moody Bible Institute, 1975), p. 77.
3. Jensen, p. 81.
4. Yates, p. 63.
5. Ibid., p. 60.
6. Ibid., p. 64.
7. The passages related to the reasons behind Israel's exile and the promises of God to regather the Jewish people back to the land of Israel once more can be found in Deuteronomy 28:64-67; Isaiah 11:11,12; 60:21; Jeremiah 16:14-16; Ezekiel 36:24-28; Hosea 6:1; Amos 9:14-15; Romans 11; and 2 Peter 3:9.

## FAITH JOURNEY 2 – JOEL: FAITH THROUGH DEVASTATING LOSS

1. "The 2011 Earthquake Off the Coast of Japan," (March 2011), http://crisisreliefcentre.org/2011japan/.
2. "The 2011 Earthquake Off the Coast of Japan."
3. Source unknown.
4. Walter C. Kaiser, Jr. & Duane Garrett (Eds.), *NIV Archaeological Study Bible* (Grand Rapids, MI: Zondervan, 2005), p. 1432.
5. Jack P. Lewis, *Minor Prophets* (Austin, TX: Sweet Publishing Company, 1966), pp. 79-80.
6. "Locusts," *National Geographic*, (2014), http://animals.nationalgeographic.com/animals/bugs/locust/
7. James Montgomery Boice, *The Minor Prophets: An Expositional Commentary, Volume 1, Hosea-Jonah* (Grand Rapids, MI: The Zondervan Corporation, 1983), p. 101.
8. Kaiser & Garrett, p. 1438.

9.  "Locusts."
10. Yates, p. 191.
11. Lewis, p. 83.
12. Mariano Di Gangi, *The Book of Joel: A Study Manual* (Grand Rapids, MI: Baker Book House, 1970), p. 35.
13. Boice, p. 107.
14. Ibid., p. 124.
15. Kaiser & Garrett, p. 1442.
16. W. MacKintosh MacKay, *The Goodly Fellowship of the Prophets* (New York, NY: Richard R. Smith Inc. Publishers, 1929), p. 259.
17. G. Campbell Morgan, *The Minor Prophets: The Men and Their Messages* (Old Tappan, NJ: Fleming H. Revell Company, 1960), p. 39.

# FAITH JOURNEY 3 – AMOS: FAITH THROUGH THE FIRES OF INJUSTICE

1.  Joseph Ignatius Kraszewski, *The Project Gutenberg EBook of the Jew* (New York, NY: Dodd, Mead & Company Publishers, 1890), http://www.gutenberg.org/files/37621/37621.txt.
2.  Kaiser & Garrett, p. 1444.
3.  Boice, p. 134.
4.  Yates, p. 33.
5.  Ibid., p. 33.
6.  MacKay, p. 38.
7.  David Allan Hubbard, *Will We Ever Catch Up with the Bible?* (Glendale, CA: G/L Regal Books, 1977), p. 38.
8.  Jensen, p. 45.
9.  MacKay, p. 13.
10. Kaiser & Garrett, p. 1445.
11. Boice, p. 23.
12. Morgan, p. 34.
13. John. E. Hunter, *Major Truths from the Minor Prophets* (Grand Rapids, MI: Zondervan Publishing House, 1977), p. 34.
14. D. Stuart Briscoe, *Taking God Seriously: Major Lessons from the Minor Prophets* (Waco, TX: Word Books, 1986). p. 49.
15. Yates, p. 52.
16. Hunter, p. 30.
17. Boice, p. 163.
18. Hubbard, p. 37.

## FAITH JOURNEY 4 – OBADIAH: FAITH WHEN IT SEEMS LIKE GOD HAS FORGOTTEN

1. Daniel I. Block, *Obadiah: The Kingship Belongs to YHWH* (Grand Rapids, MI: Zondervan, 2013), p. 21.
2. Some of that familiarity might come from other authors, not just personal observation. Obadiah might be leaning heavily on the language of Jeremiah here. Jeremiah 49:7, 9-10, 14-16 makes a prophecy against Edom and the wording is very similar. See Daniel Block's commentary for further discussion (p. 39).
3. C. Brand, C. Draper, A. England, S. Bond, E. R. Clendenen & T. C. Butler (Eds.), "Edom," *Holman Illustrated Bible Dictionary* (Nashville, TN: Holman Bible Publishers, 2003), p. 459.
4. C. E. Armerding, "Obadiah," *The Expositor's Bible Commentary: Daniel and the Minor Prophets (Vol 7)*, ed. F. E. Gaebelein, (Grand Rapids, MI: Zondervan Publishing House, 1986), p. 338.
5. Armerding, p. 344.
6. J. E. Smith, *The Minor Prophets* (Joplin, MO: College Press, 1994), p. 52.
7. J. Vernon McGee, *Thru the Bible Commentary: The Prophets (Amos/Obadiah – Vol 28)*, Electronic ed., (Nashville, TN: Thomas Nelson, 1991), p. 132.
8. David A. Dorsey, *The Literary Structure of the Old Testament: A Commentary on Genesis-Malachi* (Grand Rapids, MI: Baker Books, 1999), p. 288.
9. Some Bible prophecy teachers believe this passage ties into a war described in Psalm 83 where Israel subjugates their neighbors before the time of the Tribulation. If so, Edom's ultimate destruction would still be in the future. For practical purposes, though, Edom was no longer in the picture as a nation to be considered.
10. Block, p. 101.
11. Armerding, pp. 354-355.

## FAITH JOURNEY 5 – JONAH: FAITH WHEN YOU DON'T FEEL LIKE IT

1. H. L. Ellison, "Jonah," *The Expositor's Bible Commentary: Daniel and the Minor Prophets (Vol. 7)*, ed. F. E. Gaebelein, (Grand Rapids, MI: Zondervan Publishing House, 1986), p. 361.

2.  James Bruckner, *The NIV Application Commentary: Jonah, Nahum, Habakkuk, Zephaniah* (Grand Rapids, MI: Zondervan, 2004), pp. 28-29.
3.  Smith, p. 38.
4.  Ellison, p. 378.
5.  Dorsey, pp. 290-291.

# FAITH JOURNEY 6 – MICAH: FAITH WHEN GOVERNMENT HAS FAILED

1.  "Horrors of North Korea: Oppression, Corruption Define Life in Hermit Kingdom," *The Asahi Shimbun*, (March 18, 2014), http://ajw.asahi.com/article/asia/korean_peninsula/AJ201403180068.
2.  M. Pearson, J. Hanna & M. Park, "'Abundant Evidence of Crimes Against Humanity in North Korea,' Panel Says," *CNN World*, (February 18, 2014), http://www.cnn.com/2014/02/17/world/asia/north-korea-un-report/.
3.  "The Frightening Rise of Christian Persecution: Christians Around the World Are Being Shot, Burned, Hanged, Tortured and Stuffed Into Metal Shipping Containers," *Voice of the Martyrs*, (2014), http://www.persecution.com/public/restrictednations.aspx?country_ID=%3d3338.
4.  "The Frightening Rise."
5.  R. J. Behn, "America's Founding Drama," *The Lehrman Institute*, (2014), http://www.lehrmaninstitute.org/history/founders-optimism.html.
6.  Ibid.
7.  Hubbard, p. 75.
8.  Kaiser & Garrett, p. 1483.
9.  MacKay, p. 45.
10. Yates, pp. 107, 113.
11. Ibid., p. 110.
12. Hubbard, p. 73-74.
13. Morgan, p. 80.
14. Ibid., p. 80.
15. Briscoe, p. 100.

## FAITH JOURNEY 7 – NAHUM: FAITH IN CERTAIN VICTORY

1. "NCAA Men's Division I Basketball Championship Upsets," (April 16, 2015), http://en.wikipedia.org/wiki/NCAA_Men%27s_Division_I_Basketball _Championship_upsets.
2. Chris Tomlin, "Romans 16:19" from *Authentic*, Independent label, (1998), compact disc.
3. Smith, pp. 376-377.
4. Bruckner, pp. 138.
5. Ibid., p. 147.
6. Armerding, p. 472.
7. Bruckner, p. 166.
8. Ibid., p. 167.
9. E. Randolph Richards & Brandon J. O'Brian, *Misreading Scripture with Western Eyes* (Downer's Grove, IL: InterVarsity Press, 2012), p. 113ff.
10. Walter A. Maier, *The Book of Nahum* (Grand Rapids, MI: Baker Books, 1959), p. 318.
11. Armerding, pp. 482-483.
12. Dorsey, p. 304.

## FAITH JOURNEY 8 – HABAKKUK: FAITH WHEN YOU'RE CONFUSED

1. Lori Rackl, "Meet Bud Light's Ian Rappaport, Who's Up for Whatever," (February 2, 2014), http://voices.suntimes.com/arts-entertainment/the-daily-sizzle/meet-bud-lights-ian-rappaport-whos-up-for-whatever/.
2. Bruckner (2004), pp. 202-203.
3. J. K. Bruckner, "Book of Habakkuk," *Dictionary of the Old Testament Prophets*, eds. Mark J. Boda & J. Gordon McConville, (Downer's Grove, IL: InterVarsity Press, 2012), p. 295.
4. Ibid., p. 214.
5. Bruckner (2012), p. 297.
6. R. Harrison & W. Williams et al., "Habakkuk 2:6-20," *The NIV Study Bible* (Grand Rapids, MI: Zondervan Bible Publishers, 1985).

7. Wiersbe, Warren, *Be Amazed: Restoring an Attitude of Wonder and Worship* (Colorado Springs, CO: David C. Cook, 2010), p. 134.
8. Bruckner (2004), p. 256.
9. Bruckner (2012), p. 299.
10. Bruckner (2004), p. 237.

## FAITH JOURNEY 9 – ZEPHANIAH: FAITH UNDER PEER PRESSURE

1. J. Foxe & The Voice of the Martyrs, *Foxe: Voice of the Martyrs* (Bartlesville, OK: VOM Books, 2007), pp. 324-328.
2. G.E. Ryder, "Church Dropouts: Why Are Young People Skipping Out on Church?," *The Christian Post*, (October 11, 2011), http://www.christianpost.com/news/church-dropouts-why-are-young-people-skipping-out-on-church-57853/.
3. J.T. Chirban, "Age of Un-innocence: Confronting Difficult Topics with Kids," *Psychology Today*, (March 30, 2014), http://www.psychologytoday.com/blog/age-un-innocence/201403/appearance-and-peer-pressure.
4. Lewis, p. 36.
5. Ibid., p. 36.
6. Jensen, p. 73.
7. MacKay, p. 107.
8. Morgan, p. 112.
9. Yates, p. 164.
10. Hubbard, p. 105.
11. MacKay, p. 104.
12. Briscoe, p. 140.
13. Kaiser & Garrett, p. 1517.
14. Hubbard, p. 108.

## FAITH JOURNEY 10 – HAGGAI: FAITH WHEN YOU'RE GUILTY

1. Smith, p. 478.
2. Mark J. Boda, *The NIV Application Commentary: Haggai, Zechariah* (Grand Rapids, MI: Zondervan Publishing House, 2004). p. 86.
3. Ibid., p. 91.

4. R. L. Alden, "Haggai," *The Expositor's Bible Commentary: Daniel and the Minor Prophets (Vol 7)*, ed. F. E. Gaebelein, (Grand Rapids, MI: Zondervan Publishing House, 1986), p. 582.

5. Smith, p. 503.

6. Boda, p. 130.

7. For example, if a piece of bacon touches your lips, the ceremonially unclean food can cause you, a ceremonially clean person, to become ceremonially unclean, too. In other words, the "clean" status does not extend to the "unclean" object; the "unclean" status is contagious. This example is ceremonially unclean, but still delicious.

8. Smith, p. 510.

9. J. Kessler, "Haggai," *Dictionary of the Old Testament Prophets*, eds. Mark J. Boda & J. Gordon McConville, (Downers Grove, IL: IVP Academic, 2012), p. 305.

10. Smith, p. 513.

11. Andrew Bergmann, "World's Largest Economies," (April 9, 2015), http://money.cnn.com/news/economy/world_economies_gdp/.

12. Ben Leubsdorf, "Decline in Church-Building Reflects Changed Tastes and Times" (April 30, 2015), http://www.wsj.com/articles/decline-in-church-building-eflects-changed-tastes-and-times-1417714642.

# FAITH JOURNEY 11 – ZECHARIAH: FAITH WHEN THE FUTURE LOOKS BLEAK

1. Peter Marshall & David Manuel, *The Light and the Glory* (Tarrytown, NY: Fleming H. Revell Company, 1977), p. 106.

2. Ibid., p. 117.

3. Ibid., p. 126.

4. Kaiser & Garrett, p. 1332.

5. Hubbard, p. 125.

6. Fred H. Hartman, *Zechariah: Israel's Messenger of the Messiah's Triumph* (Bellmawr, NJ: The Friends of Israel Gospel Ministry, Inc., 1994), pp. 7-9.

7. Kaiser & Garrett, p. 1528.

8. One, the burning of Temple. Two, the murder of a former governor named Gedaliah. Three, the beginning of the siege by the Babylonians. Four, Jerusalem's capture.

9. Lewis, pp. 60-62.

10. G. Coleman Luck, *Zechariah: A Study of the Prophetic Visions of Zechariah* (Chicago, IL: Moody Press, 1957). p. 11.
11. Ibid., p. 11.
12. Morgan, p. 144.
13. Briscoe, p. 173.
14. Yates, pp. 210-211.

# FAITH JOURNEY 12 – MALACHI: FAITH WHEN YOU'RE QUESTIONED

1. George H.W. Bush, quoted in Maureen Dowd, "'I'm President,' So No More Broccoli!" (May 16, 2015), http://www.nytimes.com/1990/03/23/us/i-m-president-so-no-more-broccoli.html.
2. A.E. Hill, "Book of Malachi," *Dictionary of the Old Testament Prophets*, eds. Mark J. Boda & J. Gordon McConville, (Downers Grove, IL: IVP Academic, 2012), p. 526.
3. Smith, p. 484.
4. R. L. Alden, "Malachi," *The Expositor's Bible Commentary: Daniel and the Minor Prophets (Vol. 7)*, ed. F. E. Gaebelein, (Grand Rapids, MI: Zondervan Publishing House, 1986), p. 704.
5. Smith, p. 486.
6. Andrew Hill, "Malachi 1:2-5 Note," *NLT Study Bible* (Carol Stream, IL: Tyndale House, 2008), p. 1546.
7. Similar threats are made elsewhere in Scripture, such as in Nahum 3:6. These are somewhat shocking to hear, but God was willing to use harsh and surprising words to get the listeners' attention.
8. Smith, p. 642.
9. Christians see fulfillment of these promises in the New Testament. Malachi 3:1 refers to "my messenger," which Jesus identifies as John the Baptist (Matthew 11:10). Descriptions of the Lord coming to the Temple are fulfilled several times in the life and ministry of Jesus.
10. Smith, p. 649.
11. Carol Harris-Shapiro, *Messianic Judaism: A Rabbi's Journey through Religious Change in America* (Boston, MA: Beacon, 1998), http://en.wikipedia.org/wiki/Messianic_Judaism#cite_note-FOOTNOTEHarris-Shapiro1998177-133.
12. "Israeli Court Rules Jews for Jesus Cannot Automatically Be Citizens," *Associated Press*, (December 27, 1989),

http://www.nytimes.com/1989/12/27/world/israeli-court-rules-jews-for-jesus-cannot-automatically-be-citizens.html

13. Cathy Lynn Grossman, "Christians Drop, 'Nones' Soar in New Religion Portrait," *USA Today*, (May 16, 2015), http://www.usatoday.com/story/news/nation/2015/05/12/christians-drop-nones-soar-in-new-religion-portrait/27159533/.

## IN CLOSING

1.  Eleanor Doan, *Speaker's Sourcebook* (Grand Rapids, MI: Zondervan Publishing House, 1960), p. 101.

2.  Robert J. Morgan, *Nelson's Complete Book of Stories, Illustrations & Quotes* (Nashville, TN: Thomas Nelson Publishers, 2000), p. 283.

3.  Ibid., p. 288.